C Contents

Introduction

For many people, the prospect of reading a book about economic principles is not attractive, even when the focus is on their own industry, or even their own state. *California Real Estate Economics* attempts to address this widespread "econo-phobia" by presenting classic and substantive information in a timely, engaging and understandable way.

Features

This book was designed to take advantage of a variety of instructional design principles and content features, all of which are intended to make it more accessible to students. Page layouts are clean and easy to read, with generous right margins for note-taking and "floating" headings that make it easy to find the material you're looking for. There are numerous illustrations, and all graphic elements have been designed for the greatest possible clarity. Throughout the book, we have tried to ensure that the language is as clear and direct as it can be.

This book has fifteen chapters, organized into six modules. The modules are arranged in a logical order, from broadest principles down to specific investment applications:

GENERAL

FUNDAMENTAL ECONOMIC PRINCIPLES

REAL ESTATE IN THE U.S. ECONOMY

THE CALIFORNIA REAL ESTATE ECONOMY

GOVERNMENT REGULATION OF
THE REAL ESTATE ECONOMY

REAL ESTATE FINANCIALS

ECONOMIC ANALYSIS OF PROPERTY

SPECIFIC

However, it is not necessary to adhere to the module format: the chapters are flexible enough to be taught in virtually any order.

In addition to this book's innovative content and structure, other features have been included to enhance the learning experience:

Objectives

Learning objectives tell readers what they should get out of each chapter's discussion.

A Closer Look ...

This feature provides relevant real-world, historical or background information that helps enhance readers' understanding of sometimes difficult issues.

The Next Step

Sometimes, a chapter's focus will shift to a different direction. This feature alerts readers to such changes within a chapter, and provides a preview of the next chapter's coverage.

In California

Several chapters of this book are dedicated to California's unique economy. In more general chapters, however, information about California is sometimes included. This icon lets readers easily locate California-specific information.

Chapter Review

Each chapter includes a comprehensive, highlighted summary of its most important information, provided to both reinforce learning and help make studying and review easier.

Chapter Quiz

Each chapter ends with a quiz covering its material. The questions have been completely revised to reflect the information covered in a challenging and yet constructive way. An **ANSWER KEY** is included in the back of the book, including page references for each correct answer.

Glossary
California Real Estate Economics also features an extensive glossary that includes both economic and real estate terms.

Appendix
We've included some interesting and valuable material at the end of the book, too:

- **Appendix I** is a report from the United States Census Bureau that provides detailed projections and statistical analysis of national and state demographic changes over the next twenty-five years. California-specific information is highlighted.

- **Appendix II** is adapted from a Bureau of Labor Statistics publication that explains the Consumer Price Index (CPI): how it is derived and how it can be used and interpreted. Again, information of particular interest to Californians is highlighted.

Our goal throughout this book is to provide you with the most current, complete and relevant information about basic economic principles and the real estate economy. We've tried to make what can be dry information come alive by showing how economic theory is played out in the real world.

TO THE INSTRUCTOR:

California Real Estate Economics is accompanied by a complete Instructor's Manual. The IM includes a lecture outline and overhead transparency masters based on the text material. It also includes two 50-question midterm exams and two 100-question finals.

TO THE STUDENT: WHY STUDY REAL ESTATE ECONOMICS?

The fundamental question for you right now is, "Why should *I* study real estate economics?" For real estate professionals, the answer is clear: real estate is a constantly changing market that is formed, defined and manipulated by economic forces on a local, regional, state, national and even worldwide level. In a highly competitive environment, the players who understand what the rules are that govern the game, how the rules work and how they can be manipulated will be the ones who not only survive, but prosper. Real estate economics is not a dry, theoretical field of academic study for Nobel laureates only: it's the world in which you work and live.

Acknowledgments

Like a real estate transaction, this textbook is the product of teamwork and cooperation among skilled and knowledgeable individuals. The authors, the publisher, instructors and other professionals have worked together to help make *California Real Estate Economics* the best introductory real estate economics textbook in California. The participation of these professionals, and their willingness to share their expertise and experience, is greatly appreciated.

Thurza B. Andrew
Mortgage Broker
Associate Professor of Real Estate, Butte College
Oroville, California

Ignacio Gonzalez
Real Estate Instructor, Mendocino Community College
Land Use Planner, Mendocino County Planning Department

Levin P. Messick
Professor of Real Estate, Mount San Antonio College
Walnut, California

Nancy E. Powers
Director of Education, Anthony Schools

1 | Introduction to Economic Systems and Principles

 Objectives:

- Distinguish among different types of historical and modern economic systems

- Understand how capitalism evolved into its present form

- Explain how the U.S. economy operates

▦ WHAT IS AN ECONOMIC SYSTEM?

An **economy** is any system designed for the production, distribution and consumption of necessary and desired goods and services. Economics is the social science that studies, describes and analyzes that process.

As we'll see later in this chapter, there are a wide range of **economic systems** operating in the world. Regardless of their differences, however, all economic systems share these three basic functions:

- *Production*
- *Distribution*
- *Consumption*

Those three words form the basis of all economic systems, and are the central focus of the science of economics.

Operation

Economic activities draw on the special capabilities of the human species. The means and arrangements that support the operation of economic systems include

- *tools* — Humans are inventive tool-makers and tool-users. The creation and use of tools makes the production and distribution of goods and services more efficient.

- *techniques and knowledge* — Human beings are learners: we learn from experience, develop techniques in response to what we learn and that's how we build bodies of knowledge. The progressive evolution of human knowledge creates both greater efficiencies of production and greater demand for new and better goods and services.

- *social arrangements* — Humans are social animals. We accomplish tasks by organizing ourselves, by cooperating, by taking on specialized roles and by acting in accordance with rules that the group has agreed upon.

A Closer Look . . .

The people of a South Sea island depend on fish in their diet. The fish are caught in a lagoon, using canoes and nets (*tools*). They have developed a method of throwing the nets (*technique*) to ensure the greatest catch. The islanders have accumulated a detailed understanding over many generations (*knowledge*) about which fish are desirable. Traditional social arrangements govern who does the fishing (*roles*) and how the catch is shared by the community (*rules*).

The satisfaction of needs and wants almost always requires more than tools, techniques, knowledge and social arrangements, however. Human effort is required, because most of the things needed and wanted are not immediately at hand and freely available. Planning, cooperation, skill and effort are required to make any economic system function.

Wealth

In economic terms, the word **wealth** does not refer merely to riches. Rather, wealth is anything that contributes to human comfort and enjoyment. Strictly speaking, wealth can only be obtained through some form of labor, and is characterized by being desirable by others. That is, wealth is something that is perceived by others as having value, which is evidenced by being sold or exchanged for other goods or services. Wealth, then, requires a community of at least two people, and an object that is owned by one and desired by the other.

Adding Value

Wealth is not limited to what currently exists. Human productive activities can create wealth by *adding value* to existing goods or services. Often a productive process has many steps, and value is added at each step, as illustrated in Figure 1.1 on the next page.

In Figure 1.1, we see how a tree is cut down, the log is cut into lumber, and the lumber is used to build a house. Note how the value of the same material (wood) rises at each stage of the process. After it is cut down, its value increases only slightly. At this point, the wood's value is only *potential value*: it is a raw material waiting to become something else.

Once the log is milled into lumber, however, the value of the wood more than doubles. And once the lumber is assembled into a house, its value skyrockets. We are speaking here, of course, in purely economic terms: the tree may have other value besides economic — it has aesthetic value in its appearance, environmental value in its biological functions, and other intangible values that are real, but of less interest to an economist.

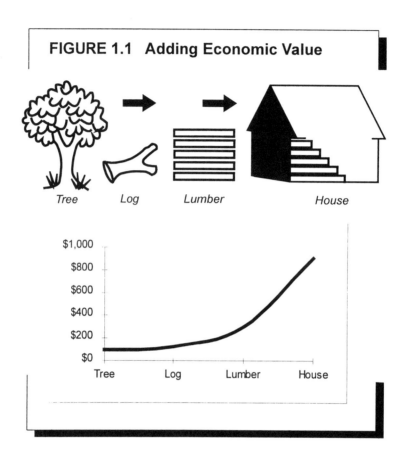

FIGURE 1.1 Adding Economic Value

Goods and Services

Wealth is used to obtain goods and services. This trading of wealth — whether composed of beads or coins or stock certificates — for goods or services defines economic activity.

The term **goods** usually refers to material things that are perceived to have monetary or exchange value. Here again, as in the case of wealth, perception is everything. Clothing, automobiles and wheat have economic value only if they are perceived as desirable.

Services, on the other hand, are immaterial. The term *service* refers to activities that are perceived as having monetary or exchange value. Examples of services include legal advice, health care, education and entertainment. If you are paid a wage, salary or commission for doing your job, you are receiving money in exchange for your services.

Needs and Desires

The goods and services that are created and distributed through the economy can be classified as those that are necessary for *survival* and those that are desirable for *quality of life*.

Biological Needs. Certain resources are absolutely necessary for human biological survival. These are

- food,
- air,
- water and
- shelter.

A person who lacks these essential needs for any significant length of time will not survive. They are necessary to life.

Socially Defined Needs. There are other needs, however, that are not vital to an individual's physical survival. Nonetheless, they are still necessary. These are the needs that are dictated by the society in which one lives. Clothing, for example, may not be strictly required for physical survival in some climates, particularly in parts of California. However, social conventions in many societies (including our own) demand that individuals wear clothing when walking around in public places. Failure to comply with such a rule will not be tolerated by the society, so clothing is a socially defined need: while not necessary to biological survival, it is necessary to social survival.

Socially Defined Desires. In any society, but especially in consumer cultures such as our own, individuals may want things that are not necessary to their social or physical survival. This may or may not be a natural human condition. In Western industrial societies, people are taught to desire many of the goods and services they purchase. Through advertising and marketing, consumers are shown how desirable a product is, and are encouraged to possess or use it.

Modern industrial economies derive much of their energy from creating and then supplying consumer wants. Throughout the industrialized world, "quality of life" is equated with material prosperity and leisure.

Such a view is not, of course, universal. Throughout history, groups and individuals throughout history have rejected materialism and consumer-style culture, and have attempted to build simple communities based on ensuring the minimum essentials of life for their members. Such societies, however, have rarely been popular on a mass scale.

Rules

Rules are established principles of behavior. They are guides or regulations agreed upon by groups of individuals among themselves or imposed by an authority. Rules define the rights and responsibilities of people in society. At their best, rules express a social agreement about what is right, what is fair, what is wrong and what is permitted. Rules also establish mechanisms for their own enforcement.

All economies are governed by rules established and enforced by the society in which they operate. The social rules that govern the functioning of economic systems may be customary and informal, or they may be written into formal law. They may be enforced by individuals, by social pressure or by the state.

▦ A BRIEF HISTORY OF ECONOMIC SYSTEMS

An *economy* is a system designed for the production, distribution and consumption of necessary and desired goods and services. Throughout history, a variety of economic systems have been invented, tried and rejected in favor of new systems. Some have been successful, others have been disastrous failures.

Human history is not a simple timeline. The overview provided here is not intended to be a complete history of the world, or even to offer a substantive view of economic history. It is provided, however, to give you some idea of how economic theories and systems have evolved over time, specifically with regard to the U.S. economy.

Hunter-Gatherer Economies

The fossil record shows us that the earliest humans lived by hunting and foraging for food. Foraging bands had to cover a wide territory — as much as a 20-mile radius — in order to sustain the small nomadic communities.

Agriculture

A revolutionary development took place between about 10,000 B.C. in the Middle East: some of the nomadic people settled down. Here, people began to develop agricultural technologies to control the production of their food, rather than simply gather it. Agriculture requires planting, and planting meant that people stayed in one place, tending crops and, eventually, domesticating animals.

While the hunter-gatherers had congregated in small bands, the agricultural communities tended to be much larger, supported by the surpluses that resulted from controlled food production.

By 4000 B.C. populous societies with centralized governments had emerged. With a settled life and economic surpluses, complex political structures grew. With the end of subsistence farming, literacy, specialized occupations, art and architecture flourished.

Trade and Conquest

As agricultural technologies improved and surpluses fed rapidly growing populations, communities found it necessary to expand their geographical boundaries. Exploration gave rise to increased trade with neighboring agrarian cultures.

Economies based on agriculture and trade were easy prey for the armies of a succession of empire-builders, who gained control of large expanses of territory through military force. The empires and expansionist nation-states such as ancient Egypt, Greece, Phoenicia and Rome served as resource allocators for their neighbors by providing established markets for local natural resources like dyes, cedar logs and shellfish, as well as agricultural products. As the empires grew, the variety of products available rapidly expanded.

Feudalism

Following the collapse of the Western Roman Empire, a complex economic system called feudalism developed and flourished. Based on a complex hierarchy of loyalties, services and land grants originating with the king and supported by a large mass of landless peasantry, feudalism dominated Europe through the end of the thirteenth century. So deeply did feudalism influence the society and culture of medieval England that modern real property law in both Britain and the United States still reflects much of its terminology and principles (see Figure 1.2).

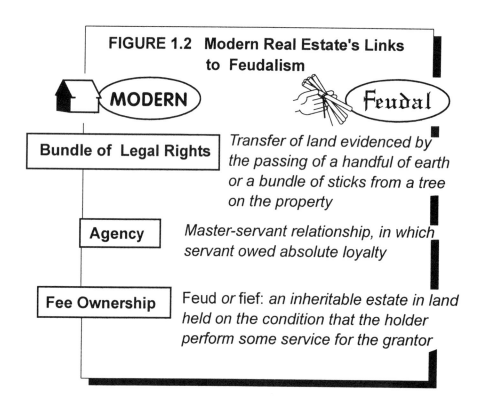

FIGURE 1.2   Modern Real Estate's Links to Feudalism

MODERN — Feudal

Bundle of Legal Rights
Transfer of land evidenced by the passing of a handful of earth or a bundle of sticks from a tree on the property

Agency
Master-servant relationship, in which servant owed absolute loyalty

Fee Ownership
Feud *or* fief: *an inheritable estate in land held on the condition that the holder perform some service for the grantor*

Rise of the Merchants

As urban culture slowly reemerged during the late middle ages, it was accompanied by a growth in the urban merchant class: a new member of a feudal society formerly composed strictly of the aristocracy, the clergy and peasants. The new merchant class had little need for the land-based relationships of feudalism, and was more interested in maintaining a stable climate in which trade could operate freely. As the strength of the urban merchant class grew, the traditional agrarian feudal hierarchy weakened in the face of this new **mercantilism**.

Exploration and Colonialism

The search for new markets for a growing surplus of goods led to global exploration. The colonial policy was based on creating self-sustaining markets by importing raw materials and valuable resources from the colonies to be converted to finished goods for resale back to the colonies and to other trading partners. As the American Revolution demonstrated, however, there were limits to the colonies' willingness to be exploited without sharing in the economic benefits of international trade.

Adam Smith. 1776 was not only the year of the American Revolution. It also marked the publication of one of the most influential books in economic history, Adam Smith's *The Wealth of Nations*. Written as a reaction against the dominant economic theory of his time, mercantilism, Smith's book essentially marks the foundation of modern capitalism.

Mercantilism, according to Smith, was flawed in its assumption that a country's wealth was measured by the amount of gold and silver in the government's treasury. Rather, wrote Smith, wealth should be measured by a nation's annual production. Smith's ideal economic system was governed by two forces: the participants' self-interest and the demands of competition. The action of those two forces Smith called "the unseen hand of the market." Smith was convinced that the highest good of both the nation and the individual was best served by permitting the unseen hand to operate freely, with a minimum of intervention by government. This approach, called *laissez faire* or "hands off" economics, assumes that a free marketplace will be self-policing and maximally profitable.

The Industrial Revolution

Between about 1750 and 1850 the adaptation of fossil fuels for industrial use and a flurry of new mechanical inventions turned Europe from a collection of farms and small cities into a humming mechanized metropolis. Factory-building surged, and smoke from what the poet William Blake called the "dark, Satanic mills" darkened the skies and rained soot on the cities. The new industrial merchant class of factory owners prospered, while the factory workers' quality of life declined. Wages were low as mechanization reduced the number of necessary workers, and conditions in the new factories and factory towns were far from pleasant or healthy.

Political Revolutions

A combination of social and economic factors — the excesses of industrialization, the disparity between owners and workers, and the erosion of monarchies — led to wide-ranging social changes sparked by the Industrial Revolution.

The rise of democracy and the labor movement led to a more equitable allocation of resources among workers, and an improvement in working conditions and wages. These reforms were far from universal, however, and in many countries the tensions created by industrialization led to more violent reactions.

Karl Marx. The author of the *Communist Manifesto* (1848) and *Das Kapital* (1867) is another significant figure in economic history. While Adam Smith had prophesied the free-market capitalism that flourished during the Industrial Revolution, Marx observed the darker side of the reality. Industrialization, according to Marx, exaggerated the normal fluctuations in the economy, creating bigger, more frequent and, for workers, more disastrous depressions. Because wages did not accurately reflect the owners' profits, Marx felt that the surplus value that the workers added to goods was being exploited by the capitalists for their personal profit. Marx's view was not pretty: according to his theory of *dialectical materialism*, capitalism would inevitably create greater and greater burdens for workers until they rose up in revolution, seized the means of production and ended their exploitation by establishing collective ownership in a socialist society.

Roots of the Modern U.S. Economy

Prior to the colonization of North America by Europeans, the native population of the continent did little to disturb the abundant natural resources that this country possessed. The quantity of resources available for exploitation made for rapid settlement and expansion by Europeans.

The colonial movement was led by England, France and Spain during the 17th and 18th centuries. Raw materials from this continent were exchanged for finished goods from the occupying nations, in keeping with the prevailing mercantile theory. Cleared fields, villages and roads soon replaced much of the wilderness. The exploitation of the English colonies by the home government led directly to the American Revolution.

The New Nation. Economic activity had its first restraints under the provisions of the United States Constitution, established in 1791. Following the Revolution, the former colonies had remained independent of one another, only loosely tied by the Articles of Confederation. After the enactment of the Constitution, the former colonies were unified, with a common currency and without taxes or tariffs between states: a true common market was created.

Certain economic powers were granted to the central government: the regulation of foreign trade and commerce, the printing of money and the granting of patents and copyrights. A central postal authority ensured continuous and reliable communication.

Divergent Philosophies. The Founders were, however, not entirely unified in their vision of the new nation. There was considerable disagreement among the ranks of the framers of the Constitution about what form the new society should take. The argument was personified by two divergent points of view:

- *Thomas Jefferson* believed in small farms, an independent press, and a weak decentralized government.

- *Alexander Hamilton* looked toward an industrialized society bolstered by high tariffs and a strong centralized government.

The debate between the Jeffersonians and the Hamiltonians was intense and long-lived. Today, however, it is clear that Hamilton's view, in large part, prevailed.

Expansionism. In the 19th century, land surveys were undertaken to stake out new territories in anticipation of admission of new states when adequate population had settled in the area. An infrastructure of canals, roads and railroads facilitated the westward transport of goods and people, and the abundance of land lured settlers to seek their fortune beyond the Appalachians.

The continuing conflict between visions of the nation was played out in the movement west. Many of the pioneers shared the Jeffersonian distaste for large cities and pervasive government regulation of commercial activities. The move west was partly spurred by the settlers' desire for isolation, for a more pure freedom from social and economic constraints on their behavior.

Industrialization. In the 19th century, the United States began to industrialize. Cotton from the south was made into finished goods by mills in New England. Iron ore mining began in the 1850s in the Great Lakes area, followed at the end of that decade by the discovery of oil in Pennsylvania.

Since there was little control of the production, allocation and distribution of wealth within the country, enterprising individuals were able to seize control of key economic resources. At the top of the pyramid were Andrew Carnegie who had a stranglehold on the steel industry, John D. Rockefeller in oil, and Leland Stanford in the railroad business. The rise of monopolies spurred greater government regulation of the American economy through enactment of antitrust laws and the breaking up of monopolistic enterprises. The government was concerned that the growing power of the monopolies created a concentration of wealth and influence in a few people and severely hindered competition and a free market.

Labor Movements. As was the case throughout the industrialized nations, the rise of factories and industry also spurred the growth of organized labor. The American labor movement grew in visibility and power with establishment of the American Federation of Labor (A.F. of L.) in the 1880s by Samuel Gompers, and the Congress of Industrial Organizations (CIO) in the 1930s.

The Great Depression and the New Deal. The stock market crash in October 1929 and its aftermath was probably the darkest economic period in American history. Unemployment rose to catastrophic levels, and the nation's social structure was severely tested. Through a series of reforms initiated by the *New Deal* program of President Franklin D. Roosevelt, a variety of new government agencies and programs were established as a means of stabilizing and revitalizing the economy. These included the Federal Deposit Insurance Corporation (FDIC) to regulate savings, the social security programs and the Federal Housing Administration (FHA). The Civilian Conservation Corps and the Public Works Administration were examples of activities undertaken by the government to provide employment in various works projects that are still enjoyed by our citizens today.

The Second World War not only defeated fascism in Europe, it elevated the U.S. economy to a position of preeminent strength in the world. The nation experienced unprecedented prosperity in the years after the war, and was lifted out of the lingering effects of the Depression.

Modern Economics

The second half of the 20th century in the U.S. has been defined by two rival, but related, economic theories: **Keynesian** and **monetarist**.

In 1936, the British economist **John Maynard Keynes** published the *General Theory of Employment, Interest and Money*. Essentially, Keynes rejected the conventional wisdom that full employment was the natural state of a stable economy. Left alone, Keynes wrote, the economy could operate in a stable state that tolerated a significant level of permanent unemployment. Keynes argued in favor of government intervention to stimulate the economy in order to create full employment. This was a radical rejection of traditional capitalist theory. It dominated American economic policy through the 1960s.

The monetarists, on the other hand, continued to advocate an unfettered free market. Led by economists such as **Milton Friedman** and **Arthur Laffer**, monetarists contend that the only legitimate role of government is to create and preserve an environment in which a free market can operate with complete freedom. Monetarists, as their name suggests, look to a steadily increasing supply of money as the key to economic stability. They reject any government actions that interfere with the supply of money (such as raising or lowering interest rates to achieve certain social, political or economic goals). The monetarists and supply-side economists of the 1980s view the free market as the best tool for defining and creating social good.

The Next Step

In this brief historical discussion, we've already alluded to the principal tension underlying economic theory and history: the role of government in defining or controlling the operation of a free market. In the next section, we'll examine the distinction between the two prevailing economic systems in the world today, capitalism and socialism, as they exemplify this tension.

▦ CAPITALISM AND SOCIALISM: THEORY AND PRACTICE

In the modern world, there are a variety of economic systems, ranging from simple barter economies in which goods and services are traded directly to complex international market economies. They all lie, however, on a broad spectrum between two fundamental economic theories (Figure 1.3):

1. *Pure capitalism*: the complete freedom of individuals to engage in the three essential economic activities without interference from regulatory authorities; and

2. *Pure socialism*: the ownership, management and control of all means of production and distribution by the community.

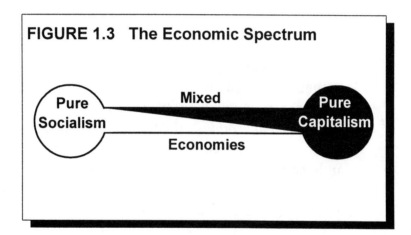

FIGURE 1.3   The Economic Spectrum

Capitalism

Hand in hand with the industrial revolution, the concept of capitalism took shape. **Capitalism** is a market-driven economic theory, driven by the independent forces of supply and demand (discussed in detail in Chapter 2). The major components of this system in its purest form are

- *private ownership* of the means of production and distribution;

- *individual enterprise*;

- the *profit motive*;

- *free competition* with no restraints; and

- *unregulated markets*.

As we've seen, capitalism's basic philosophy of free and open, unregulated markets was formalized by Adam Smith in *The Wealth of Nations*.

Capitalism is based on free economic interaction between individuals. The **capitalist** assumes the *risk* of competition, and is entitled to reap the *rewards* of market success. On the other hand, capitalism can be viewed as "hard-hearted" in its tolerance of economic failure and inequality.

Socialism

This economic system was the direct result of the excesses of unregulated capitalism experienced by impoverished and exploited workers during the industrial revolution. In its purest form, **socialism** is a *command economy*: the fundamental economic decisions are made not by the "unseen hand" of the marketplace, but by a central authority.

The major defining components of socialism are

- *public or collective ownership* of the means of production and distribution;

- *regulated enterprise*;

- economic policies reflect *social/political policies*;

- *economic equality* as a goal; and

- resources that are administered and distributed in the *common interest*

Because it relies on central planning, socialism is referred to as a **command economy** (the market responds to commands from above). As a result, it is better suited to focusing on and achieving specific social goals than is capitalism. On the other hand, it is often difficult for central planners to anticipate all the possible outcomes of decisions once they're played out in reality. There is frequently a lack of motivation to innovate, improve and grow in an economy in which there is little risk and little personal reward.

Mixed Economies

So pure capitalism breeds inequality, pure socialism's equality stifles innovation: what's the answer? The answer, as it has developed in the modern world, is the mixed economy — neither socialism nor capitalism, but a mix of elements of both. In today's world, there are no pure market economies and no pure command economies.

Look at Figure 1.4 on the next page. The vertical axis defines a spectrum of government intervention in an economy, from total control to laissez-faire. The horizontal axis describes whether the market is based on socialism's policy of protected equality or on capitalist principles of individual responsibility and risk-taking.

The old Union of Soviet Socialist Republics (USSR) might have been placed in the upper left quadrant, the U.S. economy in the lower right. Note that both of them, being mixed economies, are pulled toward the center rather than toward the extremes of the spectrums. Also, note that communism and capitalism are both on the same end of the government intervention axis. This is because under the theoretical economic system of communism there is no government authority: all property is held and administered communally by a wholly self-directed society. In pure capitalism, all property is held by individuals, but also in the absence of any government intrusion. This similarity between these two "opposed" economic systems is interesting.

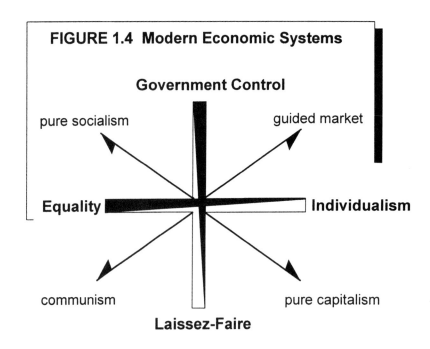

FIGURE 1.4 Modern Economic Systems

The Next Step

That completes our overview of economic theory. In the final pages of this chapter, we will present a general outline of the U.S. economy as it operates today.

▦ THE U.S. ECONOMY TODAY

By examining the components of production, consumption, employment and income, we can outline a profile of our national economy.

A Snapshot

In recent years, the United States has been a nation of consumers, with only a small percentage of personal income kept in savings. Figure 1.5 illustrates how Americans dispose of their income today.

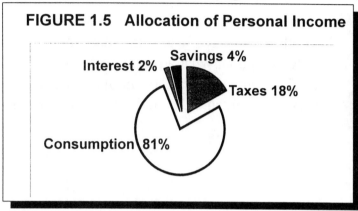

SOURCE: U.S. Bureau of Economic Analysis NIPA Report for July 31, 1997

Note that income can be examined either as national income (employee compensation, proprietors' income, rental income, corporate profits and net interest), or as personal income (after taxes, and including transfer payments such as social security and public assistance, as well as wages, dividends, interest and rents). The first is somewhat analogous to national product, and the second translates more directly into purchasing power.

Employment. As mentioned previously, the U.S. economy has been moving away from manufacturing as it becomes more service-oriented. Figure 1.6 illustrates how U.S. employment patterns are changing.

SOURCE: U.S. Bureau of Labor Statistics, 1997

The Next Step

Now that you have a general idea about the history of economic theory and about what a market economy is, you're ready for more specific economic ideas. In the next chapter, we'll look at how the forces of supply and demand interact in a market economy.

Chapter 1
REVIEW

■ An **ECONOMY** is *any system designed for the production, distribution and consumption of necessary and desired goods and services.* Economics is the social science that studies, describes and analyzes that process.

■ The word **WEALTH** describes *anything that contributes to human comfort and enjoyment*, that is *perceived by others as having value*, evidenced by being *sold or exchanged for other goods or services.* This *trading of wealth for goods or services* defines **ECONOMIC ACTIVITY**.

■ The **GOODS** and **SERVICES** that are created and distributed through the economy can be classified as those that are *necessary for survival* and those that are *desirable for quality of life.*

■ Throughout history, a variety of **ECONOMIC SYSTEMS** have been invented, tried and rejected. Some have been successful, others disastrous failures. Some historical systems include hunter-gatherer, agricultural, feudal, mercantile, colonial, industrial and monetarist.

■ Modern economic systems lie on a spectrum between **CAPITALISM** (a *market-driven* economic theory based on *private ownership* of the means of production and distribution) and **SOCIALISM** (a theory that calls for a *command-economy*, with *public or collective ownership* of the means of production and distribution). Most world economies are **MIXED ECONOMIES**: a combination of these two theories, with one or the other tending to dominate.

Chapter 1 QUIZ

1. An economy is:

   A. the social science that studies, describes and analyzes any system of production, distribution and consumption.
   B. any system designed for the production, distribution and consumption of necessary and desired goods and services.
   C. anything that contributes to human comfort and enjoyment.
   D. any system based on a complex hierarchy of loyalties, services and property transfers.

2. The trading of wealth for goods or services defines which of the following?

   A. Feudalism
   B. Production cycles
   C. Redistribution of wealth
   D. Economic activity

3. All of the following represent modern real estate's links to feudal economies, *EXCEPT*:

   A. agency.
   B. fee ownership.
   C. escrow closings.
   D. the bundle of legal rights.

4. Which of the following is considered to be the founder of modern capitalism?

    A. Karl Marx
    B. Adam Smith
    C. Thomas Jefferson
    D. John Maynard Keynes

5. Who is the author of the *General Theory of Employment, Interest and Money*?

    A. Adam Smith
    B. John Maynard Keynes
    C. Karl Marx
    D. Milton Friedman

6. Which of the following is a market-driven economic theory?

    A. Socialism
    B. Communism
    C. Capitalism
    D. Command economy

7. Which of the following argued in favor of free and open, unregulated market economies?

    A. Karl Marx in *Das Kapital*
    B. John Maynard Keynes in the *General Theory of Employment, Interest and Money*
    C. Thomas Jefferson in the *Preamble* to the *Declaration of Independence*
    D. Adam Smith in *The Wealth of Nations*

8. Economic equality is the goal of which type of economic system?

   A. Capitalism
   B. Socialism
   C. Feudalism
   D. Mercantilism

9. The dominant economic system in the world today is best characterized as:

   A. capitalist.
   B. communist.
   C. laissez-faire.
   D. mixed.

10. The fastest-growing sector of the U.S. economy is which of the following?

    A. Goods producing
    B. Manufacturing
    C. Service providing
    D. Real estate

2 Supply and Demand

◎ Objectives:

- Distinguish the characteristics of supply and demand

- Explain the interaction of supply and demand forces in shaping the real estate market place

- Discuss supply and demand curves, and explain how they respond to changing circumstances

---

▦ SUPPLY AND DEMAND IN THE REAL ESTATE MARKET

Supply and demand are the two principal economic forces that drive an open market. *The function of any market place is to provide a setting in which supply and demand can operate to establish price.* First, we'll consider supply factors and demand factors separately. Note that some of the same factors define both forces, although in different ways. Then, we'll look at how they interact to create a dynamic market place.

The operation of supply and demand in the market is how prices for goods and services are set. Essentially, when supply increases and demand remains stable, prices go down; when demand increases and supply remains stable, prices go up. Greater supply means producers need to attract more buyers, so they lower prices. Greater demand means producers can raise their prices, because eager consumers will compete for the product.

Uniqueness and Immobility

Two characteristics of real estate govern the way the market reacts to the pressures of supply and demand factors: uniqueness and immobility. **Uniqueness**, as we've discussed, means that no two parcels of real estate are ever exactly alike. **Immobility** refers to the fact that real estate cannot be moved to some other location where demand is high. For these reasons, real estate markets are **local markets**: each geographic area has a different type of real estate and different conditions that drive prices.

Because of real estate's uniqueness and immobility, the market generally adjusts slowly to the forces of supply and demand. Though a home offered for sale can be withdrawn in response to low demand and high supply, it is much more likely that oversupply will result in lower prices. When supply is low, on the other hand, a high demand may not be met immediately, because development and construction are lengthy processes. Developers may be wary of responding to a sudden surge in demand by committing to risky construction projects right away. As a result, development tends to occur in uneven spurts of activity that lag behind other economic indicators.

Even when supply and demand can be forecast with some accuracy, natural disasters, such as hurricanes and earthquakes, can disrupt market trends. Similarly, sudden changes in financial markets or local events such as plant relocations, civil disturbances or environmental factors can dramatically disrupt a seemingly stable market.

▦ VALUE

Because the objective of the owner-occupant is different from that of the investor who seeks a return on investment, valuation concepts differ among the two groups. An investor would rarely pay as much for an income property as would a person who intends to live in the house. The financial return serves as the principal investor criterion (see Chapter 12), while the emotional return is the driving force for most owner-occupants.

Money

Like most other products in the U.S. today, real estate cannot be purchased for a handful of beads, shells or colorful stones. Money is the force that drives the transaction. According to the U.S. Bureau of Engraving and Printing, if all the currency notes ($1, $5, $10, $20, $50 and $100 bills) were laid end to end, they would circle the equator twenty-four times. (Money is discussed in greater detail in Chapter 4.) Despite all that cash, however, credit availability is always a primary concern on the demand side of the real estate market place.

Interest Rates. As interest rates rise due to restrictions on the overall availability of capital, the affordability index will decrease accordingly. The **affordability index** measures the percentage of potential buyers who can afford a median priced home. For instance, a 1997 report from the California Employment Development Department showed that the median annual income for a white-collar high-tech worker in Contra Costa is $56,000 less than the qualifying income needed to purchase a median-priced home there.

Inflation. Providers of credit are as conscious of the impact of inflation as the consumer of real estate. In times of high inflation and interest rates, the lending community shifts the risk to the borrower by basing loan products on a variable rate structure. When interest rates are low, consumers will be more likely to demand fixed-rate mortgages. This allows the lender's risk to adjust to the cost of money for mortgage investments.

There is no orderly supply of or demand for real estate funds. Demand for funds may occur when the availability is at its lowest, or there may be little interest in real estate at a time when funds are easily obtained.

▦ SUPPLY FACTORS

Factors that tend to affect the supply side of the real estate market's supply and demand balance include the *labor force, construction and material costs* and *government controls and financial policies*.

Labor Force and Construction Costs

A shortage of skilled labor or building materials or an increase in the cost of materials can decrease the amount of new construction. High transfer costs (such as taxes) and construction permit fees can also discourage development. Increased construction costs may be passed along to buyers and tenants in the form of higher prices and increased rents, which can further slow the market.

Government Policies

The government's **monetary policy** (discussed in Chapter 4) can have a substantial impact on the real estate market. The Federal Reserve Board establishes a discount rate of interest for the money it lends to member commercial banks. That rate has a direct impact on the interest rates the banks in turn charge to borrowers. These interest rates play a significant part in people's ability to buy homes. Such government agencies as the Federal Housing Administration (FHA), the Government National Mortgage Association (GNMA) and the Federal Home Loan Mortgage Corporation can affect the amount of money available to lenders. Real estate financing issues are discussed in Chapter 11.

Virtually any government action has some effect on the real estate market. For instance, federal environmental regulations may increase or decrease the supply and value of land in a local market.

Real estate **taxation** is one of the primary sources of revenue for local governments. Policies on taxation of real estate can have either positive or negative effects. High taxes may deter investors. On the other hand, tax incentives can attract new businesses and industries to areas in desperate need of economic development. Of course, along with these enterprises come increased employment and expanded residential real estate markets. Wisely spent, real estate tax revenues may also contribute to higher values for properties, if the local amenities, infrastructure and schools, for instance, are well-funded and of good quality.

Local governments also can influence supply. Land-use controls, building codes and zoning ordinances help shape the character of a community and increase real estate values. The dedication of land to such amenities as forest preserves, schools and parks helps shape the character of the market. Zoning and land-use controls are discussed in greater detail in Chapter 9.

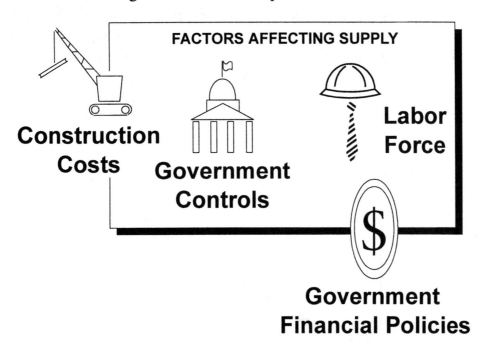

FACTORS AFFECTING SUPPLY

Construction Costs

Government Controls

Labor Force

Government Financial Policies

▦ MEASURING SUPPLY

The easiest way to understand how supply is measured is through an example. Suppose the proprietor of a candle shop is willing to offer a certain number of candles for a certain price. The shopkeeper might produce a supply schedule. A supply schedule is a table of quantities of a given product that sellers are willing to offer at various prices at particular times:

Sales Price	Candle Stock
$30	30
$35	40
$40	49
$45	57
$50	64

Supply Curve

A supply curve is a distinctive portrait of supply of a particular product or service, indicating the quantity that would be supplied at various prices. When the supply schedule is plotted on a graph with price on the vertical axis (*y*) and quantity on the horizontal axis (*x*), the line that joins the points slopes upward to the right. This is the characteristic direction of the supply curve (see Figure 2.1).

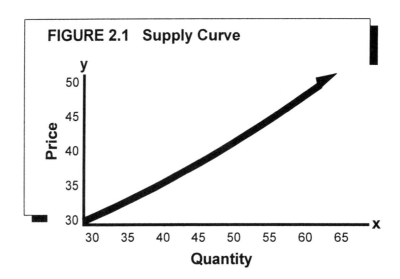

FIGURE 2.1 Supply Curve

If the number of products or services offered at each price increases, the whole supply curve shifts to the right (see Figure 2.2).

Similarly, if the number decreases, the curve shifts to the left (see Figure 2.3).

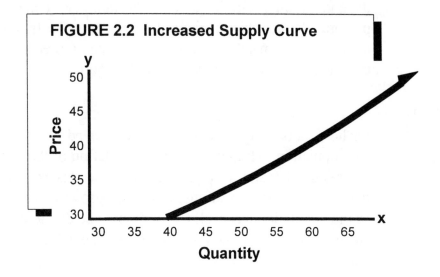

FIGURE 2.2 Increased Supply Curve

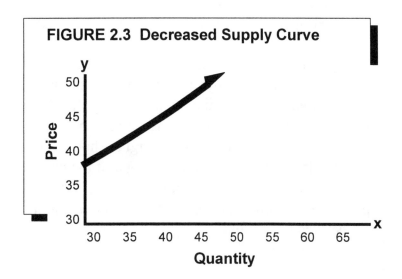

FIGURE 2.3 Decreased Supply Curve

Note that the use of the vertical axis for independent variable (price) and horizontal for dependent (demand) is the reverse of most graphs. However, this is the conventional practice for displaying both supply and demand curves.

▦ DEMAND FACTORS

Demand refers to the amount of goods or services people are willing and able to buy at a given price. In the real estate market, demand is dependent on a single factor: *affordability*. Unless this factor is present, demand has no way of manifesting itself. Factors that tend to affect the demand side of the real estate market include population, demographics and employment and wage levels.

Population

Shelter is a basic human need, so the demand for housing grows with the population. Although the total population of the country continues to rise, the demand for real estate increases faster in some areas than in others. In some locations, however, growth has ceased altogether or the population has declined. This may be due to economic changes (such as plant or military base closings), social concerns (such as the quality of schools or a desire for more open space) or population changes (such as population shifts from colder to warmer climates). The result can be a drop in demand for real estate in one area, matched by a correspondingly increased demand elsewhere.

The two basic components of population as a consideration of real estate economics are **net migration** (the number of people coming into an area divided by the number of people who leave) and **natural increase** (the number of births divided by the number of deaths). This can be measured on a neighborhood, community, state or national level, depending on the scope of the economic investigation. It is important to remember, however, that although increased population figures may indicate a *potential* demand, they may not reflect *actual* demand.

Demographics

Demographics is the study and description of a population. The population of a community is a major factor in determining the quantity and type of housing in that community. Family size, the ratio of adults to children, the ages of children, the number of retirees, family income, lifestyle and the growing number of both single-parent and "empty-nester" households are all demographic factors that contribute to the amount and type of housing needed.

Employment and Wage Levels

Decisions about whether to buy or rent and how much to spend on housing are closely related to income. When job opportunities are scarce or wage levels low, demand for real estate usually drops. The market might, in fact, be affected drastically by a single major employer moving in or shutting down.

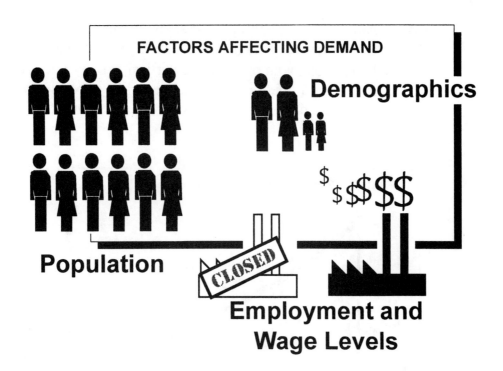

FACTORS AFFECTING DEMAND

Demographics

Population

Employment and Wage Levels

▦ MEASURING DEMAND

The easiest way to understand how demand is measured is through the same example we used for supply. Here, the shopkeeper might produce a demand schedule. A demand schedule is a table of quantities of a given product that are desired at various prices:

Sales Price	Candle Sales
$50	25
$45	29
$40	37
$35	47
$30	65

Demand Curve

A demand curve is a graphic display of demand for a particular product or service. When the candle shop's demand schedule is plotted on a graph with price on the vertical axis (*y*) and quantity on the horizontal axis (*x*), the line that joins the points slopes downward to the right. This is the characteristic direction of the demand curve (see Figure 2.4).

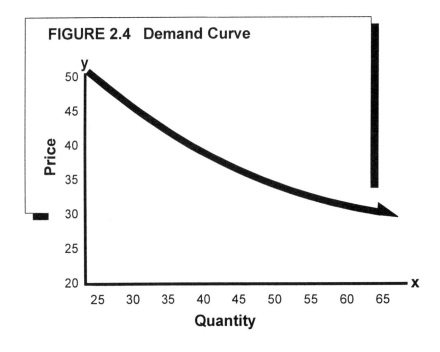

FIGURE 2.4 Demand Curve

Again, note that the use of the vertical axis for independent variable (price) and horizontal for dependent (demand) is the reverse of most graphs. However, this is the conventional practice for displaying both supply and demand curves.

The curve's slope is determined by the degree to which price affects demand. This reflects the elasticity of demand. When price has a relatively small effect (such as with necessities), the curve will be close to vertical. When price has a strong effect on demand (as with luxury items), the line or curve will be closer to horizontal.

Changes in Income

If the disposable income of the average household increases, the quantity desired of various products at each price will go up and the demand curve will shift to the right (Figure 2.5). If disposable income decreases, the quantity demanded of various products at each price will go down and the demand curve will shift to the left.

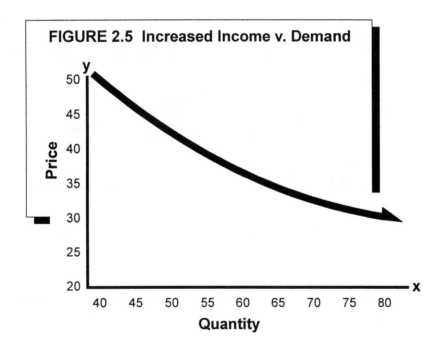

FIGURE 2.5 Increased Income v. Demand

▦ EQUILIBRIUM

The primary objective in any market driven economy is to reach the stage at which supply and demand are in balance. This is referred to as the **point of equilibrium** (see Figure 2.6). When a market is *in equilibrium*, it is balanced: enough product is provided to meet the exact demand for that product and the price is satisfactory to both producers and consumers.

On a supply and demand chart, a line drawn from the point of equilibrium to the vertical (price) axis indicates the equilibrium price. Similarly, a line drawn to the horizontal (supply or demand) axis indicates the equilibrium quantity. Figure 2.6 shows the point of equilibrium for our candle store example. For the shopkeeper, a price of $40 for just under fifty units will achieve an acceptable balance. That is, the point of equilibrium for this one product in one shop at one time is roughly eighty cents.

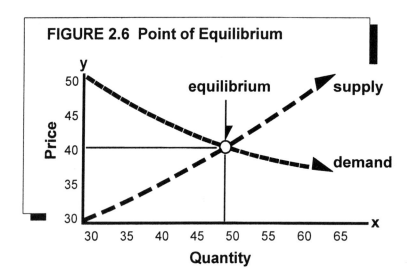

FIGURE 2.6 Point of Equilibrium

A Closer Look . . .

Here's how one broker describes market forces: "In my 17 years in real estate, I've seen supply and demand in action many times. When a car maker relocated its factory to my region a few years back, hundreds of people wanted to buy the few higher-bracket houses for sale at the time. Those sellers were able to ask what seemed like ridiculously high prices at the time for their properties, and two of my listings actually sold for substantially more than the asking prices! On the other hand, when the naval base closed two years ago and 2,000 civilian jobs were transferred out, it seemed like every other house in town was for sale. The new developments were standing empty, and we were practically giving houses away to the few people who were willing to buy. *That's* supply and demand for you."

▦ LOCAL ECONOMIC STRENGTH

In economics, one must always look at the macro (big picture) issues as well as the micro (localized picture) ones when considering factors that influence demand. International events and local conditions can both have a serious impact on the real estate sector. Some of the macro- and micro-factors that may affect the health of the community include net exports, population diversity, infrastructure and mobility of investment.

Net Exports. If the community produces more than it consumes, it is in an excellent state of economic health. A community that consumes more than it produces (that is, whose imports exceed its exports) is putting itself in a risky economic position.

Diversity. Like a healthy investment portfolio, a healthy economy will not have all its economic eggs in one basket. Towns that exist solely for the employees of the local mill, factory or military base are extremely vulnerable. In recent years, the closing of numerous military bases across the country sent many local economies into collapse. This was particularly true where the community had become wholly dependent on business generated by the base and had failed to diversify its economy.

Supporting Facilities (Infrastructure). Community amenities that have a tendency to enhance value include

- *educational opportunities* — public and private schools, colleges and universities;

- *public transportation* — bus and train transportation within a community and between neighboring communities;

- *streets, highways and freeways* — well-maintained roads and bridges;

- *utilities* — sufficient water, sewerage, gas and electricity capacity to meet expanding requirements; and

- *sports, cultural and recreational facilities* — important for residents as well as attracting out of town visitors for special events.

Diversion of Local Capital to Other Areas (Investment Mobility). Local investment may be discouraged if rates of return or risk levels are more favorable in other areas. Nations with rising incidents of terrorism and cities with increasing crime rates often suffer when wary investors divert their investments to safer places.

Taxes. As the federal government continues to experiment with capital gains, depreciation, allowable investment expenses, passive income definitions and other tax policies, demand can be stimulated or stifled in the process. Recent tax laws have sought to encourage home ownership by providing incentives through tax reforms. Investment property is particularly vulnerable to shifts in tax policy.

Elasticity

The interrelationship between demand and price is referred to as **elasticity**. Luxury items such as electronics tend to have a high elasticity, since demand can increase significantly with a significant decrease in price. On the other hand, a lowering of the price of necessities, where demand is fairly constant, will produce little increase (other than some possible hoarding). In other words, the demand for many basic products is relatively inelastic.

Chapter 2
REVIEW

- The operation of **SUPPLY AND DEMAND** in the market is *how prices for goods and services are set*. Essentially, when supply increases and demand remains stable, prices go down; when demand increases and supply remains stable, prices go up.

- Two characteristics of real estate govern the way the market reacts to the pressures of supply and demand factors: **UNIQUENESS** and **IMMOBILITY**.

- Because of real estate's uniqueness and immobility, the *market generally adjusts slowly to the forces of supply and demand*. Even when supply and demand can be forecast with some accuracy, natural disasters, sudden changes in financial markets or local events such as plant relocations can dramatically disrupt a seemingly stable market.

- Factors that must be takent into consideration in determining **VALUE** include *money*, *interest rates* and *inflation*.

- Factors affecting **SUPPLY** are *labor force, construction and material costs* and *government controls and financial policies*.

- Tools that measure supply include *supply schedules* and the *supply curve*.

- Factors affecting **DEMAND** are *population, demographics* and *employment and wage levels*. Demand is dependent on a single general factor, however: *affordability*.

- The *primary objective* of any market driven economy is to reach *the stage at which supply and demand are in balance*. This is the **POINT OF EQUILIBRIUM**.

- Elasticity refers to the responsiveness of supply or demand to price.

Chapter 2
QUIZ

1. The function of any market place is to provide a setting in which supply and demand can operate to establish:

    A. affordability.
    B. inflation.
    C. natural increase.
    D. price.

2. When supply increases and demand remains stable, which of the following usually occurs?

    A. Prices go down.
    B. Prices go up.
    C. Market equilibrium is achieved.
    D. Inflation

3. Which of the following is true of real estate markets?

    A. They are immune from supply and demand.
    B. They are primarily local in nature.
    C. They are national markets.
    D. They are characterized by uniqueness and mobility.

4. All of the following are factors that tend to affect the supply side of the market, *EXCEPT*:

    A. labor force.
    B. material costs.
    C. government financial policies.
    D. demographics.

5. On a graph illustrating the supply curve, what characteristic is measured on the *y* axis?

    A. Quantity
    B. Sales
    C. Price
    D. Profit

6. The amount of goods and services that people are willing and able to buy at a given price is:

    A. value.
    B. demand.
    C. supply.
    D. equilibrium.

7. What is the single most important factor in determining demand in the real estate market?

    A. Population
    B. Demographics
    C. Construction costs
    D. Affordability

8. The number of people coming into an area, divided by the number of people who leave, is the way of determining which of the following?

   A. Natural increase
   B. Net migration
   C. Demographics
   D. Local economic strength

9. The characteristic direction of the demand curve is:

   A. upward, from right to left.
   B. downward, from left to right.
   C. upward, from left to right.
   D. downward, from right to left.

10. The interrelationship between demand and price is referred to as:

    A. elasticity.
    B. equilibrium.
    C. supply.
    D. affordability.

3 Economic Change Analysis

 Objectives:

- Recognize types of economic trends and fluctuations, how to use them for decision making and to generate an economic forecast

- Describe the components of the business cycle and the cycle's larger implications for the economy as a whole

- Understand the types of data generated by the CPI, GDP and stock market indicators

---

THE INEVITABILITY OF CHANGE

In any vibrant economic system, change is a constant factor. As we've seen in previous chapters, the forces of supply and demand are constantly adjusting to market conditions. Adam Smith's "unseen hand" of the market place does not stay still. In the real estate market, too, the ability of participants to adapt and adjust to change is often what separates success from failure. Much of what defines success in the real estate market, in fact, is the ability to read the early warning signals of change, and prepare for coming market shifts. This is the analysis of economic trends.

Trends

An **economic trend** is a change in a market in a consistent direction. A measurement of economic activity over the course of a single day, for instance, would not be a trend. A *collection* of such measurements over several days, however, would be more likely to signal a general market direction. If the measurements were consistent over a significant period of time, they would constitute a trend. Economic trends are either **long-term** or **short-term**. A long-term (or *secular*) trend is made up of short-term changes.

In Figure 3.1, for instance, notice how the long-term trend is made up of somewhat less obvious short-term fluctuations. It's similar to how a newspaper photograph that appears to be a single image is actually made up of hundreds of thousands of tiny dots of ink. Looked at up close, they're only specks; viewed from a distance, they blend together and make more sense.

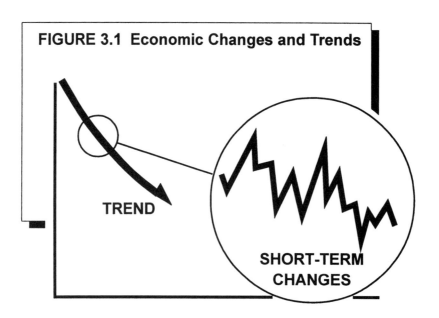

FIGURE 3.1 Economic Changes and Trends

TREND

SHORT-TERM CHANGES

Examples of long-term or secular trends in the U.S. include

- mechanization of production from the 19th to the 20th centuries and

- shift from goods production to a service economy in the second half of the 20th century.

Fluctuations

When levels of economic activity go up and down, rather than grow steadily or decline steadily, they are said to **fluctuate**. There are four kinds of fluctuation: periodic, irregular, random and cyclical.

Periodic Fluctuations. Some changes in the market happen regularly: they can be predicted with precision because their pattern has been documented over time. For example, oceanside communities dependent on tourism know very well that the summer's business boom will end abruptly after Labor Day. Similarly, department stores prepare months ahead for the rush of back-to-school and Christmas buying seasons.

Irregular Fluctuations. Other changes are predictable, even though they do not occur with any regularity. The effects of certain one-time events on business activity can be forecast because the events are scheduled and their impact can be estimated based on past experience. For example, a city may never have hosted the Olympic Games before, but the event can be expected to provide a temporary lift to the local economy. Businesses in and around the venue can prepare for a short-term boom, knowing in advance that once the torch is extinguished, the market will return to normal.

Random Fluctuations. Some fluctuations occur as a result of unpredictable events, however, such as epidemics, wars, international trade embargoes and crop failures (or unexpected surpluses). A particular product may become unexpectedly popular, causing short-term fluctuations in the market as supply races to catch up with demand. In 1996, for instance, a stuffed toy based on a popular Sesame Street character named Elmo became wildly in demand as a Christmas season purchase. Shelf stock was suddenly depleted, and the few dolls available were re-sold at outrageously high prices for a few weeks. By the time the manufacturer caught up with the heightened demand, however, the frenzy had subsided and the toy became a clearance item.

Cyclical Fluctuations. Experience has shown that the level of overall economic activity and performance rises and falls fairly regularly in a relatively long cycle of several years. However, the same is not true of the economy's periodic behavior. The onset of a periodic rise or fall is influenced by a virtually infinite number of economic and noneconomic factors, alone or in combination, and simply cannot be predicted. The longer-term fluctuation, however, is known as a business cycle.

Business Cycles

A **business cycle** is characterized by a general, simultaneous expansion or contraction in a number of different economic activities. These broad expansions and contractions reflect the health of the larger market, the region, or the nation as a whole. While the cycles are recurring, they are not periodic: their length, and the direction they take, cannot be predicted with accuracy. The cycles are long term: they vary in duration from one year to a dozen or more. Figure 3.2 illustrates a complete business cycle (the area within the dotted box).

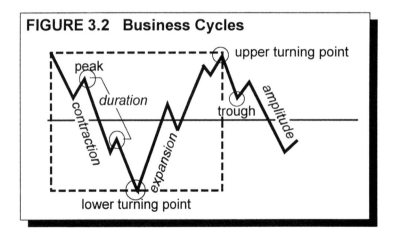

FIGURE 3.2 Business Cycles

A technical language has evolved to describe phases of and points on the business cycle. The most important terms are defined below.

Peak. The top segment of the cycle, a period during which productivity and employment are higher than the preceding or succeeding period. There are many peaks illustrated in Figure 3.2. Remember, however, that "higher" is a relative term: a peak does not necessarily mean prosperity. In Figure 3.2, if the horizontal line represents the number of people living at poverty level, a peak below that line may be of little comfort.

Upper Turning Point. The point of the cycle at which contraction of the economy begins. In Figure 3.2, that point is at the upper right hand corner of the dotted box.

Contraction. The segment of the curve that reflects a decline in economic activity. The contraction in Figure 3.2 begins in the upper left, and ends at the center of the lower dotted line.

Trough. The point at which a contraction becomes an expansion. A trough may be the low point of the entire cycle (in which case it is referred to as the lower turning point), or it may simply be another part of an overall trend. In Figure 3.2, there are many troughs.

Lower Turning Point. The point at which contraction ends and expansion of the economy begins. This point is at the center of the dotted bottom line in Figure 3.2.

Expansion. The segment of the curve that reflects a rise in economic activity. In Figure 3.2, the portion of the cycle from the lower turning point to the upper right hand corner is an expansionary period.

Duration. Usually stated in months, this term refers to the length of a contraction, expansion, the period from trough to trough, or the period from peak to peak.

Amplitude. A measure of highness and lowness: the difference between trough and peak.

Economic Conditions

The duration and amplitude of phases in the business cycle translate into terms commonly applied to ongoing economic conditions (see Figure 3.3).

Recession. A recession is usualy defined as at least *two successive quarters of contraction*, characterized by cautious spending, an increase in saving, and a decline in gross domestic product (GDP).

Depression. A period of very low use of productive capacity combined with very high unemployment.

Recovery. The process of an economy recovering from depression.

Prosperity. The ideal state of a healthy economy: high employment, productivity and income combine to create a general sense of stability.

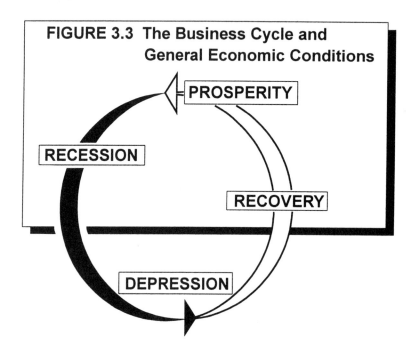

FIGURE 3.3 The Business Cycle and General Economic Conditions

Boom. A period of unusually strong demand for goods and services, accompanied by rapidly rising prices. In a boom time, employment and productivity exceed the stable levels of normal prosperity. The psychological climate of a boom is one of high optimism, often greater than is actually justified. In a sense, a boom represents an economy in a state of intoxication: some innovation or temporary, artificial condition creates the illusion of limitless opportunity for growth. The classic example of a boom is the California Gold Rush of the 1850s. In the space of a few years, whole towns were established, grew, prospered and were abandoned when the lure of fast wealth proved elusive.

A Closer Look . . .

The stock market crash of October 19, 1987 did not have the far-reaching effects of its counterpart in 1929. This was in part because of the regulatory safeguards created during and after the Great Depression of the 1930s. The Dow fell 508 points in a single day, and many stockholders and traders sustained tremendous losses. Nonetheless, two days after the crash the stock market enjoyed its fourth-best gain ever. Ten years after the crash of '87, the stock market was achieving record highs. Until...

On October 27, 1997, the market fell over 554 points in one day. While a numerically bigger drop than its 1987 counterpart, and while it certainly caused financial losses and emotional strain, the 1987 crash was still the biggest drop in stock market history: nearly 23 percent. By contrast, the 1997 crash was only a 7.2 percent fall. The reason: on August 25, 1987, the market hit an all-time high of 2,722; ten years later, on August 6, trading was almost 8,260. Bigger market, bigger drop, but a smaller percentage of the whole.

What Do Business Cycles Mean?

Business cycles describe economic activity in a very broad sense, over a period of time. The cycles themselves are made up of a combination of smaller cycles: changes and circumstances that, viewed together from an informed distance, suggest trends. Just as no single symptom will tell a doctor how healthy the patient is, no single set of data can indicate the level of business activity or condition of the economy. Economists and business people rely on a number of economic "symptoms," called **indicators**, to make informed judgments about the economy's current and prospective condition. Even economists, however, do not always agree on what the figures mean or how they should be interpreted.

Common indicators in use today include quarterly and monthly data on gross domestic product (GDP), employment, income and spending. The level of activity in the housing construction industry is also a common indicator of overall economic health. An enormous compilation of statistics on the nation's economy is available from federal government sources, including the Bureau of Economic Analysis, the Bureau of Labor Statistics, the Commerce Department and the Department of Housing and Urban Development.

Early Warning Indicators

In addition to the formal indicators relied on by economists and the business community, a number of general economic conditions serve as "warning signs" of impending changes.

Employment and Inflation. Abrupt changes in local or national unemployment figures can indicate that the economy is either overactive or stagnant. For instance, full employment in an area raises the possibility of inflation. For an investor, a time of full employment and impending inflation would be a good time for a home purchase with a fixed rate mortgage. In cooling economies, where purchasers are likely to find bargains, the best bet may be variable rate financing for a short-term hold until the upsurge begins.

Population Shifts. Shifts in population can also serve as stimulators or inhibitors. For example, the departure or arrival of a major employer in the area will have long-term effects on local economies. Many communities have been devastated by the closing of military bases: a result of peacetime economics that removes an enormous employment and consumption factor from the local economy. On the other hand, communities in southern and western states have long been benefiting from the steady emigration of businesses, industries and jobs from northern and eastern cities.

Saving vs. Spending. Savings and consumer expenditures each have widespread economic effects. The savings of investors allow the housing market to expand by making funds available for financial institutions and the secondary mortgage market. Consumer expenditures at a high level, on the other hand, stimulate local retail activity, providing jobs and potential consumers in the local housing market.

Repair vs. Replace. The level of activity in remodeling is an indicator that the new housing market is either robust or soft. In any economic downturn consumers will defer expenditures for "big ticket" items such as houses and vehicles. Accordingly, auto parts and repair businesses flourish as consumers attempt to preserve the family car for a year or so longer. At the same time, manufacturers and dealers of new cars languish. The same attitude prevails in the housing market, where the owner of a two bedroom house who has an expanding family opts to add to the existing residence rather than buy a new, larger home.

A Closer Look . . .

It's important for participants in the real estate market to be able to anticipate and adapt to economic change:

- First, learn to **chart cyclical activity** and recognize the early warning signals. The critical period in the entire cycle is when it is approaching the peak and through the entire contraction period, since this is the time that an investor in real property is most vulnerable to losses.

- Second, **anticipate change** rather than just letting it happen. Understanding the mechanics of cyclical activity in the real estate market can be a definite advantage to the investor who, like the stock investor, aims to buy low and sell high.

- Finally, **avoid overextending**. A wise investor who has property can adequately service his or her debt with either the property's own income stream (income property) or personal income is in a much better position to weather an economic storm than one who tends to reach out beyond his or her personal capabilities by overleveraging.

The Next Step

From looking for and describing patterns in past and present economic activity, it is a natural step to forecasting the future. Toward the end of this book, in Part Six, we'll apply the principles of economic forecasting to real estate investment analysis. It's important to have a general understanding of those principles early on, however, to help you analyze the markets, trends and issues we'll be examining throughout this book

⊞ ECONOMIC FORECASTING

In some ways, we know our future with certainty (the classic inevitables, death and taxes, for example). In most aspects of our lives, however, the future is unknown. But there are ways we can, with a reasonable degree of confidence, predict and anticipate the probable course of future events. In daily life, this type of clairvoyance is known as "thinking ahead." In economics, it's called **forecasting**.

The Nature of Forecasting

In any modern economy, businesses are constantly engaged in future-oriented decisionmaking. For a business to be successful, it must be able not only to adjust to conditions as they are now but to anticipate conditions as they are likely to be.

Prediction vs. Forecast. The most important quality of a forecast is that it is not a prediction. A prediction asserts that certain events will definitely occur. A forecast, by contrast, is an estimate of future events, stated in terms of probabilities. A meteorologist forecasts the weather; he or she does not predict it.

Implicit vs. Explicit Forecasting. To the extent that decision making is based on assumptions about the future, a business is engaged in implicit forecasting. An example is an automatic assumption that the present growth in demand for a product will continue indefinitely into the future. To the extent that decisionmaking is based on purposely developed and consciously considered estimates about the future, the business is using explicit forecasting.

Uses of Forecasting

Both business and government need a basis for planning their actions. In the business world, a competitive edge goes to firms with the ability to correctly anticipate changes in

- general business *conditions*;

- *demand* for the firm's products or services;

- *labor* costs and needs;

- supply and price of *materials*;

- *production and distribution*, including new technologies and procedures;

- *money supply* and *interest rates;*

- *competitors'* prices, new products and reactions; and

- *government* policies.

Similarly, the responsibilities of modern governments require massive and accurate economic forecasting on a variety of fronts.

Budget Preparation. Those who prepare federal and state budgets base them on assumptions about tax receipts. Those assumptions, in turn, are based on forecasts of general economic activity in the months ahead.

Business Cycle Crisis Management. Recessions are politically damaging but tolerable. But it has been assumed for the last half century that governments would not permit another deep depression to develop. Governments use forecasting (with varying degrees of success) to contain and manipulate economic contractions once they are under way.

Agricultural Controls and Price Supports. Government controls on production and levels of price support require forecasts of domestic and world production and consumption. Such forecasts also rely on weather forecasts, anticipated natural and social disasters and political events.

Defense Spending. Budgets for military spending must take account of economic prospects in the nation, especially when an administration's policies call for continued growth in such budgets. Economic conditions in the countries of allies and adversaries also figure into military planning.

Approaches to Forecasting

Forecasting can be based on general patterns (periodic events, cycle theories) or on specific clues to what is coming next. The most commonly used approach, the use of leading indicators, is an example of the latter.

Data Collection. Like physicians attending a patient in intensive care, private organizations and government agencies constantly monitor the workings of the American economic system. As discussed previously, huge amounts of data are collected on employment, prices, sales, savings, inventories, and producer and consumer intentions. Each set of data is an indicator of the level of activity in a particular segment of the economy.

Types of Indicators. Experience has shown that various types of data bear different relationships to the economic cycle.

- **Coincident.** Some indicators closely reflect the present state of the economy. These are called coincident indicators.

- **Lagging.** Some indicators trail the business cycle, continuing to rise for several months after a downturn has started. These are termed lagging indicators.

- **Leading.** Leading indicators warn in advance of changes in business activity. These leading indicators are the key to accurate economic forecasting.

Use of Leading Indicators

Leading indicators will start to fall before the business cycle has peaked. And they will start to rise before the trough of a contraction has been reached. Thus they assist in forecasting the behavior of the economy as a whole.

Major Leading Indicators. The U.S. Department of Commerce publishes a monthly composite index based on eleven economic indicators. The composite index assumes an average 48-month business cycle. The Commerce Department's Bureau of Economic Analysis (BEA) is the primary source of information on economic indicators. Some 300 indicators are studied by the BEA and classified as leading, coincident, or lagging.

Information on economic indicators is available from several sources:

- **Federal government publications and websites**, including the Department of Commerce, the Bureau of Labor Statistics, the Bureau of Economic Analysis, and others.

- **State government publications and websites**, such as the

California Trade and Commerce Agency's "About California" website at `commerce.ca.gov/california/economy`.

- **News media.** Radio, television, newspapers and the Internet are quick to report changes in the federal government's Index of Leading Economic Indicators, as well as other economic activities. More detailed analyses often show up in the weekly news magazines.

Diffusion Indexes

A diffusion index indicates the percentage of items or characteristics in a given population that are rising or falling. This is a broad measure of the direction of change in economic activity.

For example, a report on the percentage of stocks that rose on a given day or over a specified period is a diffusion index. Surveys are often used to generate diffusion indexes. For instance, if 65 percent of textile manufacturers polled say they intend to employ more workers in the next quarter, the diffusion index is 65.

Diffusion indexes often signal changes in activity before they occur: they are leading indicators. The following table shows the percentage of nonfarm industries reporting declining employment during six historical economic contractions. Note that the report leads the trough by several months.

TABLE 3.1

Declining Employment Anticipating Economic Troughs		
Date of Report	*Percentage of Industries*	*Date of Trough*
February 1949	90%	October 1949
September 1957	88%	April 1958
January 1975	90%	March 1975

▦ MAJOR ECONOMIC INDICATORS

Consumer Price Index (CPI)

The **Consumer Price Index**, or **CPI**, is a general average of changes in consumer prices, or the "cost of living," maintained by the Department of Labor's Bureau of Labor Statistics (BLS). Consumer expenditures are categorized as food, housing and fuel. These major categories are further subdivided into about 400 items (milk, bread, beef; gas, coal, electricity, etc.). These items make up what is called the CPI's **market basket** for comparing the current and base periods. The CPI measures the cost of living for wage-earning, salaried, self-employed and unemployed urban consumers, representing about 80 percent of the population. The consumer price index, then, is *a statistical measure of the average change in the prices paid by urban consumers for a fixed market basket of goods and services*.

Calculation of CPI. The CPI is calculated using an index number formula called the *Laspeyres formula*. The Laspeyres formula uses the quantity of goods and services purchased by urban consumers during a specific (base) period as the weight for prices, to ensure that the market basket's value is constant. The present weighted cost of the items in the CPI market basket is then compared with the price of the same items during the base period. The current base period is 1982-1984; in 1998 the base period will be 1993-1995. The Laspeyres formula asks, "What is the value of the base-period market basket in today's prices?" The answer indicates the extent to which the cost of living has risen over time.

The BLS relies on a monthly survey of 7,300 housing units and 22,500 retail and service establishments. Two hundred and six item categories are constructed for 44 different urban areas. A sample of 24,000 families in a point-of-purchase survey tells BLS where the market basket items are being purchased. Twenty percent of the data is revised annually, and the entire sampling of item prices is revised every five years.

Table 3.2 lists the CPI market basket expenditure categories.

TABLE 3.2

CPI Market Basket Expenditure Categories

❑ **Food**
cereals and bakery products
meat, poultry, fish and eggs
dairy products
fruits and vegetables
sugar and sweets
fats and oils
nonalcoholic beverages
prepared food
food away from home
alcoholic beverages

❑ **Housing**
residential rent
other rental costs
owners' equivalent rent
household insurance
maintenance/repair services
maintenance/repair commodities

❑ **Fuel and Other Utilities**
fuel oil and household fuel
gas (piped) and electricity

❑ **Household Furnishings and Operation**
house furnishings
housekeeping supplies/services

❑ **Apparel and Upkeep**
men's and boys'
women's and girls'
infants' and toddlers'
footwear and apparel

❑ **Transportation**
new cars
new vehicles
used cars
motor fuel
gasoline
maintenance and repair
other private transportation
public transportation

❑ **Medical Care**
medical care commodities
medical care services
professional medical services

❑ **Entertainment**
entertainment commodities
entertainment services

❑ **Other Goods and Services**
tobacco and smoking products
toilet goods and personal care
appliances
personal care services
school books and supplies
personal/educational services

Obviously, this calculation is not a simple one. The quality of products changes over time, and other economic and noneconomic factors may be at work, including changes in consumers' shopping habits. Although BLS goes to great lengths to ensure objectivity, interpretation of the raw data depends in part on the assumptions, prejudices and biases of the interpreter. As a result, CPI data is sometimes the subject of controversy. The BLS has responded over the years by building various adjustments into the CPI calculation, including new standards for product quality improvements and the introduction of new products. A detailed question-and-answer discussion about CPI from the BLS is provided in Appendix III.

Interpretation. A CPI of 110 means that consumer prices are 110 percent of what they were in the base year. The *annualized rate* translates a monthly rate of increase into annual terms: a monthly rise of 1 percent is an annual rise of 12 percent).

Local CPI

Regions, states and cities often differ markedly in their CPIs (as anyone can tell you who has moved from a small town to a large city) and CPIs vary over time. For example, in March 1988, the Los Angeles area CPI was 120.6, and the San Francisco area CPI was 119.1. For the same month in 1997, the Los Angeles area CPI was 159.8, and the Bay Area CPI was 159.2. That is, in early 1997 the average cost of the market basket items in San Francisco was $159. Figure 3.4 illustrates the change in California's CPI since 1953.

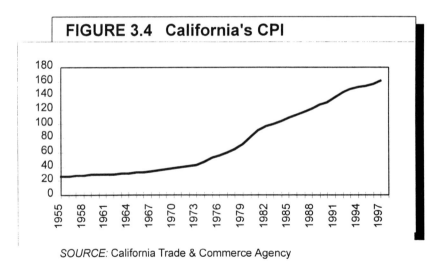

FIGURE 3.4 California's CPI

SOURCE: California Trade & Commerce Agency

Until the mid-1980s, the California CPI was essentially in line with the national CPI. Since 1985, however, California's CPI has been consistently higher than the national average. In Part Three, we'll focus on California's unique economy in detail.

Gross Domestic Product (GDP)

The principal indicator of the total output of goods and services in this country is the **gross domestic product (GDP)**. GDP measures the economic effect resulting from the production of wealth by labor and property physically located within the nation's borders. (You will recall from Chapter 1 that this is the basis for evaluating wealth proposed by Adam Smith back in 1776). GDP is also the standard international measure of economic accounting, so nations share a standard against which to gauge their productivity.

GDP measures four major components:

1. *Individual consumption*

2. *Investment spending*

3. *Government spending*

4. *Net exports*

Figure 3.5 illustrates how much of the current U.S. GDP is composed of each factor.

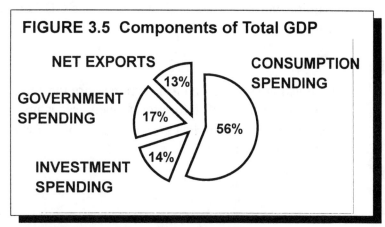

FIGURE 3.5 Components of Total GDP

NET EXPORTS 13%
CONSUMPTION SPENDING 56%
GOVERNMENT SPENDING 17%
INVESTMENT SPENDING 14%

SOURCE: Bureau of Economic Analysis, 1997

Individual Consumption Spending. This element of GDP is composed of specifically defined elements:

- **Durable goods** — products that are expected to last more than three years, such as cars or major appliances

- **Nondurable goods** — products with a shorter life span, such as clothing or food

- **Services** — activities with a monetary exchange value

Investment Spending. GDP's investment spending measurement includes:

- **Nonresidential investments** — expenditures on such capital investments as factories and equipment

- **Residential investment** — single- and multi-family homes

- Changes in **business inventories**

Government Spending. GDP takes into account the amount of money spent each year by the national government on such things as defense, highways, schools and social programs.

Net Exports. Finally, GDP includes the nation's **net exports**. Net exports is the amount remaining after total imports are deducted from total exports. If a nation has a trade deficit, for instance, that means that it imports more than it exports. A trade deficit will reduce GDP and reflect a less-wealthy national economy.

Using GDP

By tracking GDP, economists can measure the relative health of a national economy. If the GDP figure for a given year is up, over the previous year, the nation's economy has grown. Figure 3.5 illustrates the changes in the U.S. GDP since 1960.

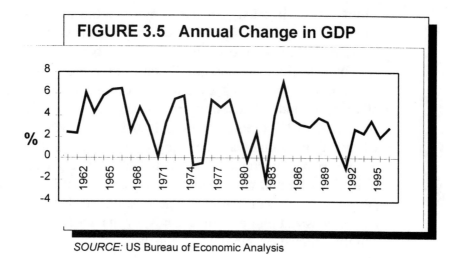

FIGURE 3.5 Annual Change in GDP

SOURCE: US Bureau of Economic Analysis

Unemployment Rate

The **unemployment rate** is a percentage used to characterize the employment situation in specified areas. Its calculation is simple: the number of unemployed persons divided by the total civilian labor force. The Bureau of Labor Statistics defines an unemployed person as anyone over the age of 16 who is available to work but who has not worked at a paying job during the past week and who has sought employment at some time during the previous four weeks. "Unemployed persons" also includes people who are waiting to be called back from a layoff or who are waiting to report to a new job sometime in the next 30 days.

The **labor force** is defined as every person over age 16 who is either working at a paying job (full-time or part-time) or who fits the definition of unemployed. Those not in the labor force include anyone over age 15 who is neither employed nor unemployed and those persons who are retired. The Bureau of Labor Statistics releases unemployment figures every month. Figures are reported for different categories, such as gender, race, ethnicity and geographic location

Data. Like the CPI, a sample is used to obtain data. A rotating sample of 50,000 households is contacted each month and asked whether each person worked at all during the week and whether nonworking members have been recently laid off or are looking for work. Of course, if they do not meet those tests, they are considered no longer in the labor force. They are, therefore, not counted as unemployed.

Limitations. Because of the limited definitions used in compiling employment statistics, the true extent of joblessness in the economy is very likely higher than the official reported number. For instance, the official employment figures exclude "discouraged workers"— people who have given up hope of finding a job and have stopped actively looking. On the other hand, individuals who are participants in the U.S. "underground economy" of bartered services and undeclared income from cash-paying work may be counted as unemployed, even though they are not. Further, the government unemployment figures may not be giving a truly qualitative reflection of employment conditions: they do not take into consideration people who are working part-time jobs out of desperation, or who have been downsized into part-time status, or the underemployed. Workers are simply counted as employed, whether or not society (or the worker's family) is receiving the full benefit of his or her skills.

The Stock Market as Indicator

The **Dow-Jones Industrial Average** is a measure of the prices that are paid for shares in major industrial corporations in the stock market. The *Nasdaq, New York Stock Exchange Index* and *Standard & Poor's 500* are other similar measures. The Dow-Jones is based on a group of thirty stocks, considered representative of the market as a whole. The Dow-Jones average on a single day says very little; what matters is its direction over a period of time. Table 3.3 shows the current Dow-Jones 30.

TABLE 3.3

The Dow-Jones 30	
General Electric	Eastman Kodak
Coca Cola	Hewlett-Packard
Exxon	American Express
Merck & Co.	Allied Signal
Philip Morris	Sears, Roebuck
IBM	J.P. Morgan
Procter & Gamble	United Technologies
AT&T	Caterpillar
E.I. DuPont de Nemours	International Paper
Walt Disney	Aluminum Company of America
General Motors	Johnson & Johnson
Chevron	Goodyear
3M	Union Carbide
Boeing	Travelers Corp.
McDonald's	Wal-Mart Stores

The **Nasdaq 100 Index** is another commonly relied-on measure of the stock market and the nation's general economic health. The Nasdaq 100 represents the one hundred largest nonfinancial domestic companies listed on the Nasdaq market, across industry groups. The *Willshire 5000* index measures the daily performance of the nation's 5,000 largest companies.

Limitations. Fluctuations in stock prices reflect the expectations of people who trade in stocks. The greater their confidence that business will be good, the more likely they are to buy shares. The more demand for a particular share, the higher its price. When investor confidence in a particular company or in the market as a whole is low, the more likely investors are to sell their shares and cause prices to drop.

The stock market has obvious limits resulting from its character as an arbitrarily processed nonrandom sample representing a very specialized part of the economy. The Dow-Jones index is heavily skewed toward blue chip stocks (those which consistently show solid growth and reliable dividends). It does not look at either less successful stocks or the sharply rising glamour stocks associated with a new process or product. Nasdaq is frequently accused of emphasizing high-tech stocks, and the *American Stock Exchange* is thought to be weighted in favor of natural resource companies. As an indicator of economic performance, the stock market offers a wealth of information, but significant limitations as well.

(In the first quarter of 1998, Nasdaq and the American Stock Exchange entered into merger negotiations. The proposed merger was seen as a move to create more effective competition against the New York Stock Exchange.)

The Next Step

In the next chapter, we'll devote our full attention to a subject that is of great interest: *money*. In addition to considering the evolution of paper money as a medium of exchange, we'll look at the Federal Reserve System, the money supply and inflation.

Chapter 3
REVIEW

- An **ECONOMIC TREND** is a *change in a market in a consistent direction, over time.* Trends may be classified as **LONG TERM** or **SHORT TERM**.

- There are four types of economic fluctuations: **PERIODIC** (*predictable and regularly occurring*), **IRREGULAR** (*predictable but not regularly occurring*), **RANDOM** (*unpredictable and irregular*) and **CYCLICAL** (*predictable and regular over a long period of time*).

- A **BUSINESS CYCLE** is characterized by a *general, simultaneous expansion or contraction in a variety of different economic activities*, reflecting the broader economic health of the nation, region or local market. Business cycles are *recurring, but very long term*. Business cycles are composed of periods of *prosperity, recession, depression* and *recovery*.

- **ECONOMIC INDICATORS** provide analysts with the data necessary to make informed judgments about the current and future economic health of a market. Indicators may be *coincident, lagging* or *leading*.

- The **CONSUMER PRICE INDEX (CPI)** is a major economic indicator prepared by the *U.S. Department of Labor*. The CPI relies on analysis of the changing prices of a **MARKET BASKET** of typical consumer items.

- The *principal indicator of the nation's total output of goods and services* is the **GROSS DOMESTIC PRODUCT (GDP)**. GDP measures *individual consumption, investment spending, government spending* and *net exports*.

- The **UNEMPLOYMENT RATE** and the **STOCK MARKET** are two other indicators that provide valuable current information about a local, regional, state or national economy.

Chapter 3
QUIZ

1. A market change in a consistent direction over a period of time is referred to as an economic:

    A. expansion.
    B. fluctuation.
    C. trend.
    D. amplitude.

2. All of the following types of economic fluctuations are predictable, *EXCEPT*:

    A. periodic.
    B. irregular.
    C. random.
    D. cyclical.

3. In a business cycle, the period between two peaks is referred to as a(n):

    A. contraction.
    B. duration.
    C. expansion.
    D. amplitude.

4. The point on a business cycle at which a decline in economic activity reaches bottom is referred to as the:

   A. trough.
   B. contraction.
   C. amplitude.
   D. lower turning point.

5. Two successive quarters of contraction, characterized by cautious spending and increased saving, is a:

   A. boom.
   B. recovery.
   C. depression.
   D. recession.

6. All of the following terms accurately describe characteristics of an economic forecast, *EXCEPT*:

   A. prediction.
   B. explicit.
   C. implicit.
   D. estimate.

7. Which of the following major economic indicators uses a "market basket" of consumer goods?

   A. GDP
   B. CPI
   C. BEA
   D. Nasdaq

8. In 1999, the CPI is 115. What does this mean?

   A. The Consumer Price Index has risen 115 percent since 1998.
   B. The average price of the most expensive item in the market basket is $115.
   C. Consumer prices are 115 percent of what they were in 1993-1995.
   D. Consumer prices are 115 percent of what they were in the 1982-1984 base period.

9. In a GDP analysis, a refrigerator would be considered which of the following?

   A. Durable goods
   B. Nondurable goods
   C. Investment spending
   D. Household furnishings

10. Which of the following stock market indicators relies on a sample of one hundred nonfinancial domestic companies across industry groups?

   A. Dow-Jones
   B. Nasdaq
   C. Willshire
   D. American

4   Money and Monetary Policy

 Objectives:

- Understand how money evolved as a form of exchange, from simple barter economies to modern electronic funds transfers

- Explain the structure and importance of the Federal Reserve System in the U.S. economy

- Define the economic measurement terms M1, M2 , M3 and L

- Describe the role of inflation and the impact of government monetary policies on the real estate market

---

▦ THE EVOLUTION OF MONEY

Money is any medium of exchange adopted by a society as a means of acquiring goods and services. Money may or may not have any intrinsic value of its own — gold coins, for instance, have an independent value; paper money, which is merely ink and paper, only *represents* value. The value assigned to money is dependent on a variety of political, economic, commercial and psychological factors.

Figure 4.1 is a timeline highlighting some of the more significant moments in the history of money.

FIGURE 4.1 Important Moments in Money

c 2500 BC	Banking invented in Mesopotamia
c 1700 BC	Code of Hammurabi includes banking laws
c 1000 BC	Cowrie shells used as money in China
c 500 BC	Gold and silver coins produced in Lydia, Asia Minor
c 400 BC	Silver-coated bronze coins minted in Athens
c 250 BC	Romans circulate silver coins
c 100 BC	Chinese issue leather money
10 AD	Augustus establishes sales, land and poll taxes
410	Fall of Rome to Visigoths; end of European banking
c 430	Use of coins ends in Britain
c 550	Use of coins resumed in Britain
c 800	China introduces paper money
c 11th-13th Century	Crusades stimulate reemergence of European banking
1156	First foreign-exchange contract (Genoese *pounds* for Byzantine *bezants)*
1292	Marco Polo, returning from China, introduces paper money to Europe
1455	China abolishes paper money
1545	In England, King Henry VIII legalizes charging interest on loans
c 1600	Tobacco is legal currency in the Virginia Colony
c 1630	Wampum shells are legal currency in Massachusetts Bay Colony
1661	Bank of Sweden issues first European paper money
1690	Massachusetts Bay Colony issues paper money
1764	Britain forbids use of paper money in American Colonies
1776	Adam Smith praises paper money
1789	U.S. Constitution empowers Congress to issue paper money
1861 - 1865	U.S. Civil War: Confederate notes become worthless
1900	U.S. adopts the gold standard
1944 - 1971	Bretton Woods Agreement attempts to standardize international trade
1973	U.S. abandons gold standard
1984	U.S. courts legalize national ATM networks
1992	Maastricht Treaty calls for common European currency by 1999
c 1995	Over 90% of transactions in the U.S. involve electronic transfers
2002	*euro* coins and noted to be adopted by European Union

Money Through History

Early Barter Economies. In early human commercial transactions, money was not an issue. In a **barter economy**, goods or services are traded directly for other goods or services. A cow, for instance, might be traded for so many bushels of corn, or a cobbler might agree to make a pair of shoes in exchange for a quilt. A barter economy values **commodities** (goods and services) both for their own usefulness and for their potential in exchange.

While often thought of as an ancient relic, barter economies are not confined to prehistory. Even in the modern U.S. economy, barter is alive and well in the **underground economy**, where individuals commonly trade goods and services as a way of avoiding income taxation or of obtaining goods or services they could not otherwise afford.

Primitive Money. There is, obviously, a limit to the number of cattle or bushels of corn a person can reasonably be expected to cart around. Just as our concept of numbers may have arisen out of the convenience of using abstract symbols to represent physical quantities, so too the idea arose over time of using a particular commodity as the basic means of exchange. If a cow, for instance, was worth seventeen bushels of corn, then a bead or shell might just as easily *represent* seventeen bushels of corn, making the transfer somewhat more convenient. In various parts of the world, the common means of exchange has taken many forms: amber, beads, cowries, eggs, feathers, ivory, jade, leather, nails, quartz, oxen, rice and salt have all, at one time or another, been somebody's "money."

This system of exchange only works, however, if it is agreed upon by a larger society. The person who receives the bead or shell only receives value for the cow if he or she can, in turn, exchange the bead or shell for seventeen bushels of corn's worth of blankets or chickens or legal advice. The development of money, then, is closely linked to the development of interdependent social structures.

The whole history of money can be viewed as the refinement of this basic abstraction: a monetary unit may represent a certain fixed value in gold or some other standard. That standard has value only because the society agrees that it does. Its value is reflected in what it can buy: a coin may be worth three ounces of gold, and three ounces of gold may buy a dozen cows or two hundred bushels of corn, bringing us right back where we started: it all boils down to barter.

Early Civilizations. As society became increasingly urbanized, merchants, writers and skilled craftsmen played a larger role in the economy. As a result, more sophisticated exchange systems were possible, and metal became a prominent medium of exchange.

Prior to the development of a minting process, metal was measured out by weight. A Greek *drachma* originally represented six obols, and each obol represented a handful of nails. Other currencies today that started out as metal measurements are the English *pound*, Russian *ruble* and Italian *lira*.

Gold and silver were especially favored as a medium of exchange, because they were scarce and durable, and small amounts could command large amounts of goods and services.

Development of Coinage. Due to the inconvenience of measuring out metal for each transaction, coinage appeared as a sort of preweighed medium of exchange in Europe. The first coins were solid precious metals, such as gold or silver; later, less expensive metals, such as bronze or copper, were covered with a thin layer of gold or silver.

In the New World, the Mayas and Aztecs used measured gold dust held in hollow, transparent quills, as well as large sacks of cocoa beans, for money. (The Incas, interestingly, did not develop a monetary system despite their high degree of civilization. This unusual situation may have resulted from the intensity of their centralized state planning.)

Medieval to Early Modern Era. With the fall of the Roman Empire, a general cultural regression occurred, including a return to the use of metal in bulk as a form of payment.

Paper Money. An early form of paper money was developed in China around the ninth century, in large part due to a shortage of copper. Marco Polo reported the innovation to Europeans with the publication of his travel journals in 1295. The new medium of exchange was viewed with suspicion, and was slow to catch on among Europeans: paper money was not in general use by merchants until the late 1600s. In the meantime, China had abandoned the use of paper money by the middle of the fifteenth century.

Goldsmiths' Notes. The use of currency backed by metal started in England in the 1600s when merchants stored their gold with goldsmiths, receiving receipts for their deposit. These receipts, in turn, gained acceptance as a means of exchange, since the recipients were confident that they could be redeemed in gold.

Eighteenth and Nineteenth Centuries. Paper money gained acceptance and sophistication during this period, and the banking industry flourished throughout Europe. With this financial boom, however, came confusion. Without a centralized monetary authority, private individuals, companies, and banks of varying reliability issued **fiduciary money**: notes promising to pay gold or silver.

The promises associated with fiduciary money were not always kept, however, and trust in paper money was often low. Even in respectable banks, such notes were fractionally rather than fully backed by precious metal. This ordinarily sufficed, since only a few individuals at a time wanted to redeem their notes. But if even a few too many depositors asked for **specie** (coin), bank resources might be strained and rumors of inadequate reserves to back the issued notes would sweep through the streets, setting off a "run on the bank," in which frantic depositors closed their accounts. Banks often failed, with depositors losing everything. The recurrent pattern of bank failure was a strong argument for the development of central banks.

Central Banks. It soon became apparent that only large, centralized banks, with enormous, reliable reserves of precious metals to back their notes, could support smaller banks in times of stress. Initially, the central banks were not always government-owned; eventually, however, they became so. Gradually, central banks became the main issuers of paper money. But even the central banks did not fully back paper money with gold or silver.

Much of the paper money issued in the 18th and 19th centuries was backed by precious metal, however fractionally or unreliably. Governments, however, could issue paper money or coins whose value was simply decreed. Because another word for an official order or decree is *fiat*, such money is called **fiat money**.

Paper Money Debate in America. Although paper money had long circulated in some sectors of European commercial life, the widespread use of paper money in America was strongly resisted. A bitter debate between the "paper money men" and the "gold bugs" lasted through most of the 19th century.

If suspicion was aroused by fiduciary money (which at least promised redemption in precious metal), the level of trust in money unsupported by precious metal reserves was intense. The debate in America over whether or not to abandon **bimetallism** (the use of gold and silver to back currency) and adopt the international gold standard divided the largely urban, eastern interests who favored the standard from the rural westerners who opposed it. The **gold standard**, which theoretically limited the amount of money in circulation to the value of gold held in reserve by the issuing government was adopted in 1900, however, and remained the basis for valuing the U.S. dollar until 1973. In the years between World Wars I and II, most of the world's countries gave up the gold standard.

A Closer Look . . .

William Jennings Bryan's famous "cross of gold" speech, delivered at the Democratic party convention in Chicago on July 8, 1896, is an example of the intensity of feeling created by the gold standard debate:

. . . We do not come as aggressors. Our war is not a war of conquest; we are fighting in the defense of our homes, our families, and posterity. We have petitioned, and our petitions have been scorned . . . we have begged, and they have mocked when our calamity came. We beg no longer; we entreat no more; we petition no more. We defy them. If they dare to come out in the open field and defend the gold standard as a good thing, we will fight them to the uttermost. Having behind us the producing masses of this nation and the world, supported by the commercial interests, the laboring interests, and the toilers everywhere, we will answer their demand for a gold standard by saying to them: You will not press down upon the brow of labor this crown of thorns, you shall not crucify mankind upon a cross of gold.

Forms of Modern Money

Money today consists of four main categories:

1. **Currency.** Governments issue **legal tender** in paper form to be acceptable in payment of all obligations by law.

2. **Coins.** Fractional currency is stamped in metallic form by governments or their central banks. This minting process in the United States is under the authority of the Secretary of the Treasury. The actual metallic value of coins is usually far less than their face value. The difference between the cost of minting and the face value of the coin is called **seigniorage**.

3. **Checks.** Although not considered a form of legal tender, checks are a demand to pay upon a depository, which may be backed by government deposit insurance. A check is not reduced to legal tender until such time as the depositing institution pays the item and allows credit for it.

4. **Electronic Funds.** The current trend is toward fewer checks of the paper variety and more electronic transfers, through the use of debit cards at retail establishments and automatic funds transfer (ATM) transactions. In 1984, a U.S. federal court cleared the way for interstate ATM networks, and by 1995, 90 percent of the value of all transactions in this country was transferred electronically. That includes everything from electronic trading of soy bean futures to withdrawing cash from an ATM machine in a convenience store miles from the nearest bank.

Today, there are more than 200 forms of currency used in the world. Table 4.1 provides a sample.

TABLE 4.1

Some Representative Currencies of the World		
Afghanistan	*afghani*	**Af**
Venezuela	*bolivar*	**B**
Nicaragua	*cordoba*	**C$**
Germany	*deutsche mark*	**DM**
United States	*dollar*	**$**
Greece	*drachma*	**D**
Portugal	*escudo*	**$**
France	*franc*	**F**
Peru	*sol*	**S**
Malawi	*kwacha*	**K**
Italy	*lira*	**L**
Mozambique	*metical*	**Mt**
Bhutan	*ngultrum*	**Nu**
Mexico	*peso*	**$**
United Kingdom	*pound*	**£**
Guatemala	*quetzal*	**Q**
Russia	*ruble*	**R**
Israel	*shekel*	**IS**
Bangladesh	*taka*	**Tk**
South Korea	*won*	**W**
Japan	*yen*	**¥**
Zaire	*zaire*	**Z**

▦ U.S. MONETARY POLICY AND THE FEDERAL RESERVE SYSTEM

The traditional, long-term goals of U.S. monetary policy are:

- Growth in productive capacity
- High employment
- Stable prices
- Stable foreign exchange

Attaining and maintaining economic conditions that reflect those goals obviously calls for more than a monetary policy; just saying it won't make it so. Productive and organizational efforts in the private sector are required. But private efforts depend on sound and available financial resources and a business climate unmarred by panic and crisis. The **Federal Reserve System** was created with the precise aim of reducing the risk and severity of financial crises.

Short-Term Goals. Stated goals often yield to special circumstances. A stable exchange value for the dollar may be a long-term goal, but the exchange value of the dollar is sometimes allowed to fall in order to encourage foreign purchases of American goods. This way, progress toward a long-term goal is sacrificed in order to address trade deficits.

History of the Federal Reserve System

As we've seen, the need for a strong, reliable central bank was recognized in Europe as early as the 1600s. Americans, however, with their deep cultural distrust of concentrated power and central authority, were slow to accept a central bank. In the 19th century, certain central banking functions were handled by the partly government-owned First and Second Banks of the United States and by the Treasury Department. However, growing demands for agricultural credit in the latter part of the century often outstripped bank reserves, and repeated cycles of booms and busts led to financial panic. These crises eventually forced recognition of the desperate need for a central bank in the United States.

Founded by Congress in 1913, the **Federal Reserve** is the central bank of the United States. The *Fed*, as it is known, is responsible for ensuring a sound banking industry and a strong economy. But unlike other nations' unitary central banks, the Fed consists of twelve independent regional banks that together process more than a third of the nation's $12 trillion in checks. The Fed's electronic network handles $200 trillion: more than the U.S. gross domestic product. All together, there are over a thousand state-chartered banks in the Federal Reserve System, representing 11 percent of all U.S. insured commercial banks and a quarter of the nation's commercial bank assets.

Structure of the Fed

The **Federal Reserve Board** is composed of seven governors, appointed by the President and confirmed by the Senate. The governors regulate the entire system and set reserve requirements for member banks.

Each of the twelve regional Federal Reserve banks is in turn governed by a nine-member board of directors. The regional banks are largely independent and responsible for monitoring economic conditions in their regions and for setting regional discount rates (subject to approval by the governors).

The governors and directors form the **Federal Open Market Committee (FOMC)**, the body responsible for making monetary policy. Only five of the twelve directors vote (on a revolving basis), although all participate in decision-making. The decisions reached by the FOMC have a significant impact on the availability of money and credit in the U.S. Figure 4.2 illustrates the structure of the Federal Reserve System, the twelve districts and the reserve bank cities.

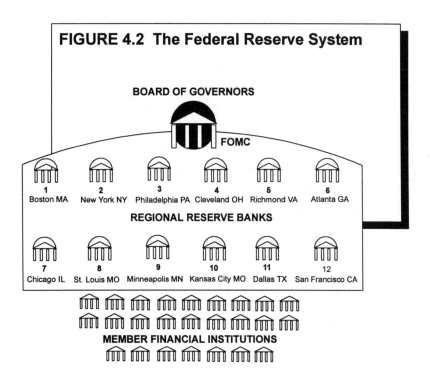

FIGURE 4.2 The Federal Reserve System

Fed's Duties

The Federal Reserve's duties fall into four general areas:

1. **Conducting the nation's monetary policy.** The Fed accomplishes this by influencing the money and credit conditions in the economy. The goal of the policy-making decisions is full employment and stable prices.

2. **Supervising and regulating the banking industry.** The Fed is responsible for ensuring the safety and soundness of the U.S. banking and financial system and for protecting the credit rights of American consumers.

3. **Maintaining the stability of the financial system.** One of the primary reasons the Fed was established in the first place was to contain the risks that arise in financial markets and prevent economic crises.

4. **Providing financial services.** The Fed is a "banker's bank," but its services extend to the U.S. government, the public, and to foreign institutions. The Fed is closely involved in operating the nation's debt payment system.

The Fed also issues U.S. coins and paper money. While the currency is actually manufactured by the Treasury Department's *Bureau of the Mint* (coins) and the *Bureau of Engraving and Printing* (paper), it is the Federal Reserve that distributes the money into circulation through the regional banks and financial institutions. The currency does, in fact, circulate: all U.S. currency eventually returns to the regional banks for inspection. Damaged, worn out or counterfeit money is destroyed; the rest is put back into circulation.

Tools of Monetary Policy

The Fed adjusts the country's money supply by buying and selling securities and by influencing the amount of money banks have available to lend to businesses and consumers.

If the Fed reduces the supply of money, the cost of credit (in the form of interest rates) will rise as a result of the operation of supply and demand. This is a **tight money policy**.

A **loose money policy**, on the other hand, will help stimulate the economy by making credit easier to obtain at lower rates.

These policies can be put into effect through one of three methods:

1. **Reserve Requirements.** All depository institutions are subject to certain requirements regarding the amount of money they must have on reserve. **Reserve funds** cannot be used for lending or investment, but must be held to cover depositors' accounts. By raising the reserve requirement, the Fed forces financial institutions to keep back more of their reserves, limiting the amount of money on hand to loan or invest (a tight money policy). The opposite is also true: a lower reserve requirement frees the institutions to lend or invest more money. Only the Board of Governors may change reserve requirements.

2. **Discount Rate.** The Fed sets the interest rate that institutions must pay to borrow money from it. A higher **discount rate** reduces the amount of money institutions are able to borrow, and so reduces the amount available to them to lend or invest. Because institutions can borrow from other sources, however, this method is not particularly effective in slowing down financial activity. Changes in the discount rate may be made by the regional banks, subject to the approval of the Fed's Board of Governors.

3. **Open Market Operations.** The Fed's buying and selling of government securities, discussed earlier, is referred to as open market operations. Open market operations are undertaken by the FOMC.

▦ THE MONEY SUPPLY

Economists agree that the quantity of money in circulation and the rate at which that quantity changes have a significant effect on the nation's economy. The specific nature of that effect, how it occurs and how it should be measured, however, are the subjects of extensive theorizing and debate.

For instance, the *Chicago School* economists (so-called because its key theorists, such as Milton Friedman, are from the University of Chicago) takes a monetarist position. **Monetarists** believe that money supply is the primary factor in a nation's economy. They pay particular attention to growth rates of money supply.

The monetarist position is that prices change in proportion to changes in money supply. Monetarists see the rate of inflation as closely tied to the rate of increase in money.

While other, nonmonetarist economists accept the influence of the money supply, they are also likely to consider other factors as well.

Measures of Supply

The size of the money supply depends, of course, on how we define what money is. If a person is asked how much money he or she has, the answer does not ordinarily describe the person's total net worth, but the total amount of his or her cash and bank deposits. This commonplace definition of money is also one of the technical definitions of money. Most economists agree that money consists of things that are spendable: that which directly drives and supports a transaction. This is called the **transactions definition of money**. The Fed uses a transactions definition in measuring the nation's monetary supply.

The Fed's transactions-based measure includes four categories. From most **liquid** (convertible into cash) to least liquid, they are:

1. **M1.** M1 is the Federal Reserve's basic measure of money supply in the nation. M1 includes

   — currency
   — coins
   — demand deposits
   — traveler's checks from nonbank issuers
   — other checkable deposits

2. **M2.** M2 includes the M1 items, plus

   — repurchase agreements issued by commercial banks
   — overnight Eurodollars
   — money market mutual funds
   — money market deposit accounts
   — savings accounts
   — time deposits less than $100,000

3. **M3.** M3 includes M2, plus

   — institutionally held money market funds
   — term repurchase agreements
   — term Eurodollars
   — large time deposits

4. **L.** L equals M3, plus

   — Treasury bills
   — commercial papers
   — liquid assets (such as savings bonds)

Money Supply and Banks. Money consists of currency held by the public and checkable deposits. If you cash a check and receive currency, the amount in deposits goes down and the amount in currency goes up but the money supply does not change. The total money supply grows when banks make loans. Banks have been creating this kind of money for several centuries.

This kind of money is called **deposit money**. It can be created in amounts substantially greater than the deposits that support it. This is because banking laws permit banks to maintain reserves that represent only a fraction of deposits.

For instance, If the reserve requirement is 10 percent, then a bank with $1 million in reserves can have deposit liabilities of $10 million. Every new deposit, by adding to the reserves of the bank, permits a multiple of that deposit to be added to deposit liabilities.

A Closer Look . . .

A small bank operates under a 10 percent reserve requirement. This bank has $500 in reserves and $4,700 in outstanding loans. These reserves and loans are the bank's assets. The bank's liabilities consist of $200 in capital and $5,000 in deposits. Under the Fed's regulations, the bank's reserves are 10 percent of its liabilities.

A depositor opens a new account, and deposits $50. The bank adds this $50 to both its assets and its liabilities. Now the bank's reserves are $550 and the deposits are $5,050. But with the additional deposit, the bank now has excess reserves. Reserves are 10.9 percent of deposits ($550÷$5,050), more than the 10 percent required.

Under the 10 percent requirement, $550 in reserves will support $5,500 in deposit liabilities ($550÷10% = $5,500). So deposit liabilities can grow by $450, from the present $5,050 to $5,500. This means the $450 can be offered in new loans.

Circulation of Deposit Money

There are about 35,000 depository institutions in the United States. A bank knows that any money it creates will be used to make payments, and those receiving the payments will almost certainly deposit them in one of those other institutions.

When payment checks return to the original bank, they draw on the bank's reserves. To protect those reserves, a bank is likely to originate loans (create money) equal only to the actual amount of excess reserves. The full amount of new money is created as the process is repeated in a number of banks and thrifts. As each institution receives new deposits, it holds a percentage in reserve, and originates loans equaling the balance of the new deposit.

As each bank receives payments and makes loans, it holds a percentage in reserve and originates loans equaling the balance. In this way, new money is created as the original loan amount is circulated through the banking system. The chart below illustrates how this works, with over $4,000 in new money created by an original loan of $1,000 from Bank A, which is deposited in Bank B, and so on. The example assumes a reserve rate of 10 percent.

BANK	DEPOSIT	RESERVE	NEW LOAN	TOTAL NEW MONEY
A	—	—	$1,000	$1,000
B	$1,000	$100	$ 900	$1,900
C	$ 900	$ 90	$ 800	$2,700
D	$ 810	$ 81	$ 729	$3,439
E	$ 729	$ 73	$ 656	$4,095

▦ INFLATION

Any rapid growth in the money supply is likely to create inflation, unless it is accompanied by a correspondingly rapid increase in goods and services. **Inflation** is a sustained upward movement of prices on a broad scale, affecting all or most goods and services. In short, inflation refers to the upward motion of prices, not to their perceived highness at any particular point.

Inflation has a number of effects on an economy, but not all of them are negative. Inflation means higher prices, which in turn means that consumers have less money to spend. Eroded purchasing power tends to destroy consumer confidence in a country's medium of exchange.

In some developing nations, for instance, skyrocketing inflation rates have rendered the local currency virtually worthless, resulting in thousand-dollar loaves of bread and widespread popular unrest. In Germany between the world wars, inflation was so far out of control that people carried cash with them in baskets and wheelbarrows, only to find that the prices of basic necessities had doubled during the time it took to walk to the store.

Inflation makes lenders wary of fixed rate yields that erode profits over the long term. On the other hand, inflation is used by real estate investors and other borrowers to pay off yesterday's purchase with today's less expensive money.

Causes of Inflation

Demand. When the money supply grows faster than gross domestic product (GDP, discussed in Chapter 3), excess demand pushes up prices. In effect, there are too many dollars chasing too few goods. Easy credit has the same effect on the economy: more money than things to spend it on.

Supply. In modern market economies, government price supports, union contracts and trade quotas may prevent prices from dropping naturally when supply is in excess. In fact, prices may continue to rise.

- **Labor.** When the supply of labor is in excess, such as in periods of high unemployment, the price of labor (manifested in wages) would naturally be expected to fall: it's basic supply and demand. But wages do not necessarily respond naturally to excess labor. Agreements between workers and employers often provide artificial wage protections that shield workers' income from the effects of actual market conditions.

- **Agriculture.** The agricultural industry in the United States has sufficient political influence to obtain and preserve government subsidies and price supports. As a result, an excess supply of agricultural goods is not necessarily reflected in reduced prices in grocery stores. Instead, surplus agricultural products fill warehouses with unused grains and dairy products. Other segments of the agriculture industry, such as tobacco farmers, are protected by artificial government subsidies from declining demand for their product.

- **Quotas.** Domestic producers often seek protection from foreign competition. One form of protection is the quota, which artificially manipulates the market by limiting consumer choice in order to pursue a social policy. Quotas often lead to higher prices.

- **COLAs.** Cost of living adjustments built into wage contracts, pensions and government social programs are designed to protect purchasing power against inflation. Automatically triggered by price rises, however, COLAs encourage prices and income to spiral up together, each driving the other.

Measuring Inflation

Inflation is measured primarily by monitoring changes in wholesale and consumer prices.

In the 20th century, governments have found it increasingly necessary to measure and report on inflation rates. Further, many private contractual arrangements now depend on price indexes, such as the CPI, discussed in Chapter 3.

Indexes are commonly used as a basis for

- early warnings of *business fluctuations* for government policy makers and the business community;

- calculating *price-support programs* and *subsidies;*

- changes in *transfer payments* such as Social Security;

- *wage adjustments* in labor-management contracts; and

- adjustments in *commercial rents*.

▦ IMPACT OF MONETARY POLICY ON REAL ESTATE

Like money itself, real estate is a measure of value. Further, monetary policy and the real estate industry are inextricably linked to one another. One of the key elements in a decision to purchase or sell real estate is the availability of money. Real estate finance and the volatility of the real estate market are influenced by a variety of monetary pressures.

Monetary Policy

As we've seen, when the Fed makes a policy decision to expand or contract the money supply, the move has a definite impact on the availability of lendable funds. The real estate industry is dependent on the availability of credit, and favorable interest rates tend to increase activity in the real estate market. The general results of a shrinkage of available money and credit are higher interest rates and a reduction in home sales. This is a simple case of supply and demand.

Fiscal Policy

The spending and revenue policies of the federal government all play a part in either stimulating or depressing real estate market activity. When the federal government decides to devote greater energies toward increasing home ownership, for instance, through such programs as tax incentives, FHA project financing and rent subsidies, the real estate market benefits. When the federal government's attention shifts to other issues — jobs creation or foreign policy — real estate receives less of the benefit.

State and Local Governments

State and local government attitudes toward such issues as **infrastructure** (transportation and utilities services), toxic waste disposal, regulation of financial institutions and property disclosure laws have a nonfinancial effect on the level of development and resale activity in the real estate market. As the impact of suburban sprawl becomes both more obvious and more unpleasant, many communities are adopting controlled-growth policies. While perhaps improving the quality of life for residents (or at least slowing the decline in quality), such policies diminish supply and create an upward pressure on value of the existing housing stock.

The Next Step

This concludes our general discussion of economic principles and tools. You should have a clearer idea now of how the market economy operates. In the next chapters, we will apply the theory to the real world as we consider more closely the real estate market and the housing industry in the United States.

Chapter 4
REVIEW

- **MONEY** is *any medium of exchange* adopted by a society as a *means of acquiring goods and services*. Money may or may not have any *intrinsic value*: the value it represents is assigned to it by its users.

- In a **BARTER ECONOMY**, goods and services are traded directly for other goods and services. Money developed from barter economies as an *abstraction*: a thing that represented something of value. Over time, money came to be seen as having value *independent* of what it represented, evolving into metal coins, paper money and electronic funds transfers.

- The **FEDERAL RESERVE** is the *central bank of the United States*. It consists of a central board of governors and twelve independent regional banks. Monetary policy is made by the *Federal Open Market Committee*, consisting of the governors and the directors. The Fed is responsible for formulating monetary policy, regulating the banking industry, maintaining financial stability in the U.S. economy and providing financial services to the federal government.

- The Fed *manipulates the money supply* through its **RESERVE REQUIREMENTS** and **DISCOUNT RATE**. **M1** is the Fed's *basic measure of money supply*.

- Inflation is a sustained upward movement of prices on a broad scale. Inflationary pressures may come from many sources.

- The **REAL ESTATE INDUSTRY** and government monetary policy are closely linked: the real estate market is dependent on availability of credit, and favorable interest rate policies tend to increase activity in the real estate market.

Chapter 4
QUIZ

1. Which of the following best describes an economy in which goods or services are traded directly for other goods or services?

   A. Feudalism
   B. Fiduciary
   C. Seigniorage
   D. Barter

2. When did the gold standard stop being the basis for valuing the U.S. dollar?

   A. 1896
   B. 1900
   C. 1973
   D. The dollar is still based on the gold standard.

3. All of the following are one of the four main categories of money, *EXCEPT*:

   A. specie.
   B. currency.
   C. seigniorage.
   D. electronic funds.

4. The central bank of the United States, founded in 1913, is the:

   A. Treasury Department.
   B. First Bank of the United States.
   C. Bureau of the Mint.
   D. Federal Reserve.

5. How many governors serve on the Federal Reserve Board, and how are they selected?

   A. Five; appointed by the Secretary of the Treasury
   B. Seven; appointed by the President
   C. Nine; elected by popular vote
   D. Twelve; elected by the FOMC

6. Interest rates and the cost of credit rise as a result of a(n):

   A. tight money policy.
   B. loose money policy.
   C. open market operation.
   D. transactions-based fiscal policy.

7. The Fed's buying and selling of government securities is referred to as:

   A. the discount rate.
   B. open market operations.
   C. a loose money policy.
   D. transactional economic policy.

8. All of the following are included in M1, *EXCEPT*:

   A. traveler's checks.
   B. currency.
   C. coins.
   D. savings accounts.

9. Money that is "created" by a bank making a loan is referred to as:

   A. deposit money.
   B. reserve funds.
   C. M2.
   D. loan money.

10. All of the following contribute to inflationary price increases, *EXCEPT*:

   A. COLAs built into wage contracts.
   B. price indexes.
   C. agricultural subsidies.
   D. trade quotas.

5   The Real Estate Market

🎯 Objectives:

- Define the term "real property" in economic terms

- Describe the unique characteristics of the real estate market

- Explain the factors that create a dynamic real estate marketplace

---

▦ THE NATURE OF REAL PROPERTY

Real property is distinguished from personal, movable property or *chattels*. The term refers to the **bundle of rights** held by a landowner. Those rights affect the land itself, as well as any improvements, appurtenances or attachments. The bundle of legal rights includes:

- *Possession* of the property

- *Control* (within the framework of the law)

- *Enjoyment* (use of the property in a legal manner)

- *Exclusion* (to keep others from using the property)

- *Disposition* (to sell, will, transfer or otherwise dispose of or encumber the property)

- *Disposition* (to sell, will, transfer or otherwise dispose of or encumber the property)

Land

Because of its fixed location, land possesses unique characteristics not normally identified with other assets. Many of these characteristics contribute to the high cost of real property and the major role it plays in our economic system. In real estate, the term **land** includes the surface and subsurface of a property, as well as the usable air space above it. **Improvements** are anything affixed to the land; **appurtenances** are the rights attached to land ownership,

Durability. Although it may be altered in shape or form, land is virtually indestructible. Similarly, improvements on the land, such as buildings, walls, fences and other structures, are designed to last for many years.

Limited Supply. The amount of land available on this planet is finite (see Figure 5.1). In addition, various local, state and federal government constraints further limit the supply. Practical considerations (such as climate, geology and location) further limit the amount of land available for development.

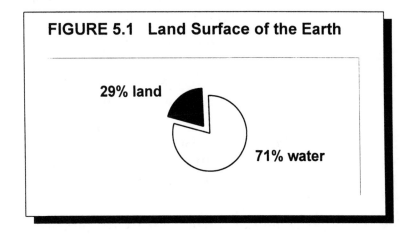

FIGURE 5.1   Land Surface of the Earth

29% land

71% water

Cost Factors. Construction technology has not experienced the revolutionary breakthroughs that occurred in other trades during the 20th century. This relative inefficiency is translated into higher costs to improve land. High improvement costs further translate into a major investment decision for the real property consumer. In turn, that translates into long-term financing to support the purchase.

Heterogeneity. Unlike products of our mechanized society that are produced in a uniform manner, real property has a unique feature: *no two parcels are exactly alike*. Each parcel of real estate is in a different location. Even though two adjacent parcels may contain exactly identical improvements, each location is different in various ways. These include:

- *Topography.* Is the parcel relatively level or is it clinging to the side of a mountain? Topographical features can definitely affect value of a property.

- *Proximity.* Is the parcel isolated or is it linked to other improved parcels in a planned pattern of development? Is it a corner or inner lot? Is it near amenities, such as shopping, recreation and schools?

- *Improvements.* Is there a uniform quality presented by the neighborhood or is it a patchwork pattern of varying quality and size of improvements?

- *Ingress and Egress.* Is the access a poorly maintained and bumpy dirt road or a well-paved street?

- *Annoyances.* Noxious or offensive activities, such as a factory, landfill site or heavy traffic near a residential area will usually have a negative effect on a property's value.

- *Panorama.* The view from a property can impact its value. A 3,500-square foot house overlooking the ocean may be far more valuable in the typical consumer's eye than the same size property with a view of a parking lot.

A Closer Look . . .

Environmental issues have a very real impact on the real estate industry. In 1995, a jury awarded $6.7 million to homeowners whose property values had been lowered because of a nearby tire company's negligent operation and maintenance of a dump site. Nearly 2,000 plaintiffs relied on testimony from economists and real estate appraisers to demonstrate how news stories about the site had lowered the market value of their homes. Nationwide, some landfill operators now offer price guarantees to purchasers of homes near waste disposal sites: a home's value may increase by as much as $6,000 for each mile of its distance from a garbage incinerator. (Environmental issues and their impact on the real estate market are discussed in Chapter 10.)

Emotional Attachment

Home ownership has a subjective worth to the consumer that is difficult to measure on a dollars and cents basis. Although the normal home purchase might not make economic sense as an investment, the satisfying *idea* of home ownership enhances a property's value.

Political Implications

The Preamble to the Code of Ethics of the National Association of REALTORS® begins with these words:

Under all is the land. Upon its wise utilization and widely allocated ownership depend the survival and growth of free institutions and of our civilization . . .

As we will see, land ownership has a wide variety of economic impacts. The proper utilization of land as an economically viable vehicle is overseen by government through the planning process as a safeguard against abuses. The political implications of home ownership cannot be overestimated, and the sense of being a home owner often has a significant impact on economic behavior.

▦ CHARACTERISTICS OF THE REAL ESTATE MARKET

The real estate market is not as organized as the stock market or other financial markets. It is a more local market, with inexperienced sellers and buyers assisted by professional real estate agents.

Components of the Market Place

A **market** is a place where goods can be bought and sold. A market may be a specific location, such as a village square. It may also be a vast, worldwide economic system for moving goods and services around the globe.

The real estate market place has its own unique set of ground rules, technical terms and specialized tasks to address the marketing process.

Complexity. Real estate is not a simple product, and its market place reflects this complexity. There are many types of real property, and an even greater number of financing strategies and valuation requirements. Individual investors have widely different expectations. Tax considerations and unique local conditions also play a significant role.

The complex nature of real estate transactions tends to encourage specialization among its professionals. Some areas of specialization include

- brokerage
- finance
- consulting
- investments
- development
- appraisal
- escrow
- title insurance
- property insurance
- pest control
- home inspections
- law
- property management

Compartmentalization. Within these broad areas of professional expertise, even further specialization is common. For example, a brokerage can specialize in only commercial or industrial properties. An escrow agency may specialize in tax deferred exchanges, or an appraiser may specialize in condemnation work. A lawyer may specialize in residential closings, and a property manager may concentrate on residential projects.

Functions of Components

In order for any economic product or service to be sold, there must be some way to expose it to the marketplace. A wonderful product has little value if no one knows it exists. In the real estate market, each component must perform certain functions to ensure that its products or services are made available to consumers.

Advertise. Potential purchasers and renters need to know that a particular property is available. This requires some form of advertisement in the media most likely to reach the desired consumers.

Inform. Consumers need specific information in order to make an informed decision. In real estate brokerage, a disclosure statement will be provided for the benefit of brokers and consumers. The federal government requires that mortgage consumers be given particular information about the costs involved in a loan.

Appraise. Consumers should be provided with a realistic, impartial estimate of the property's value.

Negotiate. The real estate brokerage community serves as a buffer between seller and buyer in price negotiations. Whichever party they represent, brokers help achieve a mutually acceptable agreement.

Arrange Financing. There must be a way to provide appropriate financing to meet the needs of the parties. Financing is an integral part of marketing real estate because it can make or break a sale.

Lenders screen prospective purchasers for their ability to manage the debt.

Transfer. There must be a reliable way of establishing that all legal and financial requirements have been satisfied. Escrow agents and title insurers work as a protective team in the transfer process, preparing the necessary transfer and loan documentation.

Respond to Consumer Demand. To meet consumers' needs in housing and other types of property, real estate developers and contractors must provide a product that combines utility, attractiveness and affordability. A range of external pressures, from escalating costs and consumer expectations to regulatory requirements and investor pressures, make this an often challenging goal.

Manage Risks. Business decisions must be made not only on the basis of sound economics but also on the basis of which approach to a project creates the least risk of financial loss, physical damage or personal injury. In a society in which lawsuits are common, the risk of litigation arising out of any project is a very real one. A variety of insurance options help deflect risk.

Interface. Real estate brokers need to be aware of all the market functions available. This includes financing plans, property insurance requirements, structural pest control requirements, home inspection procedures, comparable sales in the market, and a variety of factors necessary to market the property effectively.

Other practitioners, such as financial consultants, escrow officers, lenders, property managers, appraisers and title insurers, must apply and coordinate their specialized knowledge at various points in the process.

Market Familiarity. If any of the professionals in the marketplace are unfamiliar with a particular area, they do their customers an injustice by failing to consult with local practitioners. This is especially important in appraisal, where detailed knowledge of the area is critical.

▦ EVOLVING ISSUES

Although real estate ownership continues to be a status desired by a majority of consumers, certain issues have evolved that may affect its future investment potential.

New Laws

Consumer Protection. Consumer concern first manifested itself in Title I of the Consumer Credit Protection Act in 1969 (Truth in Lending — Regulation Z). Since then, a series of laws and court opinions have marched steadily toward increased disclosure to protect real estate consumers, particularly purchasers in the single family residential area (1-4 family dwellings).

Tax Laws. Real property ownership can be stimulated or slowed by federal, state and local tax policies. For instance, in 1997, President Clinton signed an important and wide-ranging new tax relief bill that included significant reforms designed to encourage home ownership through federal tax policy:

- A $500,000 exclusion from capital gains tax for profits on the sale of a principal residence by taxpayers who file jointly. (Single-filers are entitled to a $250,000 exclusion.)

- First-time home buyers may make penalty-free withdrawals of up to $10,000 from their tax-deferred individual retirement fund (IRA).

- The tax rate on capital gains was lowered.

Real estate taxation is one of the primary sources of revenue for local governments. Policies on taxation of real estate can have either positive or negative effects. High taxes may deter investors. On the other hand, tax incentives can attract new businesses and industries. And, of course, along with these enterprises come increased employment and expanded residential real estate markets.

Fair Housing. A commitment to equal credit opportunity has made financing available to many who had routinely been rebuffed in the past. Female heads of households, who are increasing in number, have particularly benefited. Households composed of unmarried adult partners of one or both sexes are also commonplace today. All these changes expand the need for housing.

Americans with Disabilities Act (ADA). The Americans with Disabilities Act has had a significant impact on commercial, nonresidential properties and leasing practices. Any property in which public goods or services are provided must be free of architectural barriers or must accommodate individuals with disabilities so that they can enjoy access to those businesses or services. Disabled tenants of certain residential buildings must be permitted to make reasonable modifications to a property (at their own expense), but a landlord may require that rental premises be restored to their original condition at the end of the lease term.

Ethnic Mix

The U.S. is a nation of immigrants, and that characteristic is rapidly growing today. In California, for instance, one quarter of the population is foreign-born, and a fifth of those residents immigrated to the state during the 1990s. By the turn of the century, half of the population of California will be composed of ethnic minorities. This can be good news for the real estate industry: in 1996, more than 60 percent of California's first-time new home buyers were foreign-born.

The nation's population mix continues to be steadily influenced by migration from Latin America, the Mideast, Europe, and Asia. As immigrant populations continue to be assimilated, one result is a shift in housing needs and expectations.

Architectural Fashions

Residential and commercial architecture and interior and exterior features are influenced by changes in popular taste. For example, sunken living rooms and featureless steel office buildings were once the height of architectural fashion; today, open beamed ceilings,

Jacuzzis and fanciful postmodern building facades are much more attractive to consumers. A property that is considered out-of-date or old-fashioned cannot command the same price as one that reflects the latest design.

The Next Step

This chapter has explored real property as a basic commodity, together with those forces that have a tendency to affect its value. Chapter 6 will explore the interaction of these forces in the real estate market generally.

Chapter 5
REVIEW

- **REAL PROPERTY** refers to the *bundle of legal rights held by a landowner*. The **BUNDLE OF LEGAL RIGHTS** includes *possession, control, enjoyment, exclusion, disposition*.

- **LAND** is *the property's surface, subsurface* and *usable air space*. **IMPROVEMENTS** are *anything affixed to the land*. **APPURTENANCES** are the *rights attached to land ownership*. Although it may be altered in shape or form, land is *virtually indestructible*.

- The amount of land available on this planet is *finite*. In addition, various local, state and federal government constraints further limit the supply. Practical considerations (such as climate, geology and location) further diminish the amount of land available for development.

- Unlike products of our mechanized society that are produced in a uniform manner, real property has a unique feature: *no two parcels are exactly alike*.

- **HOME OWNERSHIP** has a *subjective worth* to the consumer that is difficult to measure on a dollars and cents basis.

- A **MARKET** is a place where goods can be bought and sold. The function of a market place is to provide a setting in which supply and demand can interact. The **REAL ESTATE MARKET** is a *local market*, with inexperienced sellers and buyers.

- Real estate is not a simple product, and its market place reflects this complexity. Because of its *complexity*, real estate tends to encourage **SPECIALIZATION**.

▬ In the real estate market, each **COMPONENT** must perform *certain functions* to ensure that its products or services are made available to consumers. These include *advertising, informing, appraising, negotiating, financing, transferring, responding, managing risk* and *interfacing*.

▬ Although real estate ownership continues to be a resource desired by a majority of consumers, certain **ISSUES** have evolved that may *affect its future investment potential*. These include *new laws* (consumer protection, equal housing, ADA and tax reforms) and *changing ethnic mixes*.

**Chapter 5
QUIZ**

1. All of the following are included in a real property owner's bundle of legal rights, *EXCEPT*:

   A. possession.
   B. exclusion.
   C. proximity.
   D. disposition.

2. Which of the following is the closest approximate ratio of land surface to water on the earth?

   A. ½ : ½
   B. ⅓ : ⅔
   C. ⅔ : ⅓
   D. ¼ : ¾

3. The term *heterogeneity*, when applied to real property, refers to which of the following?

   A. Land is an interchangeable commodity.
   B. Parcels are inextricably linked to one another.
   C. No two parcels are exactly alike.
   D. Adjacent parcels are usually identical.

4. Which of the following correctly describes the real estate market?

    A. Approximately as organized as the stock market and other financial markets
    B. Involved with a simple, homogeneous product
    C. Populated by generalists rather than specialists
    D. A local market with inexperienced buyers and sellers

5. Providing consumers with a realistic, impartial estimate of the value of a specific property is a function of which component of the real estate market?

    A. Negotiation
    B. Appraisal
    C. Advertisement
    D. Risk management

6. How are single, first-time home buyers encouraged to enter the housing market by recent tax law changes?

    A. They may deduct up to $10,000 from their income taxes for the year in which they purchase a home.
    B. They are entitled to a $250,000 exclusion from their income taxes.
    C. They may withdraw up to $500,000 from their tax-deferred IRA without penalty.
    D. They may make a penalty-free withdrawal of up to $10,000 from their tax-deferred IRA for the purchase of a home.

7. By the year 2000, what percentage of California's population will be composed of various ethnic minorities?

   A. 20
   B. 50
   C. 65
   D. 80

8. All of the following are true regarding the effect of taxes on the real estate market, *EXCEPT*:

   A. high tax rates are likely to attract investors.
   B. tax incentives may attract new business.
   C. real estate taxation is a primary source of local government revenue.
   D. low tax rates are likely to encourage development.

9. What has been the major effect of fair housing laws on the real estate market?

   A. Fair housing laws have brought a once-vibrant market to a virtual standstill.
   B. Fair housing laws apply only to multifamily properties, and so have had no effect on the single-family residential housing market.
   C. Fair housing laws have made financing available to many who had been rebuffed in the past, expanding the pool of potential home owners.
   D. Fines for violations of fair housing laws are a primary source of revenue for local governments.

10. A residential property that was very fashionable in 1972 is no longer considered very attractive. However, it is in very good shape physically. Based on these facts, which of the following statements is true?

   A.   Whether or not the property is architecturally fashionable does not affect its value.
   B.   The property is likely to command a higher price in the real estate market.
   C.   The property is likely to command a lower price in the real estate market.
   D.   The property will probably be unsellable if it is considered dated or old-fashioned.

6   The U.S. Housing Market

 Objectives:

- Understand the role of residential housing in the U.S. economy and the effect of local business and financial conditions on the market

- Define the various types of housing available

- Explain the characteristics of the housing market and the demographics of U.S. home ownership

---

▦ RESIDENTIAL CONSTRUCTION

Housing is a major factor in the U.S. economy. The housing industry accounts for about 27 percent of investment spending and 5 percent of overall economic activity in the U.S., or more than $250 billion a year.

According to the National Association of Home Builders, housing stock in the United States is worth more than $9 trillion. Since the early 1970s, more than 25 million new residential units, including both owned and rented housing, have been constructed.

Once built, housing accounts for a $100 billion market in maintenance, rehabs and renovation. It's a big market, too: in 1996, the national home ownership rate was over 65 percent.

Housing is not only a big market, it's vitally important. The federal government tells us that over 50 percent of the typical home-owning family's wealth is comprised of equity in their home: the biggest source of an American family's net worth.

For economists, construction spending is an important clue to the nation's overall economic health. In 1994, for example, the value of new housing construction put in place accounted for nearly 8 percent of the total U.S. gross domestic product (GDP) for that year.

Figure 6.1 illustrates the number of existing homes in the United States, compared by value.

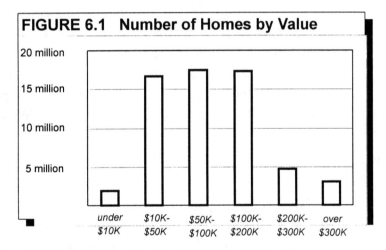

FIGURE 6.1   Number of Homes by Value

SOURCE: U.S. Census Bureau, 1993 American Housing Survey

Expenditures on Maintenance and Alteration

Annual spending on housing upkeep and alterations runs into billions of dollars. Because such spending provides jobs for people in many trades and industries, it has meaningful repercussions across the economy.

Evolution of U.S. Housing

Until the early 1800s, most quality residential construction in the United States relied on heavy posts and horizontal timbers, held together with mortise and joints. Those who did the work were craftsmen: skilled with the hand tools of the carpenter's trade. Around 1830, however, the invention of the balloon frame revolutionized the industry.

The **balloon frame** is a house built on a shell of light lumber, held together with nails. Heavy posts are not needed. The sheathing on the frame, like the skin of an airplane wing, provides strength. The term "balloon frame" derives from the fact that such light frame homes seemed to be constructed overnight: inflated like balloons.

The balloon frame spelled the beginning of the end for the highly trained construction craftsmen needed. Costs of balloon frame construction were estimated in 1865 to be less than half that of traditional building, due to the cheapness of materials and the reduced need for skilled workers. These lower costs greatly encouraged housing development in the Midwestern and Western states.

The Contractor System

Home construction in the later years of the 19th century involved specialized trades, often supervised by a carpenter. The demands of organizing and supervising a growing legion of specialists gave rise to the **contractor system**, under which a single supervisor took over responsibility for overseeing the building project. The specialists hired by the contractor are referred to as subcontractors.

Among the earliest subcontracting trades were painters, bricklayers, glaziers, stonemasons and plasterers. By the 1880s, hot water and hot-air heating systems were available. By the end of the century, public health authorities were requiring sewer connections, so plumbers were added to the building trades.

Becoming a contractor in the 19th century was not difficult. A carpenter could buy an estimator's manual and submit a bid. Staying in business, however, was another matter. Because it was so easy to break into the business, a highly competitive environment developed. Contractors were always looking for ways to cut costs and keep bids low. They experimented with new materials and labor-saving methods but often encountered resistance. The experimentation resulted in the refinement of existing materials, tools and techniques, and in the development of new technologies.

For instance, concrete rode a brief wave of popularity as the miracle material of the 1890s and early 1900s. Concrete was a favorite construction material of the visionary architect Frank Lloyd Wright. In some of his most famous buildings (such as Unity Temple in Illinois and the Falling Water residence in Pennsylvania) Wright developed a technique of building a wooden mold and casting an entire reinforced concrete structure in a single pour.

By World War I, a good contractor could build a house in one day, to the chagrin of the building-trades unions, whose members perceived threats to jobs and warned of diminished quality in housing as a possible consequence. The building trades grew increasingly organized to resist efficient new materials and technologies that threatened their livelihood. The general public, too, was wary of the more innovative construction techniques.

Nonetheless, housing construction materials, techniques and technologies have continued to evolve. Greater efficiency has resulted in quicker construction, and many new materials are far sturdier and longer-lasting than traditional ones.

Architectural Styles

Through successive styles, America's history can be traced in its housing stock. Historic styles are important in today's market because they go in and out of fashion, affecting demand and prices for a given type of house. Table 6.1 compares the characteristics of some popular housing styles.

TABLE 6.1

Popular American Architectural Styles

NAME	ORIGINAL PERIOD	KEY CHARACTERISTICS
Greek Revival	1820-1860	columns, flat roof
Octagon	1850-1860	octagonal floor plan
Italianate	1860-1890	tall, narrow, arched windows
Stick	1880s	square bays, ornamental boards
Queen Anne	1880-1900	ornate, asymmetrical, "Victorian"
Craftsman	1890-1920	exposed structural timbers
Mission Style	1890-1920	stucco walls, tile roof, arcade
Colonial Revival	1895-1910	boxy style, classical detailing
Prairie School	1900-1920	low horizonal, geometric style
Bungalow	1900-1940	small, one-story, narrow lot
Art Deco	1920-1930s	curvilinear, streamlined form
California Ranch	1950-1960s	one-story, indoor-outdoor flow
Split Level	1940s-present	floors at different levels

Today, new housing is constructed using a wide variety of styles and combinations of styles to suit the taste of individual buyers and local markets.

Housing Definitions

Like real estate, the housing industry uses some specifically defined terms. It's important to understand this professional "jargon" in order to fully engage in a discussion about the residential housing market.

Housing Unit. A **housing unit** is a general term for any place where people live. Housing units have a number of general characteristics:

- An *enclosed physical space* or structure with a *full range of living facilities*, within which an individual, group or family may live privately, separated from those in other units.

- A *single detached house*, an *apartment within or attached to a house*, a house *sharing a wall* with another house, an *apartment in a multiunit building* or *manufactured housing*. It may be one room or many rooms.

- *Rented*, *owned outright* or held in some form of *common ownership* such as a condominium, co-op or group home.

The Census Bureau defines *housing unit* as a house, an apartment, a group of rooms or a single room *occupied or intended for occupancy as separate living quarters*. "Separate living quarters" are those in which the occupants do not live and eat with other persons in the structure and that have direct access from the outside of the building or through a common hall.

Under this definition, some types of living space are specifically excluded: for instance, dormitories, bunkhouses and barracks; quarters in transient hotels and motels (except for residential hotels); quarters in institutions, general hospitals and military installations (except those occupied by staff members or resident employees who have separate living arrangements).

Single Family. Any structure used as a dwelling unit for occupancy by *one family*; a private home. A **single-family home** may be detached (free-standing) or attached (such as a townhouse).

Multi-Unit Buildings, Two- to Four-Units. For purposes of housing statistics, multi-family residential buildings are distinguished on the basis of number of units. Small multi-unit buildings include duplexes, triplexes, fourplexes, small apartment buildings and rented rooms in single-family houses.

Multi-Unit Buildings, Five or More Units. Larger multi-unit buildings include apartment towers and complexes. Individual units in multi-unit buildings may be rented (apartment buildings) or owned (as in condominiums and cooperatives).

U.S. Home Ownership

Over the past fifty years, home ownership in the U.S. has grown steadily (see Figure 6.2). So, too, has the number of available housing units (see Figure 6.3). At the same time, the *types* of homes in which Americans live have undergone significant changes.

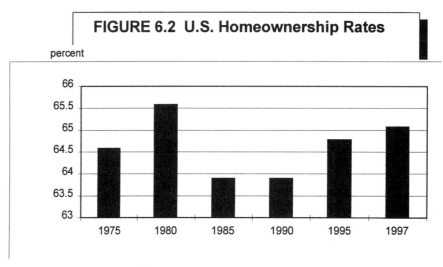

FIGURE 6.2 U.S. Homeownership Rates

SOURCE: U.S. Census Bureau, 1997

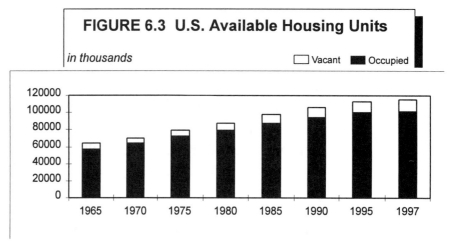

FIGURE 6.3 U.S. Available Housing Units

SOURCE: U.S. Census Bureau, 1997

According to the U.S. Census Bureau, single-family detached houses (the "American dream" home) made up more than 60 percent of the total U.S. housing inventory in 1960. Since then, this type of housing has steadily declined in popularity, and the number of multiple-unit residences has increased. In 1940, townhouse-type homes made up over 7 percent of the housing stock. By 1990, they accounted for only 5 percent. On the other hand, apartment buildings with 5 or more units have become more popular over time: they accounted for about 10 percent of the housing inventory in 1940, but for nearly 20 percent today.

The most dramatic change in Americans' housing preferences, however, has been in the popularity of mobile homes. In 1940, manufactured housing was included in the Census Bureau's "Other" category, along with boats, tents and tourist cabins. By 1990, manufactured housing accounted for over 7 percent of the housing stock.

Geographically, the north and east have seen a growth in single-family housing stock, while fast-growing southern and western regions are increasingly dominated by multi-family dwellings.

Unit Size

Statistics on unit size can be compiled for both the total housing stock and for trends in new construction. Two different measures are *number of rooms* and *square footage*.

Rooms per Dwelling. In 1960, the median number of rooms in an American dwelling was 4.9. In 1980, that had risen to 5.1, and by 1993 the average was 5.5 rooms (see Figure 6.4).

The Census Bureau counts whole rooms (such as living rooms, dining rooms, bedrooms and kitchens). A partially divided room, such as a living/dining room or dining "L" is counted as a separate room only if there is a partition from floor to ceiling.

The room count does not include bathrooms, halls, foyers or closets, alcoves, pantries, laundry or furnace rooms. Unfinished attics or

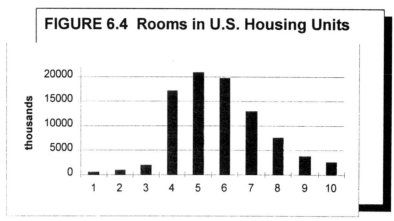

SOURCE: U.S. Census Bureau, 1993 American Housing Survey

basements, open porches, storage space, manufactured housing or trailers used only as bedrooms, and offices used only by persons not living in the unit are not counted as "rooms."

Number of Bedrooms. The Census Bureau counts bedrooms as rooms used mainly for sleeping, even if they are used for other purposes. A living room with a sofabed is not counted as a bedroom. For instance, a one-room apartment would be counted as having no bedroom (see Figure 6.5).

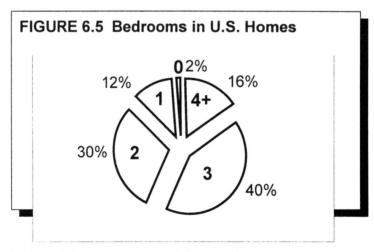

SOURCE: U.S. Census Bureau, 1993 American Housing Survey

Modes of Construction

Most of the U.S. housing stock is still built using traditional methods, many of which are more than a century old. However, various methods of prefabrication are becoming more common.

On-Site Construction. Traditional construction, built by contractors, is produced on-site from the foundation up, without significant use of factory-made modular or panelized elements. This is labor-intensive construction.

Industrialized Housing. This is housing that is factory-made or prefabricated to some degree.

- **Modular Construction.** Sections of a house — whole rooms or groups of rooms — are built in a "factory," then brought to a site and quickly assembled on a permanent foundation. Finishing work may require a month. When completed they are indistinguishable from on-site construction.

- **Panelized Construction.** Two-dimensional parts of the house (interior and exterior walls and floor panels) are factory-produced and assembled on the site, as in modular construction.

- **Manufactured Homes.** A special category of factory-built housing (commonly called "mobile homes," although the term was dropped from use by the federal government in 1980) are factory-built on a steel I-beam chassis, transported to a site and placed on a foundation that includes hook-ups for plumbing and electricity. The I-beam chassis remains a part of the structure.

  - **Regulations.** Manufactured homes must meet federal construction and safety standards, administered through HUD.

— **Real property or personal property?** Before 1980, manufactured homes were usually considered personal property: they were, after all, movable. In 1980, federal law mandated that any manufactured home affixed to a permanent foundation on privately owned land becomes real property, and can be taxed and financed as real estate.

— **Zoning.** Community acceptance of manufactured homes has been growing, as measured by changes in state law, local ordinances and public attitude.

A Closer Look . . .

In 1981 the California legislature added section 65913 to the Government Code, preventing any city from categorically prohibiting the installation of manufactured housing on lots zoned for single-family dwellings:

In no case may a city . . . apply any development standards which will have the effect of totally precluding mobile homes from being installed as permanent residences.

▦ WHO OWNS AMERICA'S HOUSING STOCK?

After a dramatic rise between 1940 and 1960, the proportion of housing units occupied by owners has been more or less on a plateau. Figure 6.6 illustrates the changing percentage of the U.S. housing stock that is owner-occupied.

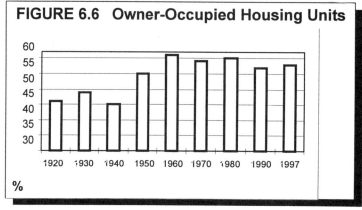

FIGURE 6.6 Owner-Occupied Housing Units

SOURCE: U.S. Census Bureau, 1997

Figure 6.7 shows how the rate of home ownership has changed in the four major U.S. geographic regions.

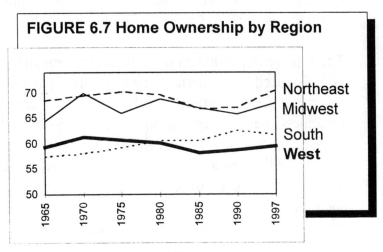

FIGURE 6.7 Home Ownership by Region

SOURCE: U.S. Census Bureau, 1997

Not surprisingly, in view of the financial means required, age is strongly correlated with home ownership. Older individuals, who were in their first home-buying phase before prices skyrocketed in the 1970s, are most likely to own their homes today (see Figure 6.8).

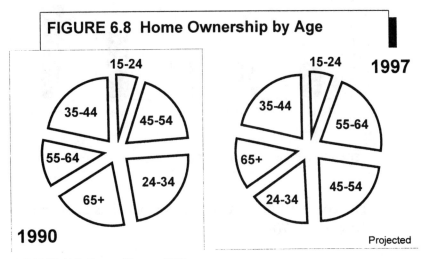

FIGURE 6.8 Home Ownership by Age

SOURCE: U.S. Census Bureau, 1996

Households

A *housing unit* is a physical structure. A **household**, on the other hand, is a social unit. It consists of all the people who live together in a housing unit, and helps define the character of the local market.

The relationship between household characteristics and housing units is influenced by marriage and divorce patterns, attitudes about independence for young adults and the elderly, costs of living separately, business conditions, available affordable housing and, of course, income levels. As lifestyles change in the United States, "traditional" patterns of two-parent, single-family, one-earner households have evolved accordingly. This process is not just of sociological interest, however: it has a real affect on the housing market, in such areas as housing needs and design.

Figure 6.9 illustrates the different average sizes of households in the four major geographic regions of the U.S., plus California.

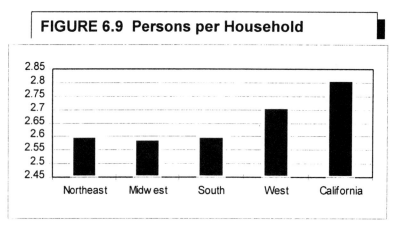

FIGURE 6.9 **Persons per Household**

SOURCE: U.S. Census Bureau, 1997

The composition of U.S. households has changed significantly since the early 1970s.

For instance, the share of households represented by families fell from about 81 percent in 1970 to 74 percent in 1980. In 1994, the number of family households reached 71 percent, or 68.5 million family households. Families have traditionally accounted for a majority of all U.S. households, but their share of the total is now significantly lower than in the past.

What is meant by **family households**? The U.S. Census Bureau defines the term as including

- *married-couple families* (approximately 53.2 million);

- families with a *female householder*, no husband present (approximately 12.4 million); and

- families with a *male householder*, no wife present (roughly 2.9 million).

A **householder** is the *designated head of household*, in whose name the home is owned or rented.

Obviously, families do not necessarily include children. Less than half of American households currently include one or more children under the age of 18. The last year in which most U.S. families included at least one child living at home was 1982.

The number of nonfamily households in the U.S. has more than doubled since 1970, from 11.9 million to nearly 30 million today. Over a third of all U.S. households are considered "nonfamily." Most of these (about 85 percent) are one-person households.

As the number of nonfamily households has grown, the number of large households has dramatically decreased. In 1970, 21 percent of U.S. households consisted of five or more persons. Today, such households account for less than 10 percent of the total. On the other hand, small households (consisting of only one or two people) have grown from under half in 1970 to almost two thirds today.

▦ CHARACTERISTICS OF THE MARKET

Certain general principles apply to the housing market and set it apart from markets for other commodities. They derive from the fact that buildings are fixed in place, durable and varied.

Housing: A Unique Product

Housing is unlike other market commodities because *every unit is unique*. The uniqueness of housing results from a variety of factors, all of which boil down to: location, location, location.

Value in Context. The value of a product such as real estate is determined only partly by its intrinsic qualities. The setting of the product is part of its value. This is a case where externalities (benefits and disabilities arising from the acts and omissions of neighbors) directly impact value. Whether these are positive or negative, the effect cannot be escaped, since a house is fixed in place. One can remove a diamond from an ugly setting, but a house is stubbornly attached to its foundation, rooted to the ground. A fine, lovingly maintained house in a decaying neighborhood may lose value (a situation referred to as regression), while a more modest house in a desirable location appreciates in value (progression).

Further, remember that housing markets are intensely local. Although local communities are influenced by national and regional circumstances, each has its own geographic setting and environment, its own demographics, its own economic structure and markets, its own policies on development — all with implications for local housing demand and supply. A community's power to draw and hold population is influenced by a number of factors.

- **Business Climate.** The fortunes of the local business community and its sustained capacity to offer jobs and good incomes, is often dependent on the degree to which the economic base is diversified.

- **Infrastructure.** The general quality of roads, utilities and transportation.

- **Amenities.** Cultural, social, environmental and recreational attractions.

- **Public Sector.** The existence in or near the community of public-supported institutions or facilities that offer employment and purchase local goods and services, such as a state university, veterans' hospital, military base or prison.

- **Specialized Services.** Industries and businesses that attract outside dollars: one city may be renowned for its hospitals and medical specialists, while another location may be synonymous with high-tech industries or aircraft manufacturing.

- **Neighborhoods.** The local nature of the housing market applies not only to the community as a whole but to its parts. Within the boundaries of a community are many submarkets, each with its own different populations and income levels. The reputation of particular neighborhoods or streets, scenic qualities, proximity to industry or airport noise and a host of other factors will affect the value and desirability of housing.

Subjectivity

No two houses are alike in every way (design, features, location and condition). Nor are any two buyers ever exactly the same. The match between house and buyer, and therefore the value of the product, will always include a large measure of subjectivity.

This does not mean that demand for housing with certain facilities, within a certain price range, cannot be estimated. Developers and investors in income properties make such estimates all the time. But a rich profusion of house and apartment types will usually be needed in the supply mix that satisfies demand.

Recent History
of House Prices

Since 1965, new house prices in the U.S. have trended steadily upward, outrunning inflation and representing one of the soundest investments an individual can make (see Figure 6.10).

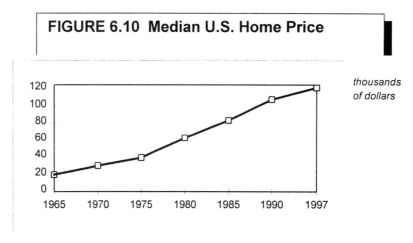

FIGURE 6.10 Median U.S. Home Price

SOURCE: U.S. Census Bureau, 1997

But behind the broad national picture of house prices are important regional differences in sale prices, illustrated in Figure 6.11.

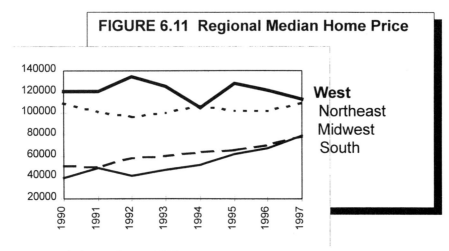

FIGURE 6.11 Regional Median Home Price

SOURCE: U.S. Census Bureau, 1997

By comparison, the median price of a single-family home in California in 1997 was about $178,000. The median price in the Los Angeles area was $170,700; in the Bay Area, $276,000; and in Northern California, the median price was $131,850. Again, these figures demonstrate that the housing market is intensely regional and microcosmic. While it might be useful to know that the median price for a single-family home in the U.S. was $88,250 in 1997, the really significant number is the most local one.

Housing Starts

Housing starts are a measurement of the number of new residential construction projects begun in the United States during a given period, typically in the form of monthly, quarterly or annual reports.

Economists look to these housing starts to catch any trends developing in the housing industry. The housing starts figures published by the federal government include units

- being built *for rent*;

- built *by a contractor* on an owner's land;

- built *by an owner* acting as his or her own contractor; and

- being built for *condominium or co-op development*.

Housing starts are an extremely important leading indicator, and are watched closely by government and private economists. Figures are usually derived from local building permits. Almost all permits lead to a construction start, usually within 30 to 60 days, with an average project completion time of 6.5 months. Figure 6.12 shows the monthly fluctuations in housing starts during a single year.

Housing Start Cycle. The *business cycle* (discussed in Chapter 3) is reflected in and influenced by the ups and downs of housing starts. The **housing starts cycle** leads the business cycle, on average, by about 13 months.

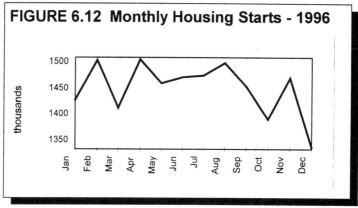

SOURCE: U.S. Census Bureau, 1997

The housing starts cycle for each type of building (single-family, townhouse, condominium, large apartment building) has its own average course, depending on differences in demand. But the curves usually show a similar direction and go up or down at roughly the same times.

Local Business Conditions

The real estate market is driven by the business climate in which it exists. As discussed in Chapter 5, the key to economic health in an urban setting is the area's economic base. There are several components of this base.

Population Growth. People are attracted by an eclectic variety of factors, among them the availability of jobs, climate, local attractions for recreation and amusement, cultural needs and educational opportunities.

Real Estate Development. Real estate development goes hand in hand with population growth. Without continuous population growth, housing development would be limited to simply replacing existing stock or even reducing overall housing stock. Another limiting factor is affordability, which has caused a reduction in development of detached housing and a surge in the development of condominiums, apartment buildings and attached residences such as townhouses.

Employment Opportunities. Employment is spurred by a variety of factors and is an indicator of the stability of the economic base. If the local economy is strongly dependent upon one component, as in a "company town," this is an extremely fragile foundation and likely to lead to large swings in employment levels, retail sales and demand for housing. Diversity in the economic base is desirable.

Diversity is the key to a strong local economy. If the economy is rooted in one industry, such as lumber in Oregon or automobiles in Detroit, it is extremely vulnerable to an overall economic downturn. If, on the other hand, there is a wide base of diversity within the industrial sector, prospects for weathering an adverse economic climate appear brighter.

Retail Sales. Retail sales are closely tied to population demographics (that is, the age, ethnicity, income, education and other factors that define a social group) and employment patterns. If the local plant that employs 2,000 people lays off 500, retail activity is affected geometrically, not just arithmetically. In other words, for every basic industry job in town, there is a corresponding number, whether on a one to one basis or even more, of service and retail jobs that support and are supported by it. The basic industry may be a factory, banking, trucking, farming, or even an educational institution. Whatever it is, the loss of basic jobs has a ripple effect, reducing demand for gyms and suntan parlors, barber and beauty shops, TV and appliance repair, shoe stores and computer stores — all the myriad goods and services that the base-industry employees consumed in their daily activities.

Interest Rates

Few people contemplating the purchase of a house can afford to buy outright. Such major purchases almost always require a loan. Buyer decisions to purchase and lender decisions to loan are both based primarily on the buyer's estimated ability to handle monthly payments, and interest rates have strong effects on monthly payments. During the early 1980s, house sales dropped off markedly when interest rates were high. The housing industry picked up again, however, when rates went down again. Figure 6.19 illustrates how interest rates for fixed, conventional first mortgages have risen and fallen over the years.

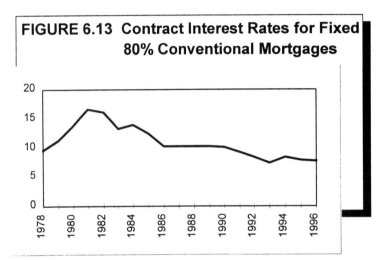

FIGURE 6.13 Contract Interest Rates for Fixed 80% Conventional Mortgages

SOURCE: Freddie Mac Lender Survey, 1997

The Next Step

This concludes our general statistical overview of the U.S. real estate economy. As we've said repeatedly, the real estate market is a local market. In the next chapters, we will focus specifically on the state of California: its economic structure and strength in general and its real estate market in particular.

Chapter 6
REVIEW

- **HOUSING** is a major factor in the U.S. economy, accounting for nearly 5 percent of the nation's overall economic activity. The U.S. home ownership rate is over 65 percent, and more than 50 percent of most home owners' total wealth is made up of equity in their homes.

- Residential construction has evolved over the years, both technologically and stylistically. Greater efficiency has resulted in quicker construction, and many new materials are far sturdier than their traditional counterparts. More cost-efficient home-building methods have made home ownership a possibility for more people.

- A **HOUSING UNIT** is an *enclosed space intended for occupancy as separate living quarters*, with a *full range of living facilities* in which an individual, group or family may live privately, *separated from others.*

- There are a variety of **CONSTRUCTION METHODS** available. The two basic forms are *on-site* (traditional) and *industrialized*, which includes modular, panelized and manufactured homes.

- A **HOUSEHOLD** is a *social unit*. It consists of *all the people who live together in a housing unit*. A **HOUSEHOLDER** is the *designated head of household*, in whose name the home is owned or rented.

- The **HOUSING MARKET** is unlike other market commodities because every unit is *unique*.

- Since 1965, the **PRICE** of a new home has *trended steadily upward*, ahead of inflation and representing one of the soundest investments an individual can make.

▪ **HOUSING STARTS** are a measurement of *the number of new residential construction projects begun in the U.S. during a given period.* The housing starts cycle generally leads the business cycle by slightly more than a year.

▪ Among the factors that drive the real estate market are **LOCAL BUSINESS CONDITIONS** and **MORTGAGE INTEREST RATES**.

Chapter 6
QUIZ

1. The housing industry accounts for approximately what percentage of overall economic activity in the United States?

    A.   3 percent
    B.   5 percent
    C.   7 percent
    D.   9 percent

2. The greatest number of existing homes in the United States are in which of the following price ranges?

    A.   Under $10,000
    B. $50,000 to $100,000
    C. $200,000 to $300,000
    D.   Over $300,000

3. Which type of residential construction earned its name based on the speed with which houses were constructed?

    A.   Modular
    B.   Overnight
    C.   Balloon
    D.   Stick

4. Which architectural style is characterized by ornate, asymmetrical detailing?

   A. Octagon
   B. Bungalow
   C. Italianate
   D. Queen Anne

5. All of the following would be included in the Census Bureau's definition of housing unit, *EXCEPT*:

   A. a rented home.
   B. manufactured housing.
   C. an efficiency apartment.
   D. a motel room.

6. Since 1960, which type of housing has increased in popularity, according to the U.S. Census Bureau?

   A. Large apartment buildings
   B. Single-family detached houses
   C. Townhouses
   D. Tourist cabins

7. Mr. and Mrs. Hopper's house has three bedrooms, a kitchen, two bathrooms, a den, a large foyer and a combination living/dining room. There is a sofabed in the den. The house also includes a separate laundry room and a large pantry off the kitchen. According to the Census Bureau's methodology and based on these facts, how many rooms are in the Hoppers' house?

   A. Five
   B. Six
   C. Nine
   D. Eleven

8. The construction method in which two-dimensional pieces of a house's interior and exterior walls and floors are factory-produced and then assembled at the building site is referred to as:

    A. panelized construction.
    B. modular construction.
    C. balloon construction.
    D. traditional construction.

9. *L*, *M* and *N* live together in an apartment. *L* and *M* are married. *L* signed the lease for the apartment, but only *M* is employed, so *M* pays the rent. *N* owns the apartment building. In this situation, who is the householder?

    A. *L* only
    B. *M* only
    C. *N* only
    D. *L* and *M* together

10. Housing is unlike other market commodities for one basic reason: because

    A. housing must usually be purchased with borrowed money.
    B. every unit is unique.
    C. there is such a variety of styles and materials available to consumers.
    D. regulations control its quality.

7 California's Economic Profile

 Objectives:

- Understand how California's diverse climates, populations and geography contribute to the state's economic condition

- Explain the importance of micro-economies to the overall economic health of the state

- Compare how California's various regions have different economic histories, conditions and expectations

---

▦ AT HOME IN CALIFORNIA

Each state has its own economy. Over the years, the people, organizations and political leadership build on the state's natural and human resources and create a culture. They develop a distinctive transportation, communication and educational infrastructure and create their own business, legal and social climate. A state builds its own agricultural, labor and trade policies and, to a significant degree, its own opportunities. The results can be impressive, as the following survey of the California economy demonstrates.

California's Diversity

Geographically, California's land area — nearly 160,000 square miles — makes it the third largest state in the country. Its thousand miles of Pacific coastline runs from the sandy Mediterranean-style beaches of the south to the rocky, fog-shrouded redwood forests of the northern part of the state. California has the highest peak in the continental U.S., Mount Whitney in the Sierra Nevada mountains, and the lowest point in North America, Death Valley. There are glaciers and deserts and 6 million acres of fertile cropland in the Central Valley where farms and orchards grow more than 250 different types of crops.

California has the largest population in the United States. Its 32 million people account for over 12 percent of the nation's total population. The state produces about 12.5 percent of the total U.S. GDP and is the port for 40 percent of all U.S. trade with Asia. Some $3 billion in imports and exports cross its coastline annually.

More than 960,000 businesses call California home. Its industries are at the forefront of the electronics revolution, and California is a leading producer of computers, memory chips, semiconductors, communications and automation. The defense industry, medical research, tourism (a $53 billion industry alone) and entertainment are vital components of the widely diversified California economy.

Demographics

There are 32 million people living in California. That number represents not only the greatest number of people in any state but a 20 percent increase over the past ten years.

California has one of the most ethnically diverse populations in the world. By the year 2000, ethnic minorities may make up more than half of the state's total population. Figures 7.1 through 7.3 illustrate the international nature of California's population.

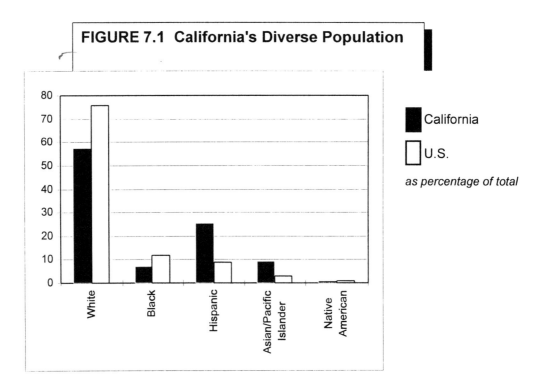

FIGURE 7.1 California's Diverse Population

California

U.S.

as percentage of total

SOURCE: California Trade & Commerce Agency, 1997 (based on 1990 U.S. Census data)

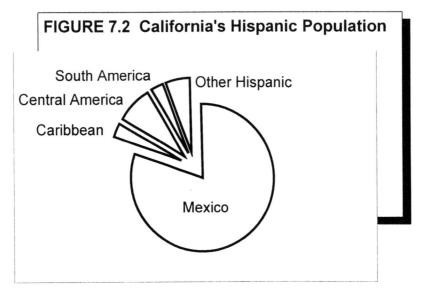

FIGURE 7.2 California's Hispanic Population

SOURCE: California Trade & Commerce Agency, 1997 (based on 1990 U.S. Census data)

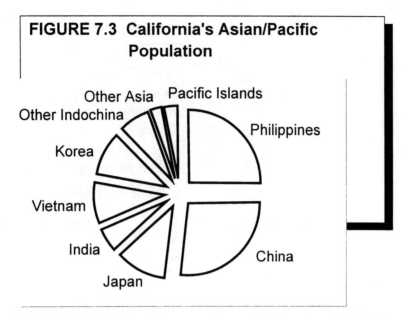

FIGURE 7.3 California's Asian/Pacific Population

SOURCE: California Trade & Commerce Agency, 1997 (based on 1990 U.S. Census data)

In the intervening fifty years between 1946 and 1996, California's population grew from 9.6 million to over 32 million. Population growth slowed in the early 1990s as the state experienced a serious economic downturn, but the state's growth trend has continued upward.

Level of Economic Activity

If California were an independent nation, it would have the world's seventh highest GDP, ahead of China, Canada and the former Soviet Union (see Figure 7.4).

Professional Workforce. Because of its physical and cultural amenities and its job opportunities, the state attracts well-educated professionals from other parts of the country and other parts of the world. Thus, California is on the receiving end of a "brain drain" which makes these people's services and abilities available to business and to the general public.

FIGURE 7.4 California's Rank: World GDP

United States
Japan
Germany
France
Italy
United Kingdom
CALIFORNIA
China
Canada

SOURCE: California Trade & Commerce Agency, 1997

Educational Institutions. Economic growth is often strongly related to the quality of a state's system of higher education. California has excellent public and private colleges and universities, staffed by renowned scholars. Their advanced research and teaching helps keep the state on the leading edge of ideas and technology.

High-tech companies often send their engineers back to school to keep abreast of the latest research. Such companies find it desirable to locate near universities and think tanks.

While recent tax and spending reforms may impact public universities' ability to continue to provide a broad, high-quality education, the perception of California's status as an educational powerhouse remains strong.

Hospitality to New Ideas. California has the reputation of being a trend-setting state. In fact, California has long had a culture that is hospitable to creativity, diversity and unconventionality. Fashion trends, religious movements, social and tax reform ideas — all of these and more find their origins in California's "social laboratory." The natural result of such a climate is that innovative and risk-taking individuals find a natural home in the state. This has beneficial economic consequences, among them a business environment that encourages entrepreneurship.

This pro-entrepreneur environment is demonstrated by California's rapidly-growing small business sector. A "small business" is defined by the Trade & Commerce Agency as any independently owned and operated company that is not dominant in its industry and has fewer than 100 employees. There are nearly 1 million small businesses in California today (see Figure 7.5). That number is more than doubled when the million and a half self-employed entrepreneurs are included.

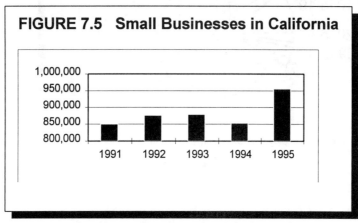

FIGURE 7.5   Small Businesses in California

SOURCE: California Employment Development Department, 1995

In 1995, more than 6.6 million Californians were working in small businesses, a number that accounts for over half of all the state's private-sector employees. Most of them worked in businesses with fewer than five employees (see Figure 7.6).

Employment in California

In California as elsewhere, employment falls into four major categories of productive activity: service-providing, goods-producing, agriculture and government (see Figure 7.7).

Quarterly state unemployment rates have fallen steadily since 1994, from 9 percent to slightly over 6 percent. Six out of every ten working Californians is employed in the service sector (see Figure 7.8).

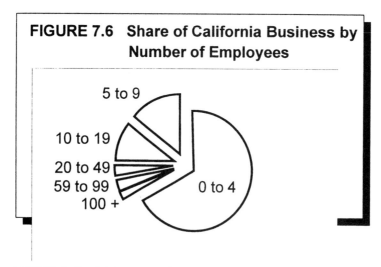

FIGURE 7.6   Share of California Business by Number of Employees

SOURCE: California Employment Development Department, 1995

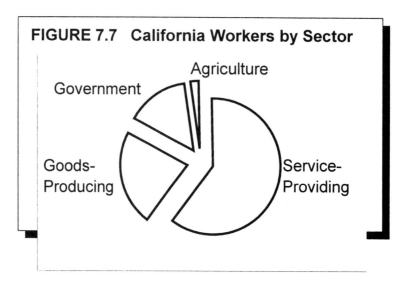

FIGURE 7.7   California Workers by Sector

SOURCE: California Employment Development Department, 1995

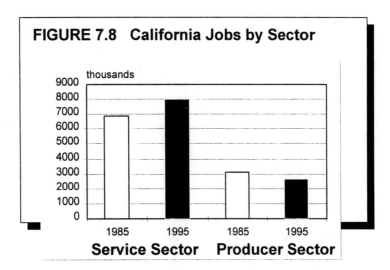

FIGURE 7.8 California Jobs by Sector

SOURCE: California Employment Development Department, 1995

California ranks first in the U.S. in its share of high-wage jobs such as management services, biomedical instruments, entertainment, computers and engineering services. As in the rest of the country, California's service sector is growing, while manufacturing, agriculture and mining are becoming less important parts of the state economy.

Major Categories of Employment. Each of the four broad categories encompasses several major categories of employment. For example, goods-producing includes manufacturing, construction and mining. Figure 7.9 shows the number and proportion of California workers in major categories of employment in 1985 and 1995.

The Service Sector. As illustrated in Figure 7.9, the service sector is the largest employer in California. Figure 7.10 shows the relative sizes of the nine major components of the state's service sector.

Manufacturing Employment. Manufacturing is the second largest category of employment in the state, after services. About 15 percent of California's jobs are in manufacturing industries, mostly those related to electronics and aerospace technologies. Figure 7.11 illustrates the major components of the manufacturing economy.

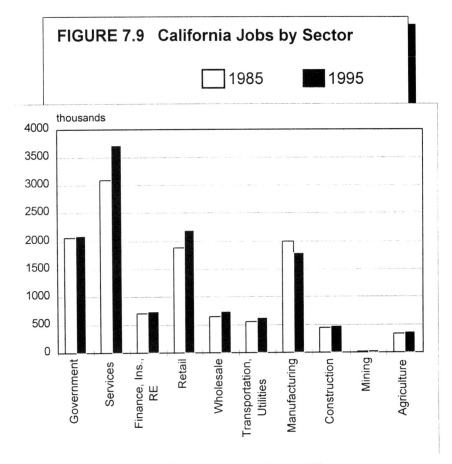

FIGURE 7.9 California Jobs by Sector

☐ 1985   ■ 1995

SOURCE: California Employment Development Department, 1995

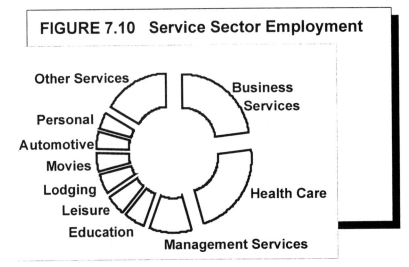

FIGURE 7.10 Service Sector Employment

SOURCE: California Employment Development Department, 1995

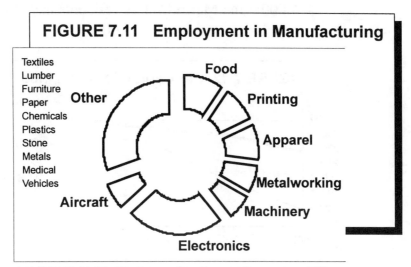

FIGURE 7.11 Employment in Manufacturing

SOURCE: California Employment Development Department, 1995

Federal Government as Buyer. As a major buyer of aircraft, missiles and electronics, the federal government supports (but does not guarantee) employment in much of the aerospace and electronics industries.

Income

Although gross product (in dollar terms) is the most common measure of a nation's or state's economic activity, personal income is another measure. California's per capita personal income has been 10 to 20 percent higher than the national average year after year. Historically, Californians' income has been appreciably higher than that of other Americans. In the 1990s, however, broad cuts in defense spending had a devastating effect on high-paying defense-related jobs. At the same time, the state has been experiencing a rapid growth in population among low wage earners. The result is that California's per capita income is no longer far ahead of the rest of the nation (see Figure 7.12).

Actual income, of course, varies widely across the state (as we'll discuss later, in the "Micro-Economies" section of this chapter). As a rule, incomes are higher in urban areas and lower in rural counties. Per capita income is particularly high in the Bay Area (about

$34,000), and Marin County residents have the nation's third-highest per capita income, over $40,000.

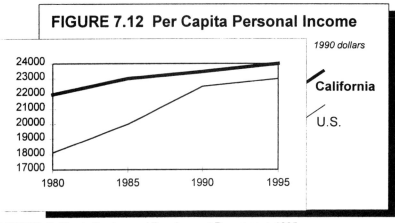

FIGURE 7.12 Per Capita Personal Income

1990 dollars

California

U.S.

SOURCE: California Employment Development Department, 1995

Sources of Personal Income. Employees earn wages and salaries. Stockholders receive dividends. Savers earn interest. Landlords receive rents. Retirees receive Social Security and pensions. Wages and salaries constitute by far the most significant source of personal income in California.

Agriculture

Although it accounts for only 2 percent of reported California employment, agriculture is still a major economic and physical presence in the state.

One of the strengths of California agriculture is that it is very diverse. This contrasts with the heavy dependence of some states on one or two crops. Because of California's extraordinarily diverse climate and geography, it offers ideal conditions for dairy farms, orchards, vegetable farms and fishing: over 250 different agricultural products are farmed in California, with no single, dominant product. California is the leading producer of 75 different crops. On only 3 percent of the nation's farmland, Californians grow over half the fruit, nuts and vegetables consumed in the US. California is also the nation's number one dairy state, and produces 95 percent of domestic wines.

Food Processing. Processing all those products is a major California industry. From food warehousing and transportation to wineries and baked goods, from producing beverages and sugar to fats and oils, California is the largest food processing employer in the United States, employing 200,000 people in over 3,000 different businesses.

Foreign Trade

Exports are a major source of earnings for the California economy. Its geographic location makes it the nation's principal western port for both domestic export products and international imports. It is the primary sea and air port for the Asian and Pacific markets, handling over 20 percent of total U.S. trade. More than 75 percent of all goods shipped through West Coast ports move through California. The ports of Los Angeles and Long Beach are the nation's busiest.

But California is more than just a passive doorway to the world. California is a major export power in its own right. Overall, one-third of the state's farm products are sent to foreign markets, principally Europe, Japan, Canada and South Korea. Significant exports are also made to Mexico and Southeast Asia. The European Economic Community (EEC) accounts for over 20 percent of California's exports. Japan alone accounts for more than 17 percent (see Figure 7.13).

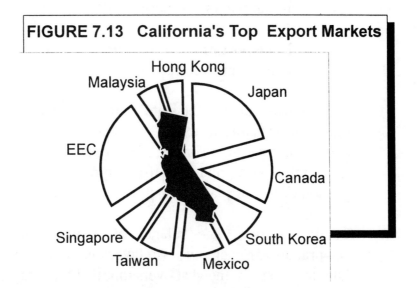

FIGURE 7.13 California's Top Export Markets

SOURCE: California Trade & Commerce Agency, 1996

California's leading commodities export products are shown in Figure 7.14, along with their percentage of US exports.

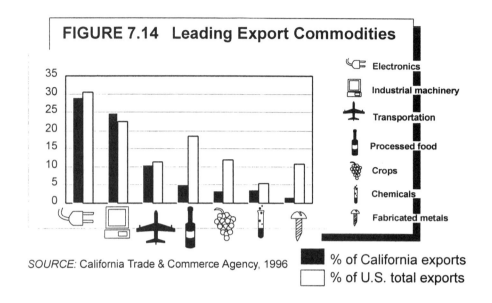

FIGURE 7.14 Leading Export Commodities

SOURCE: California Trade & Commerce Agency, 1996

█ % of California exports
☐ % of U.S. total exports

Technology. Most of California's "hard" exports fall into three categories:

- **Electronic Products:** telecommunications equipment and various electronic components

- **Industrial Machinery:** manufacturing technologies, as well as computers and peripherals

- **Transportation Equipment:** automobiles, mass-transit vehicles and aircraft

Agriculture. Beef is the state's biggest agricultural export product, but other agricultural exports include cotton, grapes, almonds, fish and — of course — oranges. Processed food, such as wine, dried fruit, milled rice and soft drink syrups, comprise a considerable portion of California's agricultural export economy.

Trade Balance. The balance of trade is classified as positive (favorable) or negative (unfavorable). While this mercantilist interpretation is somewhat oversimplified for today's global economy, a nation's ratio of imports to exports has important effects on its production and purchasing power. As we've seen, the same is true of any other economic entity.

Shipments by land, sea and air through California's ports of entry account for nearly 3 billion dollars in value. More importantly for the state's balance of trade, over 80 percent of the goods shipped through California are produced in the state.

▦ CALIFORNIA'S MICRO-ECONOMIES

Just as California is a part of the total U.S. economy, the California economy is made up of a number of micro-economic units: regions, counties, cities and even neighborhoods.

Demographics

No Mason-Dixon Line divides them, but Northern and Southern California have their own distinctive traits. Other parts of the state also have developed into clearly distinguishable micro-economies. Some of the key demographic differences include the following:

- **Population.** Almost 60 percent of Californians live in the coastal urban areas — San Francisco and Los Angeles (see Figure 7.15).

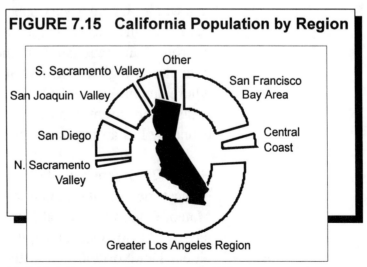

FIGURE 7.15 California Population by Region

SOURCE: California Department of Finance, 1996

- **Employment.** California experienced an enormous increase in migrants during the 1990s. Coupled with a disastrous recession in the early years of the decade, California's unemployment rate rose dramatically. For much of the mid-90s, unemployment continued high in California, even as the rate fell in the U.S. as a whole. By 1996-1997, however, unemployment in California was declining.

  California's Central Valley and northern regions typically have higher unemployment rates than the metropolitan regions to the south. This is largely a by-product of the region's seasonal job base in agriculture, lumber and tourism. State unemployment is lowest in the Bay Area, where high-tech industries provide fuel for rising employment.

  The L.A. area's unemployment tends to be higher than that of other metropolitan areas, due to its economic diversity and the strains resulting from the region's being unprepared for massive immigration.

- **Per Capita Income.** While California has historically enjoyed a per capita income higher than that of the country as a whole, incomes vary substantially in various parts of the state. For instance, incomes tend to be higher in the major metropolitan areas (such as the Bay Area) than in rural or agricultural regions. Income also tends to track employment: where unemployment is high, incomes are lower than in areas where more people are working. Of course, the local economy has an important effect on income level.

  Figure 7.16 contrasts the five California counties with the highest per capita incomes (Marin, San Francisco, San Mateo, Contra Costa and Santa Clara) with the five counties having the lowest per capita incomes (Tehama, Imperial, Yuba, Del Norte and — with California's lowest per capita income — Kings). Interestingly, the top five are all clustered in the Bay Area, while three of the bottom five are in Northern California.

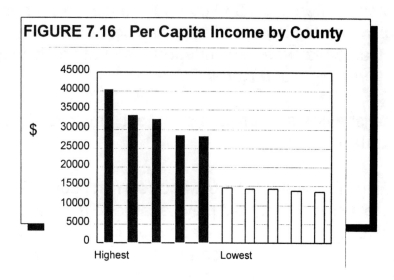

FIGURE 7.16 Per Capita Income by County

The Next Step

In the next chapter, we will focus on California's housing market. Like the state's economy in general, the housing market is highly diverse, with major differences among the various regional micro-economies.

Chapter 7
REVIEW

- **California** is the nation's *third largest state* geographically. With 32 million people, it is the *most populous and ethnically diverse state in the U.S.* It has one of the most *varied climates*, and its farms grow more than *250 different kinds of crops.*

▪ California is an **ECONOMIC POWERHOUSE**, producing *over 12 percent of the total U.S. GDP*. It is the port for *40 percent of all U.S. trade with Asia*, and home to more than 960,000 businesses, from fast-food restaurants and convenience stores to high technology, defense and entertainment giants. If California were an independent nation, it would have *the world's seventh highest national GDP.*

▪ The **SERVICE SECTOR** is the largest employer in California, followed by **MANUFACTURING**.

▪ California's **AGRICULTURAL ECONOMY** accounts for only *2 percent* of the state's employment but plays a large role in the state's economic health. California is the world's leading producer of *seventy-five different crops*. On 3 percent of the nation's farmland, California grows *half of the nation's produce*. California is the *number one dairy producer* in the country.

▪ **EXPORTS** are a major source of earnings for the California economy. The state handles over *20 percent of total U.S. trade*. The ports of Los Angeles and Long Beach are the *busiest in the nation*. California's **MAIN EXPORTS** are electronics, industrial machinery, transportation equipment, processed food, agricultural crops, chemicals and fabricated metals.

▪ California is composed of a number of **MICRO-ECONOMIES**: the northern and southern parts of the state have distinct characteristics, and other regions have their own unique economic qualities and challenges.

Chapter 7
QUIZ

1. In terms of geographical area, where does California rank among U.S. states?

   A. First
   B. Second
   C. Third
   D. Fifth

2. California accounts for what percentage of the total U.S. gross domestic product?

   A. 2.0 percent
   B. 6.5 percent
   C. 12.5 percent
   D. 18.4 percent

3. The largest ethnic group in California is:

   A. White
   B. Black
   C. Hispanic
   D. Asian

4. Yesterday, the governor signed a decree declaring California's independence from the U.S. and establishing the Republic of California. Where does this new nation rank in the world, in terms of GDP?

   A. First
   B. Third
   C. Fifth
   D. Seventh

5. The largest share of California's business community is held by employers of how many people?

   A. 0 to 4
   B. 5 to 9
   C. 20 to 49
   D. Over 100

6. Which of the following job sectors is the largest in California?

   A. Government
   B. Goods-producing
   C. Service-providing
   D. Agriculture

7. All of the following are components of the service sector, *EXCEPT*:

   A. lodging.
   B. electronics.
   C. health care.
   D. education.

8. Which of the following is the largest recipient of California's state exports?

   A. Japan
   B. Canada
   C. The EEC
   D. Mexico

9. California's leading export commodity is:

   A. processed food.
   B. electronics.
   C. chemicals.
   D. fabricated metals.

10. All of the following California counties are in the state's top five for highest per capita income, *EXCEPT*:

    A. San Mateo.
    B. Santa Clara.
    C. Contra Costa.
    D. Del Norte.

8

The California Real Estate Market

 Objectives:

- Understand the volatile history of California's real estate economy

- Describe the demographics of the California real estate market

- Explain income and affordability issues, and the way they interact with California's unique economy

- Distinguish among the characteristics and special issues of the residential, commercial and industrial real estate markets

---

▦ BUILDING A MARKET

As we've said over and over, real estate is intensely local in nature. The value of any property is completely dependent on where the property is located. That is as true for an apartment in New York or an office building in Chicago as it is for an Iowa farm or a house in any suburb. It is also true of California. As in most things, however, California occupies a unique position in the real estate market. All states are different from one another, of course, but as we saw in the last chapter, California's unique geography, demographics, income culture produce a vastly different picture from the national economy in general. The nature of California's housing market is a reflection of the state's uniqueness and diversity.

An Economic Roller Coaster

When the recession of the early 1980s ended, California underwent something of a second Gold Rush. Real estate and construction markets soared along with the rest of the state's economy. On the other hand, the Tax Reform Act of 1986 led to a steep decline in multifamily rental construction, as investors lost significant tax benefits. In the early 1990s, the economic cycle started around again: recession returned, and the real estate market once again suffered. Today, however, home sales have returned to their pre-recession levels, and both residential and commercial construction show signs of recovery. On average across the state, median home prices are lower than they've been in many years. While mixed news for sellers and developers, that's good news for affordability and increased home ownership generally (see Figure 8.1).

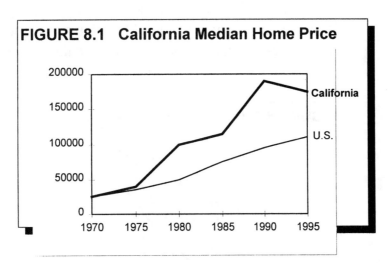

FIGURE 8.1 California Median Home Price

SOURCE: California Department of Finance, 1996

Housing Patterns

California now has in excess of 11 million dwelling units, representing a 9 percent increase since 1990. California leads the nation in housing growth, despite the slump in housing that resulted from the recession of the early years of the decade (see Figure 8.2).

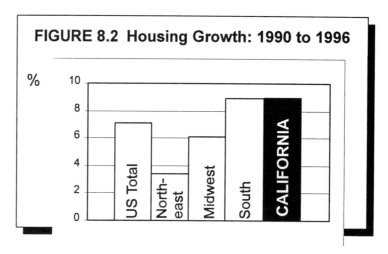

SOURCE: US Bureau of the Census, 1997

Occupancy

California has a high level of renter occupancy, due largely to high land costs in the state and the fact that many types of occupations demand a high degree of mobility. Figure 8.3 shows the relationship of owner-occupied, vacant, and renter-occupied properties in California.

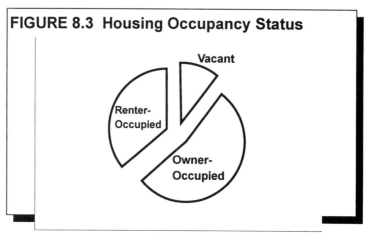

SOURCE: U.S. Bureau of the Census, 1997

Types of Housing Units

Renters are more likely to be in multiunit buildings, but the continuing trend toward condominiums (both new and conversions) has increased the percentage of owner occupied multiunit dwellings. Across California, there are a variety of types of dwellings available. Figure 8.4 illustrates the relationship among the various types statewide.

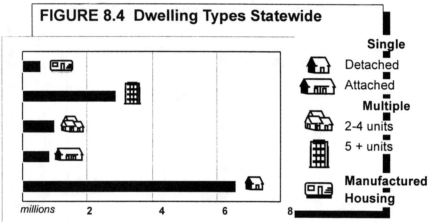

FIGURE 8.4 Dwelling Types Statewide

SOURCE: U.S. Bureau of the Census, 1997

Vacancy Rates

Housing vacancy rates in California are generally low. For any commodity, affordability and merchandise appeal affect how much of the inventory is unsold at any time; however, the significance of vacancy rates varies from place to place with economic conditions, environmental appeal, and development patterns.

Geographic Factors. Climate and scenery are important in the California mystique. Californians prefer coastal areas, other things being equal, so demand for housing in those areas tends to be high and vacancy rates generally low. In recent years, transportation cost, time and inconvenience have caused many consumers to reexamine their traditional fondness for the suburbs.

Economic Fluctuations. A community in a normally low-vacancy region may suffer high vacancy rates because of some temporary economic distress or a rash of overbuilding as occurred in the rapid growth areas of the Antelope Valley and Inland Empire (Riverside-San Bernardino County areas) in the 1980s.

Figure 8.5 shows the most recent vacancy rates for residential properties in various regions of the state.

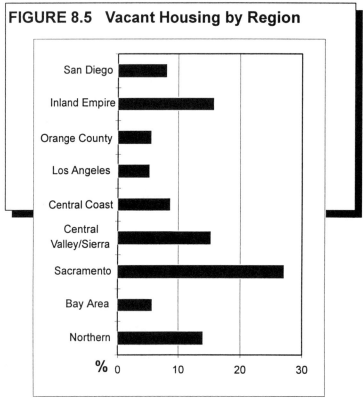

FIGURE 8.5 Vacant Housing by Region

SOURCE: U.S. Bureau of the Census, 1997

Characteristics of Households

In 1997, there were close to 32 million households in California. A household, you'll recall from Chapter 6, refers to all the people who occupy a housing unit. The demographics (factual characteristics) about these units help us better understand the California real estate marketplace.

Age. Figure 8.6 illustrates the change in the ages of heads of household in California between 1990 and 1996.

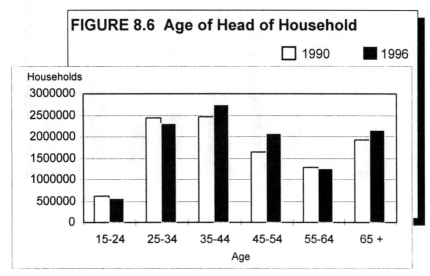

FIGURE 8.6 Age of Head of Household

SOURCE: U.S. Bureau of the Census, 1997

Another way of looking at age composition is the age distribution of total heads of households. Figure 8.6 shows a substantial percentage in the 65-plus age category, reflecting increased life expectancy, the attraction of the state to senior citizens and a continuing trend away from extended families and toward more independent living for the older age group. This has significant ramifications for future housing needs. Note, too, how the number of younger heads of household has actually declined since 1990.

Household Size. In general, the more people living together in a housing unit, the more space they will need. There are exceptions, of course, including cases of extreme poverty (in which large numbers of persons may live together in very small quarters) and extreme wealth (in which a small family may occupy a very large home). But there remains nonetheless a direct relationship between household size and housing need. Figure 8.7 compares the average number of persons per household in California with the nation as a whole and with other regions.

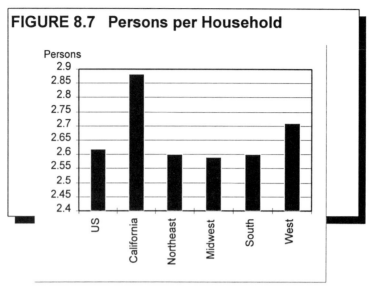

FIGURE 8.7 Persons per Household

SOURCE: U.S. Bureau of the Census, 1997

Income and Affordability

Income is obviously an important factor in shaping the California housing market: how much money buyers can afford to spend has a lot to do with establishing the fair market value of properties. As we saw in Chapter 7, per capita income in California varies a great deal, depending on which region is considered. On average, however, the state's per capita income is around $24,000: higher than the national average.

On the other hand, it's almost a necessity that California's per capita income exceed that of the U.S. as a whole: it represents one of the nation's most expensive housing markets. San Francisco, for instance, has the highest median home price in the U.S., $288,000. That's four times the median income for the Bay Area, or roughly two and a half times the 1997 national median home price ($120,000). In the interior of the state, away from coastal regions, housing affordability is slightly over 50 percent, or roughly the national average.

According to the National Association of Home Builders, five of the nation's ten least affordable metropolitan areas (and twelve of the top twenty-five), are in California. California's representatives in the "top five" are San Francisco, Santa Cruz-Watsonville, Santa Rosa, Salinas and San Jose. A computer programmer in Contra Costa, or an environmental engineer in San Diego, is likely to earn upwards of $40,000 less than the minimum qualifying income to purchase a median-priced house in his or her city.

California is one of the states in the nation where housing is the least affordable. In the early 1990s, the median priced home in an urban area could be purchased by roughly only one family in five. Affordability ratios (discussed below) as reported in local periodicals indicate a range of around 15 to 20 percent, depending upon the cost of financing at any given time.

Payment to Income Ratios. Lenders traditionally have used a "rule of thumb" formula to determine whether or not a prospective buyer can afford a certain purchase: The monthly cost of buying and maintaining a home (mortgage payments — both principal and interest — plus taxes and insurance impounds) should not exceed 28 percent of the borrower's gross (pretax) monthly income. The payments on all debts should not exceed 36 percent of monthly income. Expenses such as insurance premiums, utilities and routine medical care are not included in the 36 percent figure, but are considered to be covered by the remaining 64 percent of the buyer's monthly income. These formulas may vary, of course, depending on the type of loan program and the borrower's earnings, credit history, number of dependents and other factors.

Based on this traditional rule of thumb, many Californians are effectively barred from any hope of ever buying their own home.

Nonetheless, housing affordability has generally increased throughout California. As Figure 8.8 illustrates, only 14 percent of Californians could afford their own home in 1989; by 1997 that number rose to nearly 40 percent. This was in part due to a growth in higher-income jobs in the state, and partly due to a decline in home prices.

A Closer Look . . .

A prospective California home buyer wants to know how much house he or she can afford to buy. The buyer has a gross monthly income of $3,750. The buyer's allowable housing expense may be calculated as follows:

$3,750 gross monthly income x 28% = $1,050 **total housing expense**

$3,750 gross monthly income x 36% = $1,350 **total debt expenses**

(More lenient ratios are sometimes used for first-time home buyers.)

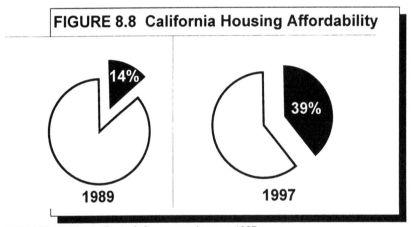

FIGURE 8.8 California Housing Affordability

SOURCE: California Trade & Commerce Agency, 1997

Sales of Existing Homes

One obvious measure of a housing market is the number of existing homes that are sold. The term "existing homes" refers to previously occupied housing, as opposed to new construction. Since 1970, the California market for existing homes has fluctuated wildly, peaking in the late 1970s at nearly 650,000 units, then falling to around 200,000 units in the early 1980s. By 1990, the market was back up near 600,000 again, only to slump in the middle of the decade to around 450,000. Toward the end of the 1990s, the market seems to be adjusting itself upward once again.

Housing Starts

As discussed in Chapter 6, one measure of the vitality of a real estate market (whether local, state or national) is the amount of residential construction activity, measured by projects started during a particular period. Despite periodic downturns, housing starts in California generally were higher by 1997 than they had been since 1989.

While local economic conditions define local housing starts, the new housing industry is not unrelated to national trends. In Figure 8.9, notice how the trend line for California's housing starts between 1978 and 1986 closely reflect the national trend line. In the early 1990s, however, California's housing industry was stifled by recession and lagged behind the national average. By the late 1990s, however, California's housing starts increased even as the national numbers showed a decline.

Rental Housing

There are many reasons why people rent their homes. Some consumers who would like to buy houses find it financially impractical to do so. Others prefer the relative freedom from maintenance and upkeep responsibilities offered by rental housing. Still others work in jobs that require frequent travel or relocation. Because the decision to rent or buy is often based on personal preferences and fluctuating economic conditions, it is difficult to make broad demographic statements about "renters" as a group. Whatever the reason for renting, rental housing is a significant part of the California real estate economy.

Roughly one-quarter of California's population live in rental housing. That's about half of all households, as defined by the Census Bureau.

By comparison, the national figure is under 20 percent. The disparity reflects the constant affordability question, and the diversity of California's economy. The number of renters as a percentage of households is highest in the southern coastal area, including Los Angeles, and the Bay Area. There are fewer renters in the central and northern parts of the state.

Disadvantages of Renting. While there are many good reasons to rent housing, there are some significant disadvantages to the choice. Primary among these is the fact that once rental payments are made, they are gone: renters do not build up equity in their homes. There are also very real tax

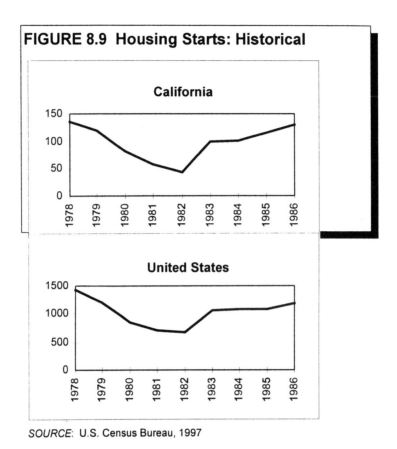

FIGURE 8.9 Housing Starts: Historical

California

United States

SOURCE: U.S. Census Bureau, 1997

advantages to home ownership that are not enjoyed by renters, principally the ability to deduct mortgage interest payments from income taxes, and to shelter gains on the sale of a primary residence. Contrary to the popular view, renters are not immune from increases in local property taxes or utility rates: the rent payment reflects prorated shares of property taxes and utilities paid by the landlord.

The California real estate rental market is growing. Nearly seven million Californians live in rental housing. In 1996, there were over 3 million occupied apartments in California, representing an 82 percent increase over 1990. Nearly 20,000 new units were built in 1996, and the construction trends indicate continued growth.

The Next Step

In focusing on the California real estate market, this chapter has emphasized residential properties up to this point. Next, we'll consider two other very important components of the California real estate market: commercial and industrial real estate.

▦ COMMERCIAL AND INDUSTRIAL TRENDS

California characteristically outstrips the rest of the country in industrial development, principally due to its attraction as a place to live and work. The California climate is famously appealing, the state's workforce is qualified and plentiful and the regulatory environment, although demanding, does not drive away business. Even without artificial incentives for relocation of new industry as used in some states, such as tax incentives or state-provided infrastructure improvements, California fares extremely well. The ability to attract new industry is in turn a major force in creating the need for more office, retail, and temporary and permanent housing.

Availability

In California as a whole, commercial construction (including offices, retail centers and hotels) exceeds industrial by a wide margin, paralleling the national pattern. Statewide, from the late 1970s to the mid-1980s and into the 1990s, measured in terms of building permit values, industrial construction activity was relatively flat, while commercial construction activity grew steadily, even during the two recessions that occurred during that period.

Figure 8.10 illustrates the pattern of industrial property vacancy in the Los Angeles metropolitan area in mid-1997. Note that the amount of vacant property declined as the recession of the early 1990s came to an end.

Figure 8.11, on the other hand, compares office vacancy rates in 1997 for the U.S. generally with five California metropolitan areas, for both suburban and downtown office space. Note how California's famous regional diversity is apparent here, too. In some cities, such as Sacramento, the downtown vacancy rate is lower than that of the outlying suburbs. In others, urban vacancies far surpass the suburban rate.

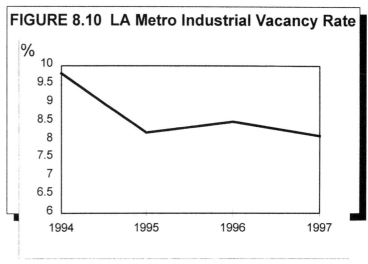

SOURCE: CB Commercial/Torto Wheaton Research, 1997

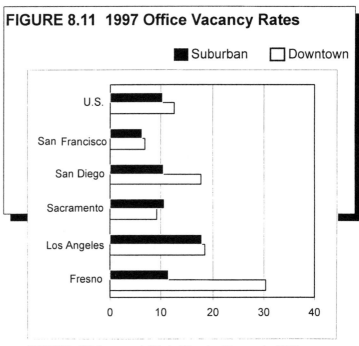

SOURCE: CB Commercial/Torto Wheaton Research, 1997

A Closer Look . . .

Silicon Valley: the phrase summons up images of high-tech industrial parks, humming with white-suited workers building computer chips and disk drives in cool, sterile factories. But Silicon Valley (the popular nickname for the Santa Clara Valley/San Jose region) is not a simple success story. While home to such technology giants as Adobe Systems, Apple Corporation, Borland International, Hewlett Packard, Hitachi, IBM, Intel, Netscape, Novell and Pacific Telesis, as well as aerospace giant Lockheed Missiles & Space Company, the Silicon Valley commercial and industrial real estate market has known its ups and downs.

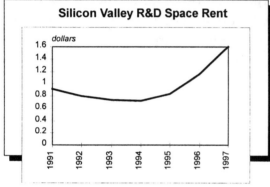

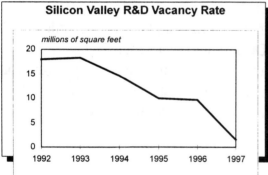

SOURCE: California Office of Economic Development, 1997

The Silicon Valley commercial real estate market (measured in the figures in terms of research and development [R&D] space) underwent a recovery in the latter half of the 1990s from a slump earlier in the decade. The area thrived during a major recession in the early 1980s, when interest rates were in the high teens, resulting in an economic bonanza followed by a sharp decline due to oversupply.

From 1987 until 1994, the real estate market stagnated and buildings stood empty, commanding only the lowest rents. The international demand for high-technology products in the mid-1990s, however, has fueled a dramatic recovery. Today, land prices are high, rent increases common, and new high-rise office buildings are once more under construction.

Building Types

Due to the constantly changing needs of the commercial/industrial market, convertibility of improvements is an important factor in preserving value. For example, former motels are now convalescent facilities; supermarket buildings have become everything from restaurants to mortuaries; office buildings have been converted to school use; warehouses become bowling alleys. In urban areas, conversions of industrial and warehouse lofts into dramatic, spacious residential properties is popular.

Specialized industrial plants use have been to some extent supplanted by huge planned multipurpose industrial parks, designed to bring the jobs to suburban areas where the people are rather than centralize industrial activity in densely populated urban areas. At the same time, businesses are tiring of suburban congestion, uncontrolled sprawl and long intersuburban commutes, and are looking back toward urban centers for solutions.

Aging of Inventory

The post-World War II building boom, from 1946 until 1960, produced a large stock of commercial and industrial buildings that are now showing their age. During the 1980s, many older structures were either replaced with more modern and functional counterparts or renovated. Part of this recycling process is due to updated building standards that have rendered older structures obsolete.

Environmental Concerns

Of all the factors involved in an aging stock of commercial, office, retail and industrial properties, perhaps the most significant for owners, managers, sellers, buyers and investors are the environmental factors involved in nonresidential properties. These issues are particularly important for existing industrial properties, although they sometimes arise in the context of other commercial buildings, too. These issues are discussed at length in Chapter 10; here, however, is a brief overview.

Asbestos. A negative factor in many older industrial buildings is the probability that asbestos was used in their construction. In the half-century between 1920 and 1970, asbestos was commonly used in the construction of commercial buildings for insulation, noise dampening and fireproofing.

Since the early 1970s, asbestos has been increasingly recognized as an environmental hazard, and the presence of the material in a building often affects the building's value.

Some large firms will not lease office space in buildings containing asbestos, fearing lawsuits brought by employees who suffer health-related injuries due to exposure to asbestos. The same anxiety affects real estate investors.

Lead. Lead was once used as a pigment and drying agent in alkyd oil-based paint. Lead-based paint may be on any interior or exterior surface, but it is particularly common on doors, windows and other woodwork, and in commercial and industrial properties built prior to 1978, the year in which the use of lead-based paint was banned.

Elevated levels of lead in the body can cause serious damage to the brain, kidneys, nervous system and red blood cells. The degree of harm is related to the amount of exposure and the age at which a person is exposed. Lead dust can be ingested from the hands, inhaled or ingested from the water supply because of lead pipes or lead solder. High levels of lead have been found in the soil near waste-to-energy incinerators.

Underground Storage Tanks. Over time, neglected tanks may decay and leak hazardous substances into the environment. This permits contaminants to pollute not only the soil around the tank but also adjacent parcels and groundwater. Underground storage tanks are a particular concern for purchasers of existing industrial properties.

Underground storage tanks are commonly found on sites where petroleum products are used or where gas stations and auto repair shops are located. They also may be located in a number of other commercial and industrial establishments, including printing and chemical plants, wood treatment plants, paper mills, paint manufacturers, dry cleaners and food processing plants, for storing chemical or other process waste. Military bases and airports are also common sites for underground tanks.

As bases close throughout California and the former military properties are converted into commercial, industrial and even residential use, the presence of buried toxic materials is an important consideration. Detection, removal and the clean-up of surrounding contaminated soil can be an expensive operation.

Components of the Market

Major sectors of the commercial/industrial real estate market are

- single commercial properties (free-standing or street-front retail properties, restaurants, professional offices or service providers as well as hotels or motels);
- retail centers and malls;
- office buildings;
- industrial buildings;

Each of these sectors has its own distinctive marketing issues, regional patterns, and economic strengths and weaknesses. Figure 8.12 shows how the different types of uses compare nationally.

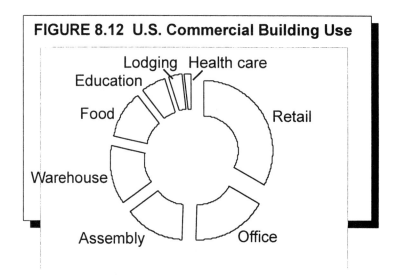

FIGURE 8.12 U.S. Commercial Building Use

Commercial Structures. Commercial structures house retail stores, offices, motels/hotels, restaurants, commercial schools, warehouse facilities, medical offices and many other businesses. About 90 percent of these structures are occupied by only one establishment.

Retail Market

The nation has largely converted from the proverbial "general store," evolving from the retail strip and downtown commercial hub to a variety of planned retail centers that fall into five general categories.

1. **Convenience Centers.** These are often found on corners formerly occupied by gas stations. During the 1970s the oil industry concluded that major retail corner locations were no longer economically viable for gasoline and car repairs. Developers improved these locations (many well under an acre in size) as small retail centers with service type tenants and fast food facilities. The principal tenant is often a liquor/deli store or a minimart. By the mid-1980s the oil companies recognized a missed opportunity and started to expand their service station facilities with minimarts, and began downplaying the auto service aspect.

2. **Neighborhood Centers.** Roughly four to ten acres in size, these centers serve a larger population than the convenience centers, which are supported by small, densely populated trading areas. In the neighborhood center, a major supermarket or drugstore is usually the principal tenant, with an array of service and specialty establishments. A recent trend finds some of the major supermarket chains providing for additional tenants within the market structure itself, such as drug stores, restaurants, banks and clothing outlets, with direct access to potential customers whose principal destination has been the supermarket.

3. **Community Shopping Centers.** These usually occupy ten to thirty acres and are anchored by a medium-sized department store or outlet of a major store. They require probably four to five times the service area needed to support a neighborhood

center. However, as regional shopping centers proliferate, the community center is often becoming what is described as a "power center" where discounters gravitate.

4. **Regional Shopping Centers.** At the end of World War II the flight to the suburbs spurred major department stores to relocate from their traditional downtown locations to the new, freeway-oriented areas where potential shoppers lived. The plot size of these basically suburban centers (which are now often multistoried and enclosed instead of single story and exposed) runs from 30 to 100 acres with a major department store as the main or **anchor** tenant.

5. **Shopping Malls.** The rise of the shopping mall during the 1970s and 1980s caused a severe drainage of resources and revenues from downtown areas, as retailers and service-providers moved out of urban areas and clustered themselves in and around the new suburban and outlying malls. Attracted by clean, pleasant, temperature-controlled environments and acres of free parking, the shoppers whose dollars had supported downtowns got in their cars and drove out to the malls, taking their dollars with them.

Downtown retailers attempted to reinvigorate themselves by supporting closed streets and pedestrian malls, but these too failed. By the mid-1990s, however, there were signs that the trend was reversing. Shopper preferences changed, and downtown areas began reattracting retailers and shoppers even as the malls began to fail. The factory outlet mall phenomenon further contributes to the troubles facing traditional malls: shoppers are often willing to travel to remote locations to enjoy particularly steep discounts.

California is home to the nation's largest number of shopping centers, according to the International Council of Shopping Centers. Three of biggest centers in the country are in California: Del Amo Fashion Center in Torrance; South Coast/Crystal Court in Costa Mesa; and Lakewood Center.

Availability. The end of the recession of the early 1990s brought a boom in retail construction, particularly in large shopping centers anchored by national discounters such as Target Greatland, Super K-mart, Wal-Mart and Home Depot. At the same time, older centers began to experience higher vacancy levels in the mid- and late 1990s, as the discounters' new "big box" developments (a reference to the warehouse-style architecture favored by major discount chains) moved into existing markets.

Office Space

The availability of office space is a significant indicator of the overall vitality of the local commercial real estate market. For instance, when office vacancy is high, rents will be forced to low levels by the forces of supply and demand. There will be little motivation for investors and developers to add to an already glutted inventory of office properties. As a result, construction jobs will decline, and employment and income will be affected across a broad range of industries. On the other hand, when office vacancy rates are low, developers will seize the opportunity to respond to increased demand by building more space. Rents will increase along with employment opportunities.

Figure 8.13 compares recent office vacancy rates in four major California markets. Figure 8.14 compares the rental price per square foot that can be demanded in high and low vacancy markets.

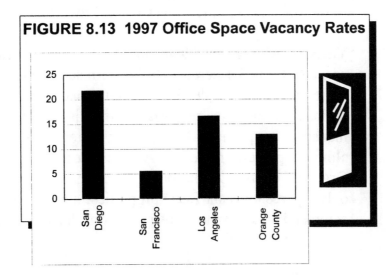

FIGURE 8.13 1997 Office Space Vacancy Rates

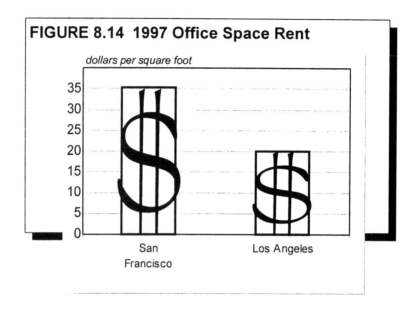

FIGURE 8.14 1997 Office Space Rent

The Industrial Market

California's industrial market includes all properties used for manufacturing and other industrial uses, such as research and development (R&D), on industrially zoned land. In the mid-1980s, 60 percent of industrial space was devoted to warehousing and distribution activities. Today, while California's vital national and international trade and commerce activities continue to drive demand for distribution centers, high-tech R&D properties are the "hot" niche as the state's economy moves toward the 21st century.

Vacancy Rates. In 1996, the U.S. vacancy rate for industrial properties was 8.1 percent. In Western states, the rate was 8 percent, representing a slight decline. In California specifically, however, the regional nature of the real estate market is reflected in the demand for industrial properties. The vacancy rate for R&D properties was almost 9 percent in the Los Angeles area, and nearly 13 percent in Orange County. On the other hand, the Silicon Valley region had only 5 percent vacant R&D properties: a record low rate that, in the commercial real estate industry, is considered the equivalent of zero.

The Next Step

Finally, we conclude our look at California real estate with an overview of the rural real estate market: agricultural properties, the lumber and mining industries, and open space protections.

▦ CALIFORNIA'S RURAL REAL ESTATE MARKET

Through the years, rural land use has experienced a far-reaching metamorphosis, largely due to two distinct forces: advances in agricultural technology and the changing demographics of expanding suburban sprawl.

Technology has increased productivity, permitting less land and fewer workers to produce even more food products. As agriculture has receded from its primary role in our economy, rural lands are increasingly converted to other uses. Orange groves are replaced by subdivisions, a ranch becomes an office park, a strawberry field becomes a shopping center. The family farm of the past has for the most part succumbed to giant agribusiness operators, replacing small generational farmsteads with corporate savvy and factory-style efficiency.

This bleak image of picturesque rural Americana being gobbled up by parking lots is not the whole story, however. Agriculture is vitally important: it's where the food comes from, after all, to feed the people in all those subdivisions, office parks and shopping centers. And in California, agriculture is still a very big business, earning the state's agricultural sector nearly $25 billion in revenue, and employing roughly 400,000 people. California's farms produce 250 different crop and livestock commodities, making the state the number one agricultural producer in the country.

The Land

California ranks as one of the leading agricultural producers in the world. Some of the reasons for this leadership position are

- **arable soil.** The productive areas of the San Joaquin, Sacramento, Coachella and Imperial Valleys are widely known for the excellent quality of their soil. Soil determines the suitable type of crop and yield per acre. Thirty million acres of California land are under cultivation.

- **extended growing season.** Due to California's mild climate, farmers can enjoy multiple harvests, increasing yields. Each crop has a particular growing cycle to reach fruition. It takes seven years for new citrus trees to produce. Considerable time, capital expenditure, effort and luck are needed before there is any return in the form of crop yield. Other crops like strawberries may produce at once and have several yields per growing season, given proper conditions. California's climate makes the long-cycle products more economical, and makes multiple yields possible.

- **water supply.** Natural water supply through adequate rainfall or irrigation by manmade systems such as agricultural canals is vital to agricultural productivity. While water is problematic in some parts of the state, the Sierra Nevada snow runoff plus Colorado and Owens River waters have sustained crop development for many years. In 1913 the Owens River was diverted by aqueduct to serve the Southern California citrus crops.

Grazing Land

Under leases from the U.S. Department of Agriculture (forest lands) and the Bureau of Land Management (usually desert areas) as well as in private ownership, twice as much agricultural land in California is devoted to grazing as to crops. The reasons are quite basic:

- Lands not adaptable to farming are still suitable for feeding livestock, particularly in the Coast and Sierra Nevada mountain ranges.

- Livestock require a large area per unit to provide adequate range feed.

- Livestock are a lower maintenance form of agriculture than crops, which generally require more human resources and attention in their tending and reaping.

Inhibitors to Agricultural Development

Both politics and economics play a role in controlling, and sometimes inhibiting, California's agricultural economy. In certain instances farmers are precluded from growing specific crops or are required to obtain permission: this is true of tobacco, cotton and sugar beets. Farms located near urban areas, particularly in the Los Angeles, Inland Empire, San Diego and, most recently, Sacramento areas have succumbed to the upward pressure on land value and the lure of developers' dollars. Environmental regulation of the use of pesticides and growth hormones, coupled with labor union activity among farm workers, has also impacted the farm community.

▦ LUMBERING AND MINING

Lumber rights alone (sold separately from the land) can be a valuable commodity in the marketplace. This resource has exerted considerable upward pressure on price levels, and thus on the desirability of timber rights, during the 1990s, due to several factors:

- **Scarcity.** There is a long "gestation" period for the product. Reforestation after harvesting requires years for replenishment.

- **Government Control.** Through the national park system, the government exerts control on the California, Oregon and Washington timber industries by limiting the stands of timber available for harvesting. Some 3 million acres may be set aside nationwide, reducing the amount of acreage available for lumbering.

- **Supply.** Timberlands are also undergoing conversion to urban, recreational and commercial applications. Just as development reduces the amount of land available for agricultural purposes, it reduces the land available for lumbering.

- **Difficult Access.** Many timber areas have difficult topography and limited road access. In these cases flumes and waterways may be used for transportation. Smaller timber stands do not warrant erection of a processing mill and therefore may not be economical for harvesting.

- **Transportation.** Because of the bulk of the product, mills are usually located close to the stands of timber, and the raw product is not transported over long distances for processing. For unfinished goods, trucks are the principal haulers. Trucks, vessels and freight trains transport the finished products, and transportation adds to cost.

- **Demand.** Housing, paper and other timber product requirements continue at brisk levels, with the current interest in recycling only slightly mitigating dependence on new timber harvests. Demand for the product is national and international in scope, with net exports from most harvesting areas far exceeding the amount of harvest required for use in the immediate area.

- **Tax Treatment.** There are special tax benefits for logging operations in California and elsewhere.

Mining

California's mining sector is relatively modest: under half a million jobs, mostly in oil and gas. The remainder of the industry is largely limited to stone extractions, such as quarries and sand and gravel operations, and some metals, such as gold (see Figure 8.15).

Once an extractive resource is removed, it does not replenish itself like timber. Therefore special tax treatment in the form of a depletion allowance (a mineral, oil and gas version of depreciation) is permitted.

Certain factors are of particular importance for land devoted to mineral, oil and gas activities. These include:

- **quality of resource.** If the resource is abundant and of good quality it will command a higher price than inferior quality in lesser amounts.

- **economic conditions.** Precious minerals (such as gold, silver and platinum) fluctuate in price based upon the degree of confidence that citizens place in their currency. As confidence wanes, prices of these metals increase: people feel that their wealth is "safer" in the form of a permanent metal. As confidence improves, prices for precious metals tend to decline. Precious metal prices are not, however, pure indicators of consumer confidence. Investors and traders can artificially manipulate the market for precious metals.

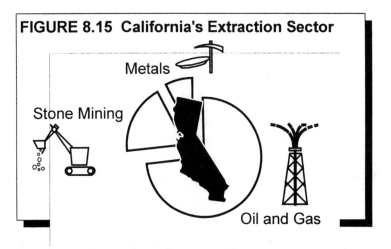

FIGURE 8.15 California's Extraction Sector

Metals

Stone Mining

Oil and Gas

SOURCE: California Department of Finance, 1997

Environmental Concerns

Extractive processes disturb the land, lumbering leaves hillsides barren and eroded and both industries produce have toxic side effects. Since 1976, stringent state and federal environmental regulations have helped diminish such negative side effects, while increasing operating costs.

▦ OPEN SPACE PROTECTION

Rural land applications are constantly under extreme pressure to convert to higher density uses. Urban sprawl is particularly evident in the so-called Sun Belt states where the climate serves as a lure to growing population. California is now the most populous state in the country. While immigration into the state has slowed over the years, a growing population continues to exert pressure on the remaining open space.

Farmland Protections

State and federal legislators have deemed it a public good to provide incentives and protections to farmers. For example, special tax laws help to preserve the present land use by keeping assessments of farm lands low, reflecting their current use instead of the highest and best use to which the land could be put. Other tax laws protect remaining family farms.

The Williamson Act. The Williamson Act (included in the Land Conservation Act of 1965) is a voluntary land conservation program administered by counties and cities, with technical assistance from the California Department of Conservation. The purpose of the act is to:

- preserve California farmland, to ensure a secure food supply for the state and nation and for future generations.

- maintain agriculture's contribution to local and state economies.

- provide economic relief to tax-burdened farmers and ranchers.

- promote orderly city growth and discourage sprawl and the loss of farmland, while preserving open space for its scenic, social, aesthetic and wildlife values.

The Williamson Act essentially creates a contract between the state and small farmers. Farm land is taxed a lower rate, using a scale based on the actual use of the land for agricultural purposes, as opposed to its unrestricted market value. In exchange, the landowners agree to restrict the use of the land to agricultural and open space uses for ten years. Counties and cities are compensated for the loss of property tax revenue. Approximately one-half of California's agricultural and open space land is currently protected under the Williamson Act.

Natural and Recreational Land

Privately funded activist groups such as the Sierra Club and the Nature Conservancy are diligent in their efforts to preserve open space, and have ongoing campaigns to acquire open space for the use and enjoyment of future generations. Public park programs also allow these lands to be preserved in their natural state.

Open space preservation efforts are generally altruistic and, to some extent, represent an ideal situation. This reverse side of this coin is that they further limit the amount of land available for future development. Since the laws of supply and demand still prevail, this puts inflationary pressure on the remaining lands and their products.

Chapter 8
REVIEW

- California's housing market is a reflection of the state's unique and diverse economy.

- California has undergone steep rises and sharp falls in its housing market from the 1980s to the present. Currently, California has more than 11 million dwelling units, and leads the nation in housing growth. Housing vacancy rates vary across the state.

- California is one of the nation's most expensive housing markets.

- Lenders use a 28/36 "rule of thumb" in determining whether a prospective borrower can afford a particular home purchase.

- While there are many good reasons to rent housing, there are also significant disadvantages. These include the lack of equity build-up and the absence of tax advantages.

- Commercial construction exceeds industrial by a wide margin in California. The industrial vacancy rate in the state varies by region: some parts of California have industrial vacancy rates at or above the national average; others are below it. Many previously vacant industrial and commercial buildings are being converted to other uses, including residential.

- Investors in commercial and especially industrial properties must be aware of potential environmental liabilities, including asbestos, lead and underground storage tanks.

- Office vacancy and rental rates vary widely among the state's regions. Office vacancy is a sign of local economic health.

▪ Agriculture, lumbering and mining are major commercial uses of California's rural land. In the mining industry, or extraction sector, oil and gas are the primary products.

▪ The Williamson Act provides incentives and protections for agricultural land use. Natural and recreational lands are preserved by state and federal laws and by the work of private activist groups.

Chapter 8
QUIZ

1. The highest housing vacancy rates in California are in which of the following areas?

   A. Los Angeles
   B. Sacramento
   C. San Diego
   D. Northern California

2. Since 1990, the number of heads of household in each of the following age ranges has increased, *EXCEPT*:

   A. 25-34.
   B. 35-44.
   C. 45-54.
   D. Over 65.

3. The average number of persons per household in California is:

   A. higher than the national average.
   B. lower than the national average.
   C. higher than the national average, but lower than the Midwest and Northeast.
   D. the same as the national average.

4. What is the average per capita income in California?

   A. Less than $15,000
   B. $21,450
   C. $24,000
   D. $32,500

5. Which of the following statements about the California residential housing market is true?

   A. California is one of the nation's most affordable housing markets.
   B. Housing affordability has declined in California since 1990.
   C. Since the mid-1980s, California's housing market has proven itself to be uniquely recession-proof.
   D. California's housing market is one of the least affordable in the United States.

6. Approximately what percentage of Californians live in rented housing?

   A. One quarter
   B. One third
   C. One half
   D. Two thirds

7. Which of the following statements is true regarding commercial and industrial properties in California?

    A. Since the mid-1990s, industrial construction has rapidly exceeded commercial construction.
    B. In the Los Angeles metropolitan area, industrial vacancy rates rose sharply after 1994.
    C. Commercial construction continued to increase during the recessionary years of the early 1990s.
    D. Commercial and industrial construction and vacancy rates are an exception to the usual regional differences among areas of California.

8. Asbestos and underground storage tanks are of particular concern to investors in which of the following types of property?

    A. New office construction
    B. Existing industrial properties
    C. Retail
    D. Existing office

9. In regional shopping centers, the main tenant, usually a department store, is referred to as the:

    A. power center.
    B. hub.
    C. anchor.
    D. "big box."

10. The purpose of the Williamson Act is to:

    A. preserve California's farmland.
    B. protect the water supply to cities.
    C. acquire open land for public parks and preserves.
    D. develop technologies to prolong growing seasons.

9

Land Use Planning and Development

 ## Objectives:

- Describe in detail the various steps involved in the planning and development process

- Explain the types of zoning, their underlying objectives and possible constitutional issues

- Understand the ways in which local governments regulate land use and the strategies available to developers to work with government agencies and community organizations in planning successful projects

---

▦ STEPS IN THE DEVELOPMENT PROCESS: AN OVERVIEW

The conversion of raw land to an improved state is the ultimate in risk taking. Success lies at the end of a long and convoluted path of regulations, due diligence reports, contractual negotiations and obligations, financial arrangements, scheduling challenges, public relations hurdles and infinite details involved in the development process. This chapter will examine how the elements of land, labor and capital are combined to bring a project to fruition.

The process begins long before ground is broken on the site. In broad outline, the stages in a development project are

- **site identification.** A site must first be identified that meets the specifications of the development. Housing developers do not normally seek sites in industrial areas, and vice versa. In order to properly identify a suitable site, locators investigate a number of aspects.

- **zoning.** The local planning department will indicate which areas are currently zoned or have the potential of being rezoned (such as agricultural to residential) in keeping with the needs of the project.

- **economic conditions.** Discussions with the local Chamber of Commerce can reveal the general economic health of the area as well as economic stratification by neighborhood.

- **real estate values.** Local real estate brokers and appraisers can provide useful, current data concerning the tiers of value by neighborhood and their relative stability or trends upward or downward.

- **availability.** Upon identification of the target development area, local real estate firms should be contacted to determine available sites for consideration.

Site Acquisition

Once a site has been identified, the negotiation process begins.

Feasibility Study. A thorough economic analysis of the area is performed to evaluate the following, as relevant to the type of project:

- Local amenities

- Utility availability

- Transportation availability

- Economic trends of the area

- Housing price levels and/or rent comparables

- Retail sales activity

- Shopping, schools and houses of worship

- Actual or potential project competition

- Financing terms available on competing projects

Sales Contract

Once a price has been negotiated with the land owner, the terms of the sales contract can be structured to reduce the developer's risk. Even when a comprehensive study indicates a project at the particular site is feasible, there are many hurdles yet to overcome. For this reason the developer should consider three possible routes:

1. **Option Agreement.** The most cautious approach is merely providing option money on the site while the due diligence process takes place.

2. **Lease with Option to Purchase.** If the transaction initially appears to be fairly solid, the developer may want more control of the land than a mere option, and this instrument is such an intermediate device.

3. **Escrow Instructions with Contingencies.** This is, in effect, another form of option, since normally these escrow instructions will call for an extended escrow period (sometimes as much as a year or eighteen months), subject to rezoning of the property, approval of a preliminary tract map; availability of utilities and satisfactory soil and geological tests. In an area such as Malibu where there are no sewers, this would include the ability of the land to accept septic discharge.

4. **Other conditions of due diligence**, such as building permits, also may be necessary to the intended use of the site.

Interim Activities

During the **option period**, certain expenditures are required in order to ascertain the viability of the project. Some of these activities are

- hiring a professional *subdivision engineer* to prepare maps and coordinate map approvals with local authorities.

- engaging an *architect* to design building plans, taking into consideration the lot configuration designed by the subdivision engineer as well as local regulations and market realities.

- obtaining appropriate *legal documentation* that may be required for the development, such as articles of incorporation, by-laws, protective restrictions and leases.

- soliciting bids from *subcontractors* for various construction elements, such as: foundation, framing, plumbing, electrical, masonry, plastering and roofing.

- preparing a project *budget*.

- preliminary arrangements for *construction financing* on the project.

- negotiating for *permanent financing*, either for qualified purchasers (in the case of residential developments), or for the developer directly if ownership is to be retained (in the case of commercial and industrial property).

Project Financing

Once the sale is complete and final subdivision maps and permits have been obtained, the construction process begins with funds impounded by the construction lender to be disbursed upon satisfactory progress.

Lender's Investigation. Before the construction lender consummates a credit extension, many of the preliminary steps that were performed by the developer will be independently repeated by the construction lender to verify the financial feasibility of the project. In addition, the condition of title will be examined for

- **restrictions.** Existing recorded restrictions may preclude the intended development unless it wins approval of architectural committees or a holder of reversionary rights.

- **easements.** Easements on the property may interfere with proposed improvements.

- **contracts.** Agreements with local authorities may not be in concert with the proposed project. For instance, a prior owner may have signed an agreement with the city reserving the site for development of low to moderate income housing, while market rate housing is planned.

- **liens.** Prior financing arrangements that affect the equity requirements of the lender may have to be paid off or subordination arranged.

- **other conditions.** Other title items may affect the ability of the lender to be in a first lien position or otherwise violate the lender's underwriting requirements.

Construction Scheduling

Once the construction loan is consummated and construction commences, the developer converts to a scheduling phase, which may be based on the Gantt charts used by manufacturers in scheduling production. A **Gantt chart** is a bar-style chart in which project activities are illustrated on a horizontal time scale. Each bar corresponds to an item in the task list. By comparing the horizontal bars to the current date, a developer can see clearly whether or not the project is on schedule. Figure 9.1 illustrates a sample Gantt chart for reviewing this book so far.

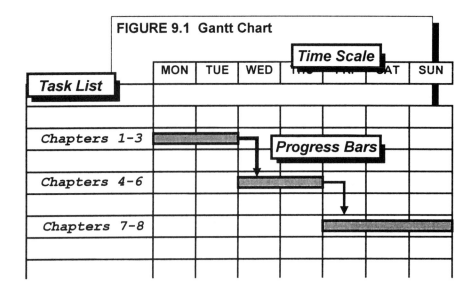

FIGURE 9.1 Gantt Chart

A successful scheduling process should bring the project to completion at or before the contemplated date. Credit checks and background investigations of the subcontractors are essential to avoid mechanics' liens and production delays, which can be disastrous.

Permanent Financing

Once construction is complete, the developer will want to convert the construction loan to permanent financing at the earliest possible date. Early conversion to a permanent loan is important to the developer because

- it *reduces overall project cost* due to the elimination of the risks involved during construction.

- it *increases the developer's profit* in the event the project is sold.

There is still some risk involved in obtaining permanent financing for a development project. Commercial and industrial loan funds have become harder to obtain since the restructuring of the financial market due to the savings and loan crisis of the early 1980s. Lenders are also reluctant to become involved in projects in which there are environmental issues involved. This concern will be discussed in Chapter 11.

▦ GOVERNMENT REGULATION OF LAND USE

In Chapter 5, we saw that an extensive *bundle of rights* goes along with owning real estate. However, those rights are not absolute. That is, a landowner's power to control his or her property is subject to other interests. Even the most complete ownership the law allows is limited by public and private restrictions. These are intended to ensure that one owner's use or enjoyment of his or her property does not interfere with others' use or enjoyment of their property or with the general welfare.

Individual ownership rights are subject to certain powers, or rights, held by federal, state and local governments. These limitations on the ownership of real estate are imposed for the general welfare of the community and, therefore, supersede the rights or interest of the individual. They represent the entry of the government into the marketplace to act as regulator and, to some extent, limiter of the functioning of a free real estate market.

Over the years, the government's policy has been to encourage private ownership of land. Home ownership is often referred to as "the American Dream." It is necessary, however, for a certain amount of land to be owned by the government for such uses as municipal buildings, state legislative houses, schools and military stations. Government ownership may also serve the public interest through urban renewal efforts, public housing and streets and highways. Often, the only way to ensure that enough land is set aside for recreational and conservation purposes is through direct government ownership in the form of national and state parks and forest preserves. Beyond this sort of direct ownership of land, however, most government controls on property occur at the local level.

In this chapter, we will look at government controls of land use that directly affect economic development of real estate. In the next chapter, we will consider more indirect regulation, such as fair housing laws and environmental regulation.

Police Power

Every state has the power to enact legislation to preserve order, protect the public health and safety and promote the general welfare of its citizens. That authority is known as the state's **police power**. The states delegate to counties and local municipalities the authority to enact ordinances in keeping with general laws. The increasing demands placed on finite natural resources have made it necessary for cities, towns and villages to increase their limitations on the private use of real estate. There are now controls over noise, air and water pollution as well as population density.

In California, the state's police power may be exercised "for the protection of the welfare, health, and peace of the people of this state." The California Constitution (Article XI, § 7) delegates police powers to counties and cities to enforce ordinances and regulations that are "not in conflict with the general laws."

Eminent Domain

Eminent domain is not a police power, it is the constitutional right of the government to acquire privately owned real estate for public use. **Condemnation** is the *process* by which the government exercises this right, by judicial or administrative proceedings. The use

- must be for the *public good*;
- *just compensation* must be paid to the owner; and
- the rights of the property owner must be protected by *due process of law*.

Public use has been defined very broadly by the courts to include not only public facilities but also property that is no longer fit for use and must be closed or destroyed.

Zoning

Zoning ordinances are local laws that regulate and control the use of land and structures. Zoning ordinances are, in effect, tools used by local governments to implement the master (or general) plan and ensure orderly growth and development. In general, zoning affects such things as

- permitted uses of each parcel of land;

- lot sizes;

- types of structures;

- building heights;

- setbacks (the minimum distance away from streets or sidewalks that structures may be built);

- style and appearance of structures;

- density (the ratio of land area to structure area); and

- protection of natural resources.

Zoning ordinances cannot be static; they must remain flexible to meet the changing needs of society. For example, in many large cities, factories and warehouses sit empty. Some cities have begun changing the zoning ordinances for such properties to permit new residential or commercial developments in areas once zoned strictly for heavy industrial use. Coupled with tax incentives, the changes lure developers back into the cities. The resulting housing is modern, conveniently located and affordable. Simple zoning changes can help revitalize whole neighborhoods in big cities.

Zoning Objectives. Zoning ordinances have traditionally divided land use into residential, commercial, industrial and agricultural classifications. These land-use areas are further divided into subclasses. For example, residential areas may be subdivided to provide for detached single-family dwellings, semidetached structures containing not more than four dwelling units, walkup apartments, high-rise apartments and so forth.

To meet both the growing demand for a variety of housing types and the need for innovative residential and nonresidential development, municipalities are adopting ordinances for subdivisions and planned residential developments. Some municipalities also use buffer zones, such as landscaped parks and playgrounds, to screen residential areas from nonresidential zones. Certain types of zoning that focus on special land-use objectives are used in some areas. These include

- **bulk zoning** to control density and avoid overcrowding by imposing restrictions such as setbacks, building heights and percentage of open area or by restricting new projects;

- **aesthetic zoning** to specify certain types of architecture for new buildings; and

- **incentive zoning** to ensure that certain uses are incorporated into developments, such as requiring the street floor of an office building to house retail establishments.

- **inclusionary zoning.** Residential projects in a number of cities have been approved on condition that a limited percentage of the purchasers buy at market prices, and the remainder at a reduced price reserved for low to moderate income buyers. The economic effect, in practice, is that the price level of the "market price" units is raised to compensate for the profit lost in offering the price reductions.

Figure 9.2 shows part of one city's zoning map.

Comprehensive (or General) Plan. Local governments establish development goals by creating a **comprehensive (or general) plan**. This is also referred to as a *master* (or *general*) *plan*. Municipalities and counties develop plans to control growth and development. The plan includes the municipality's objectives for the future, and the strategies and timing for those objectives to be implemented.

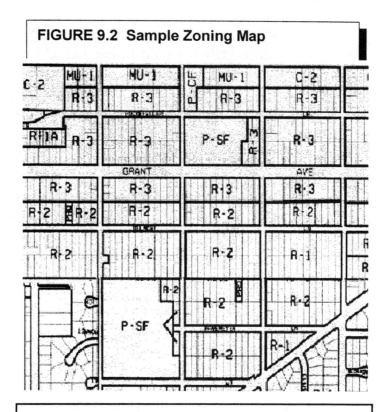

FIGURE 9.2 Sample Zoning Map

C: Commercial Zone
MU: Mixed Use Zone
P-SF: Planned Single-Family Residential Development
R-1: Single-Family Residential Zone
R-2, R-3: Low-Density Multifamily Residential Zone

For instance, a community may want to ensure that social and economic needs are balanced with environmental and aesthetic concerns. The comprehensive (or general) plan usually includes the following basic elements:

- **Land use** — that is, a determination of how much land may be proposed for residence, industry, business, agriculture, traffic and transit facilities, utilities, community facilities, parks and recreational facilities, floodplains and areas of special hazards

- **Housing needs** of present and anticipated residents, including rehabilitation of declining neighborhoods as well as new residential developments

- **Movement of people and goods**, including highways and public transit, parking facilities and pedestrian and bikeway systems

- **Community facilities and utilities**, such as schools, libraries, hospitals, recreational facilities, fire and police stations, water resources, sewerage and waste treatment and disposal, storm drainage and flood management

- **Energy conservation** to reduce energy consumption and promote the use of renewable energy sources

In California, cities and counties are required by state law to prepare and adopt a comprehensive, long-term general development plan. The plan must include basic goals and guidelines for land use, circulation, housing, conservation, open space, noise and safety.

Constitutional issues and zoning ordinances. Zoning can be a highly controversial issue. Among other things, it often raises questions of constitutional law. The preamble of the U.S. Constitution provides for the promotion of the general welfare, but the Fourteenth Amendment prevents the states from depriving "any person of life, liberty, or property, without due process of law."

Section 19, Article 1 of the California Constitution states that

> Private property may be taken or damaged for public use only when just compensation, ascertained by a jury unless waived, has first been paid to, or into court for, the owner. The Legislature may provide for possession by the condemnor following commencement of eminent domain proceedings upon deposit in court and prompt release to the owner of money determined by the court to be the probable amount of just compensation.

Any land-use legislation that is destructive, unreasonable, arbitrary or confiscatory usually is considered void.

Taking. The concept of **taking** comes from the takings clause of the Fifth Amendment to the U.S. Constitution. The clause reads, "nor shall private property be taken for public use, without just compensation." This means that when land is taken for public use through the government's power of eminent domain or condemnation, the owner must be compensated.

In general, no land is exempt from government seizure. The rule, however, is that the government cannot seize land without paying for it. This payment is referred to as **just compensation** — compensation that is just, or fair.

Of course, it is sometimes very difficult to determine what level of compensation is fair in any particular situation. The compensation may be negotiated between the owner and the government, or the owner may seek a court judgment setting the amount.

One method used to determine just compensation is the **before-and-after method**. This method is used primarily where a portion of an owner's property is seized for public use. The value of the owner's remaining property after the taking is subtracted from the value of the whole parcel before the taking. The result is the total amount of compensation due to the owner.

Nonconforming Use. Frequently, a lot or an improvement does not conform to the zoning use because it existed before the enactment or amendment of the zoning ordinance. Such a **nonconforming use** may be allowed to continue legally as long as it complies with the regulations governing nonconformities in the local ordinance or until the improvement is destroyed or torn down or the current use is abandoned. If the nonconforming use is allowed to continue indefinitely, it is considered to be grandfathered in to the new zoning.

Variances and Conditional-Use Permits. Each time a plan or zoning ordinance is enacted, some property owners are inconvenienced and want to change the use of their property. Generally, these owners may appeal for either a conditional-use permit or a variance to allow a use that does not meet current zoning requirements.

- A **conditional-use permit** (also known as a special-use permit) is usually granted to a property owner to allow a special use of property that is defined as an allowable conditional use within that zone, such as a house of worship or day-care center in a residential district. For a conditional-use permit to be appropriate, the intended use must meet certain standards set by the municipality.

- A **variance** permits a landowner to use his or her property in a manner that is strictly prohibited by the existing zoning. Variances provide relief if zoning regulations deprive an owner of the reasonable use of his or her property. To qualify for a variance, the owner must demonstrate the unique circumstances that make the variance necessary. In addition, the owner must prove that he or she is harmed and burdened by the regulations. A variance might also be sought to provide relief if existing zoning regulations create a physical hardship for the development of a specific property. For example, if an owner's lot is level next to a road, but slopes steeply 30 feet away from the road, the zoning board may allow a variance so the owner can build closer to the road than the setback allows.

Both variances and conditional-use permits are issued by zoning boards only after public hearings. The neighbors of a proposed use must be given an opportunity to voice their opinions. A property owner can also seek a change in the zoning classification of a parcel of real estate by obtaining an amendment to the district map or a zoning ordinance for that area. That is, the owner can attempt to have the zoning changed to accommodate his or her intended use of the property. The proposed amendment must be brought before a public hearing on the matter and approved by the governing body of the community.

Building Codes

Most municipalities have enacted ordinances to specify construction standards that must be met when repairing or erecting buildings. These are called building codes, and they set the requirements for kinds of materials and standards of workmanship, sanitary equipment, electrical wiring, fire prevention and the like.

A property owner who wants to build a structure or alter or repair an existing building usually must obtain a building permit. Through the permit requirement, municipal officials are made aware of new construction or alterations and can verify compliance with building codes and zoning ordinances. Inspectors will closely examine the plans and conduct periodic inspections of the work. Once the completed structure has been inspected and found satisfactory, the municipal inspector issues a certificate of occupancy or occupancy permit. A building permit is evidence of compliance with municipal regulations.

Similarly, communities with historic districts or those that are interested in maintaining a particular "look" or character (such as the "painted lady" areas of San Francisco), may have aesthetic ordinances. These laws require all new construction or restorations to be approved by a special board. The board ensures that the new structures will blend in with existing building styles. Owners of existing properties may need to obtain approval to have their homes painted or remodeled.

A Closer Look . . .

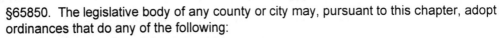

Here is a section of the California Government Code regarding zoning:

§65850. The legislative body of any county or city may, pursuant to this chapter, adopt ordinances that do any of the following:

(a) Regulate the use of buildings, structures, and land as between industry, business, residences, open space, including agriculture, recreation, enjoyment of scenic beauty, use of natural resources, and other purposes.

(b) Regulate signs and billboards.

(c) Regulate all of the following:

(1) The location, height, bulk, number of stories, and size of buildings and structures.

(2) The size and use of lots, yards, courts, and other open spaces.

(3) The percentage of a lot which may be occupied by a building or structure.

(4) The intensity of land use.

(d) Establish requirements for off street parking and loading.

(e) Establish and maintain building setback lines.

(f) Create civic districts around civic centers, public parks, public buildings, or public grounds, and establish regulations for those civic districts.

(g) (1) Regulate, pursuant to a content-neutral zoning ordinance, the time, place, and manner of operation of sexually oriented businesses, when the ordinance is designed to serve a substantial governmental interest, does not unreasonably limit alternative avenues of communication, and is based on narrow, objective, and definite standards. The legislative body is entitled to rely on the experiences of other counties and cities and on the findings of court cases in establishing the reasonableness of the ordinance and its relevance to the specific problems it addresses, including the harmful secondary effects the business may have on the community and its proximity to churches, schools, residences, establishments dispensing alcohol, and other sexually oriented businesses.

▦ REGULATION OF LAND DEVELOPMENT

Laws governing subdividing and land planning are controlled by the state and local governing bodies where the land is located. Rules and regulations developed by federal government agencies have provided certain minimum standards. Many local governments, however, have established standards that are higher than the minimum standards.

Development Plan

Most communities have adopted subdivision and land development ordinances as part of their comprehensive (or general) plans. An ordinance includes provisions for submitting and processing subdivision plats. A major advantage of subdivision ordinances is that they encourage flexibility, economy and ingenuity in the use of land.

In California the **Subdivision Map Act** and **Subdivided Lands Act** establish certain procedures for public protection that must be followed by developers. These laws regulate subdivision map processing as well as informational reports that must be provided (public report or "white report") to potential consumers detailing area amenities as well as any potential hazards (such as earthquakes or flooding) that may exist in the area.

A **subdivider** is a person who buys undeveloped acreage and divides it into smaller lots for sale to individuals or developers or for the subdivider's own use. A **developer** (who may also be a subdivider) improves the land, constructs homes or other buildings on the lots and sells them. Developing is generally a much more extensive activity than subdividing.

Before the actual subdividing can begin, the subdivider must go through the process of land planning. The resulting land development plan must comply with the municipality's comprehensive (or general) plan. Although comprehensive (or general) plans and zoning ordinances are not necessarily inflexible, a plan that requires them to be changed must undergo long, expensive and frequently complicated hearings.

Plats. From the land development and subdivision plans, the subdivider draws plats. A plat is a detailed map that illustrates the geographic boundaries of individual lots. It also shows the blocks, sections, streets, public easements and monuments in the prospective subdivision. A plat may also include engineering data and restrictive covenants. The plats must be approved by the municipality before they can be recorded. A developer may be required to submit an environmental impact report with the application for subdivision approval if the proposed development will have a significant effect on traffic, noise or pollution. This report explains what effect the proposed development will have on the surrounding area.

Subdivision Plans. In plotting out a subdivision according to local planning and zoning controls, a subdivider usually determines the size as well as the location of the individual lots. The maximum or minimum size of a lot is generally regulated by local ordinances and must be considered carefully.

The land itself must be studied, usually in cooperation with a surveyor, so that the subdivision takes advantage of natural drainage and land contours. A subdivider should provide for utility easements as well as easements for water and sewer mains. Most subdivisions are laid out by use of lots and blocks. An area of land is designated as a block, and the area making up this block is divided into lots.

One negative economic aspect of subdivision development is the potential for increased tax burdens on all residents, both inside and outside the subdivision. To protect local taxpayers against the costs of a heightened demand for public services, many local governments strictly regulate nearly all aspects of subdivision development.

Subdivision Density. Zoning ordinances control land use. Such control often includes minimum lot sizes and population density requirements for subdivisions and land developments. For example, a typical zoning restriction may set the minimum lot area on which a subdivider can build a single-family housing unit at 10,000 square feet. This means that the subdivider can build four houses per acre.

Many zoning authorities now establish special density zoning standards for certain subdivisions. Density zoning ordinances restrict the average maximum number of houses per acre that may be built within a particular subdivision. If the area is density zoned at an average maximum of four houses per acre, for instance, the subdivider may choose to cluster building lots to achieve an open effect. Regardless of lot size or number of units, the subdivider will be consistent with the ordinance as long as the average number of units in the development remains at or below the maximum density. This average is called gross density. For a subdivider and/or developer to realize the maximum economic benefit from a project, it is vital that the greatest legally allowable number of units be included.

Street patterns. By varying street patterns and clustering housing units, a subdivider can dramatically increase the amount of open or recreational space in a development. Two of these patterns are the gridiron and curvilinear patterns (see Figure 9.3).

The **gridiron pattern** features large lots, wide streets and limited-use service alleys. Sidewalks are usually adjacent to the streets or separated by narrow grassy areas. While the gridiron pattern provides for little open space and many lots may front on busy streets, it is an easy system to navigate.

The **curvilinear system** integrates major arteries of travel with smaller secondary and cul-de-sac streets carrying minor traffic. Curvilinear developments avoid the uniformity of the gridiron, but often lack service alleys. The absence of straight-line travel and the lack of easy access tend to make curvilinear developments quieter and more secure. However, getting from place to place may be more challenging.

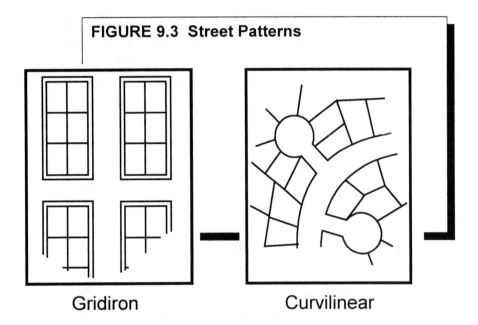

FIGURE 9.3 Street Patterns

Gridiron   Curvilinear

Clustering for Open Space. By slightly reducing lot sizes and clustering them around varying street patterns, a subdivider can house as many people in the same area as could be done using traditional subdividing plans, but with substantially increased open space.

Private Land-Use Controls

Not all restrictions on the use of land are imposed by government bodies. Certain restrictions to control and to maintain the desirable quality and character of a property or subdivision may be created by private entities, including the property owners themselves. These restrictions are separate from, and in addition to, the land-use controls exercised by the government. No private restriction can violate a local, state or federal law.

Restrictive covenants set standards for all the parcels within a defined subdivision. They usually govern the type, height and size of buildings that individual owners can erect, as well as land use, architectural style, construction methods, setbacks and square footage. Restrictive covenants cannot be for illegal purposes, such as for the exclusion of members of certain races, nationalities or religions.

Private restrictions can be enforced in court when one lot owner applies to the court for an injunction to prevent a neighboring lot owner from violating the recorded restrictions. The court injunction will direct the violator to stop or remove the violation. The court retains the power to punish the violator for failing to obey. If adjoining lot owners stand idly by while a violation is committed, they can lose the right to an injunction by their inaction. The court might claim their right was lost through laches — that is, the legal principal that a right may be lost through undue delay or failure to assert it.

▦ REGULATION OF LAND SALES

Just as the sale and use of property within a state are controlled by state and local governments, the sale of property in one state to buyers in another is subject to strict federal and state regulations.

Interstate Land Sales Full Disclosure Act

The federal **Interstate Land Sales Full Disclosure Act** regulates the interstate sale of unimproved lots. The act is administered by the Secretary of Housing and Urban Development (HUD) through the office of Interstate Land Sales registration. It is designed to prevent fraudulent marketing schemes that may arise when land is sold without being seen by the purchasers. (You may be familiar with stories about gullible buyers whose land purchases were based on glossy brochures shown by smooth-talking salespersons. When the buyers finally went to visit the "little pieces of paradise" they'd bought, they frequently found worthless swampland or barren desert.)

The act requires developers to file statements of record with HUD before they can offer unimproved lots in interstate commerce by telephone or through the mail. The statements of record must contain numerous disclosures about the properties.

Developers are also required to provide each purchaser or lessee of property with a printed report before the purchaser or lessee signs a purchase contract or lease. The report must disclose specific information about the land, including

- the type of title being transferred to the buyer;

- the number of homes currently occupied on the site;

- the availability of recreation facilities;

- the distance to nearby communities;

- utility services and charges; and

- soil conditions and foundation or construction problems.

If the purchaser or lessee does not receive a copy of the report before signing the purchase contract or lease, he or she may have grounds to void the contract.

Exemptions. The act provides a number of exemptions. For instance, it does not apply to subdivisions consisting of fewer than 25 lots or to those in which the lots are of 20 acres or more. Lots offered for sale solely to developers also are exempt from the act's requirements, as are lots on which buildings exist or where a seller is obligated to construct a building within two years.

California Subdivided Land Sales

Section 11010 of the California Business and Professions Code requires that anyone who intends to offer subdivided land within this state for sale or lease must file a notice of intention and apply for a public report with the Department of Real Estate. The notice of intention must contain certain information about the subdivided land and the proposed offering, including

- the name and address of the owner, the subdivider, and a legal description of the land.

- a statement of the condition of the title to the land, particularly including any encumbrances.

- a statement of the terms and conditions on which it is intended to dispose of the land, together with copies of any contracts intended to be used and a statement of the use or uses for which the proposed subdivision will be offered and any limits on the use or occupancy of parcels.

- a statement of any provisions that have been made for public utilities in the proposed subdivision, including water, electricity, gas, telephone, and sewerage facilities.

- a statement, if applicable, referencing any soils and/or geologic report that have been prepared specifically for the subdivision, as well as whether or not fill is proposed to be used in the subdivision.

■ ECONOMIC COOPERATION

Developers must deal with the realities of the marketplace. The ultimate input in the planning process comes from the community itself, and increasingly activist citizens have considerable influence on the development process. Even in unplanned communities, developers must deal with powerful and organized forces of public opinion.

- **Establishing Rapport.** Developing a rapport within the community as well as with the governing bodies is important. This means some form of liaison and dialogue in community and governmental forums. An understanding of the cultural, economic and political demographics of a community is vital to knowing how to communicate effectively with citizens. Look for "common ground" issues and "mutual benefit" perspectives. Consider the kind of unspoken messages that development may send and how those messages may be interpreted by the public. For instance, what does a gated subdivision say to the surrounding community?

- **Willingness to Compromise.** In order to carry out a development project, many times trade-offs must be arranged. Developers must be willing to compromise in order to see their projects to fruition.

- **Infrastructure.** Infrastructure issues have high priority in most communities: as more citizens arrive, more services are required. To alleviate some of these problems, developers often donate land for parks, schools, roads, flood control and recreation.

- **Participation in the Planning Process.** Rather than opposing a comprehensive (or general) plan after the fact, the developer might seek to become involved and thus have some control of his or her own destiny. The developer can serve as a consultant to the community in reaching its development goals.

- **Understanding Community Goals.** Ideally, site selection criteria should include ascertaining that community goals are in harmony with the developer's own. One of the areas where tension arises between the development process and the community is the "slow growth" mode that many communities have embraced in recent years. Once the developer understands that the goal of master (or general) plans of this nature is to preserve the value of existing improvements, frustration can be eased somewhat. The self-image a community promotes through zoning regulations might be an urban financial center, an industrial giant or a residential village.

Benefits to Community

The development process is indeed challenging. However, along with the challenges come both private and public rewards. Improvement of raw land provides needed housing and business structures and enhances the tax base, enabling local and state governments to provide the services their citizens need.

The Next Step

In the next chapter, we will consider the ways in which government regulations in a more "social" arena influence the real estate market and the economics of land development.

Chapter 9
REVIEW

■ The **DEVELOPMENT PROCESS** includes several distinct issues, each with its own analysis and considerations: *site identification*, *zoning*, *economic conditions*, *real estate values* and *availability*.

■ Individual ownership rights are subject to powers exercised by federal, state and local governments. A state's power to *preserve order*, *protect public health* and *promote the general welfare* is its **POLICE POWER**.

■ **EMINENT DOMAIN** is the government's *right* to acquire privately owned real estate. The *process* by which that right is exercised is called **CONDEMNATION**.

▬ A government make **TAKE** private real estate only for the *public good*. **JUST COMPENSATION** must be paid to the owner, and the owner's rights must be protected by *due process of law*.

▬ **ZONING ORDINANCES** are local laws that *regulate and control the use of land and structures*, to carry out the objectives of a **COMPREHENSIVE (OR GENERAL) PLAN** for the community.

▬ A **CONDITIONAL-USE PERMIT** allows a *special use of property allowable within a zone*. A **VARIANCE** permits a landowner to use his or her property in a manner that is *strictly prohibited by existing zoning regulations*.

▬ Through subdivision and land development laws, developers and subdividers must follow strict procedures to protect the public interest by *disclosing* specific information and following rules regarding hearings and compliance with the comprehensive (or general) plan.

▬ Developers can comply with density requirements and maximize the profitable use of land through the use of various **STREET PATTERNS** and **CLUSTERING** strategies.

▬ The *sale* of **SUBDIVIDED LAND** is regulated by both state and federal law.

Chapter 9
QUIZ

1. An economic analysis of a site, including utility availability, economic trends and competition is a:

   A. plat.
   B. feasibility study.
   C. Gannt chart.
   D. comprehensive (or general) plan.

2. All of the following steps would be taken by a developer during the option period, *EXCEPT*:

   A. engaging an architect.
   B. preparing a budget.
   C. soliciting subcontractor bids.
   D. filing an ILFDA report with HUD.

3. The process by which the government may acquire privately owned real estate for public use is:

   A. eminent domain.
   B. condemnation.
   C. police power.
   D. zoning.

4. Local laws that regulate and control the use of land and structures within designated land-use districts are:

   A. zoning ordinances.
   B. takings.
   C. conditional-use permits.
   D. subdivision plans.

5. Zoning with the primary intent of controlling density and avoiding overcrowding through setbacks, building height restrictions and limits on new construction is which type of zoning?

   A. Bulk
   B. Aesthetic
   C. Incentive
   D. Inclusionary

6. All of the following are relevant to the government's power to take private property for public use, *EXCEPT*:

   A. the 14th Amendment to the U.S. Constitution.
   B. the Preamble to the U.S. Constitution.
   C. the 5th Amendment to the U.S. Constitution.
   D. the Declaration of Independence.

7. The city of Onion Lake has passed a new zoning ordinance that prohibits all commercial structures more than 30 feet high. A developer wants to construct an office building that will be 52 feet high. Under these facts, the developer must apply for a:

   A. nonconforming use permit.
   B. zoning permit.
   C. conditional-use permit.
   D. variance.

8. A home owner would like to operate a day-care business in her home. If she lives in an area zoned for residential, noncommercial use only, she must do which of the following?

    A. Request that the zoning board declare her home to be a nonconforming use
    B. Ask a court to grant an injunction against the zoning board
    C. Seek a conditional-use permit from the zoning board
    D. Apply to the zoning board for a variance

9. A detailed map that illustrates the geographic boundaries of individual lots in a subdivision is a:

    A. plan.
    B. plat.
    C. gridiron.
    D. disclosure.

10. The California Business and Professions Code requires that anyone who intends to offer subdivided land in California for sale or lease must file a notice of intention with the:

    A. Secretary of Housing and Urban Development.
    B. California Department of Real Estate.
    C. Governor.
    D. Office of Land Use Planning and Development.

10 Fair Housing and Environmental Regulations

 Objectives:

- Understand the economic impact of fair housing laws on the real estate industry

- Identify the most common environmental considerations that influence buying and investing decisions

- Explain the liability issues arising under federal Superfund laws

---

FAIR HOUSING LAWS

The purpose of civil rights laws that affect the real estate industry is to create a marketplace in which all persons of similar financial means have a similar range of housing choices. The goal is to ensure that everyone has the opportunity to live where he or she chooses. Owners, real estate licensees, apartment management companies, real estate organizations, lending agencies, builders and developers must all take a part in creating this single housing market. Federal, state and local fair housing or equal opportunity laws affect every phase of a real estate transaction, from listing to closing. The intended effect of all these various regulations is to create a freer real estate market.

215

The California Real Estate Commission's specifically stated goal is "to achieve a 'color blind' real estate industry which can help attain peaceful equal opportunity and fair housing for society." The Commission believes the "primary attitude of a licensee should be one which is color blind and absolutely without bias."

The U.S. Congress and the Supreme Court have developed a legal framework that preserves the Constitutional rights of all citizens. However, while the passage of laws may establish a code for public conduct, centuries of discriminatory practices and attitudes are not so easily changed. Failure to comply with fair housing laws is both a civil and criminal violation, and grounds for disciplinary action against a violator.

Evolution of Equal Housing

The federal government's effort to guarantee fair and equal housing opportunities to all U.S. citizens began with the passage of the **Civil Rights Act of 1866**. This law prohibits any type of discrimination based on race.

The U.S. Supreme Court's 1896 decision in *Plessy v. Ferguson* established the "separate but equal" doctrine of legalized racial segregation. A series of court decisions and federal laws in the 20 years between 1948 and 1968 attempted to address the inequities in housing that were results of *Plessy*. Those efforts, however, tended to address only certain aspects of the housing market (such as federally funded housing programs). As a result, their impact was limited. **Title VIII of the Civil Rights Act of 1968**, however, prohibited specific discriminatory practices throughout the real estate industry.

The U.S. Supreme Court has since expanded the definition of the term race to include ancestral and ethnic characteristics, including certain physical, cultural or linguistic characteristics that are commonly shared by a national origin group. These rulings are significant because discrimination on the basis of race, as it is now defined, affords due process of complaints under the provisions of the Civil Rights Act of 1866.

Fair Housing Act. Title VIII of the Civil Rights Act of 1968 prohibited discrimination in housing based on race, color, religion or national origin. In 1974, the Housing and Community Development Act added sex to the list of protected classes. In 1988, the Fair Housing Amendments Act included disability and familial status (that is, the presence of children). Today, these laws are known as the federal **Fair Housing Act**. The Fair Housing Act prohibits discrimination on the basis of race, color, religion, sex, disability, familial status or national origin. The act also prohibits discrimination against individuals because of their association with persons in the protected classes. The law is administered by the Department of Housing and Urban Development (HUD).

A Closer Look . . .

The following are provisions of the Federal Fair Housing Act, along with examples of each:

- **Refusing to sell, rent or negotiate the sale or rental of housing**
  K owns an apartment building with several vacant units. When an Asian family asks to see one of the units, K tells them to go away.

- **Changing terms, conditions or services for different individuals as a means of discriminating**
  S, a Roman Catholic, calls on a duplex, and the landlord tells her the rent is $400 per month. When she talks to the other tenants, she learns that all the Lutherans in the complex pay only $325 per month.

- **Advertising any discriminatory preference or limitation in housing or making any inquiry or reference that is discriminatory in nature**
  A real estate agent places this ad in a newspaper: "Just Listed! Perfect home for white family, near excellent parochial school!"

A developer places this ad in an urban newspaper: "Sunset River Hollow — Dream Homes Just for You!" The ad is accompanied by a photo of several African-American families.

- **Representing that a property is not available for sale or rent when in fact it is**

  J, who uses a wheelchair, is told that the house J wants to rent is no longer available. The next day, however, the For Rent sign is still in the window.

- **Profiting by inducing property owners to sell or rent on the basis of the prospective entry into the neighborhood of persons of a protected class**

  N, a real estate agent, sends brochures to homeowners in the predominantly white Ridgewood neighborhood. The brochures, which feature N's past success selling homes, include photos of racial minorities, population statistics and the caption, "The Changing Face of Ridgewood."

- **Altering the terms or conditions of a home loan, or denying a loan, as a means of discrimination**

  A lender requires M, a divorced mother of two young children, to pay for a special in-depth credit report. In addition, her father must cosign her application. After talking to a single male friend, M learns that he was not required to do either of those things, despite his lower income and poor credit history.

- **Denying membership or participation in a multiple-listing service, a real estate organization or another facility related to the sale or rental of housing as a means of discrimination**

  The Topper County Real Estate Practitioners' Association meets every week to discuss available properties and buyers. None of Topper County's black or female agents is allowed to be a member.

Disability

A disability is a physical or mental impairment. The term includes having a history of, or being regarded as having, an impairment that substantially limits one or more of an individual's major life activities. Persons who have AIDS are protected by the fair housing laws under this classification.

The federal fair housing law's protection of disabled persons does not include those who are current users of illegal or controlled substances. Nor are individuals who have been convicted of the illegal manufacture or distribution of a controlled substance protected under this law. However, the law does prohibit discrimination against those who are participating in addiction recovery programs.

It is unlawful to discriminate against prospective buyers or tenants on the basis of disability. Landlords must make **reasonable accommodations** to existing policies, practices or services to permit persons with disabilities to have equal enjoyment of the premises. For instance, it would be reasonable for a landlord to permit support animals (such as seeing eye dogs) in a normally no-pets building or to provide a designated handicapped parking space in a generally unreserved lot.

People with disabilities must be permitted to make **reasonable modifications** to the premises at their own expense. Such modifications might include lowering door handles or installing bath rails to accommodate a person in a wheelchair. Failure to permit reasonable modification constitutes discrimination.

However, the law recognizes that some reasonable modifications might make a rental property undesirable to the general population. In such a case, the landlord is allowed to require that the property be restored to its previous condition when the lease period ends.

The law does not prohibit restricting occupancy exclusively to persons with handicaps in dwellings that are designed specifically for their accommodation. For new construction of certain multifamily properties, a number of accessibility and usability requirements must be met under federal law. Access is specified for public and common-use portions of the buildings, and adaptive and accessible design must be implemented for the interior of the dwelling units.

Exemptions

The federal Fair Housing Act provides for certain exemptions. It is important for developers, investors and licensees to know in what situations the exemptions apply. However, no exemptions involve race and no exceptions apply when a real estate licensee is involved in a transaction.

- The sale or rental of a single-family home is exempt when the home is owned by an individual who does not own more than three such homes at one time, a real estate broker or salesperson is not involved in the transaction and discriminatory advertising is not used.

- The rental of rooms or units is exempted in an owner-occupied one- to four-family dwelling.

- Dwelling units owned by religious organizations may be restricted to people of the same religion if membership in the organization is not restricted on the basis of race, color or national origin. A private club that is not open to the public may restrict the rental or occupancy of lodgings that it owns to its members as long as the lodgings are not operated commercially.

- The Fair Housing Act does not require that housing be made available to any individual whose tenancy would constitute a direct threat to the health or safety of other individuals or that would result in substantial physical damage to the property of others.

While the Fair Housing Act protects families with children, certain properties can be restricted to occupancy by elderly persons.

Equal Credit Opportunity Act

The federal **Equal Credit Opportunity Act (ECOA)** prohibits discrimination based on race, color, religion, national origin, sex, marital status or age in the granting of credit. Note how the ECOA protects more classes of persons than the Fair Housing Act. The ECOA bars discrimination on the basis of marital status and age. It also prevents lenders from discriminating against recipients of public assistance programs such as food stamps and Social Security. As in the Fair Housing Act, the ECOA requires that credit applications be considered only on the bases of income, net worth, job stability and credit rating.

Americans with Disabilities Act

The ADA requires employers to make reasonable accommodations that enable an individual with a disability to perform essential job functions. Reasonable accommodations include making the work site accessible, restructuring a job, providing part-time or flexible work schedules and modifying equipment that is used on the job. The provisions of the ADA apply to any employer with 15 or more employees. The ADA also applies to accessibility to commercial buildings.

Fair Housing Advertising Practices

No advertisement of property for sale or rent may include language indicating a preference or limitation. The media used cannot target one population to the exclusion of others. For instance, advertising property only in a Korean-language newspaper tends to discriminate against non-Koreans. Similarly, limiting advertising to a cable television channel available only to white suburbanites may be construed as a discriminatory act. However, if an advertisement appears in general-circulation media as well, it may be legal. Table 10.1 outlines HUD's various restrictions.

TABLE 10.1

CATEGORY	RULE	PERMITTED	NOT PERMITTED
Race Color National Origin	No discriminatory limitation/preference may be expressed	"master bedroom" "good neighborhood"	"white neighborhood" "no French"
Religion	No religious preference/limitation	"chapel on premises" "kosher meals available" "Merry Christmas"	"no Muslims" "nice Christian family" "near great Catholic school"
Sex	No explicit preference based on sex	"mother-in-law suite" "master bedroom" "female roommate sought"	"great house for a man" "wife's dream kitchen"
Handicap	No exclusions or limitations based on handicap	"wheelchair ramp" "walk to shopping" "non-smoking"	"no wheelchairs" "able-bodied tenants only"
Family Status	No preference or limitation based on family size or nature	"two-bedroom" "family room" "quiet neighborhood"	"married couple only" "no more than 2 children" "retiree's dream house"
Photographs or Illustrations of People	People should be clearly representative and non-exclusive	Illustrations showing a mix of races, family groups, singles, etc.	Illustrations showing only singles, black families, elderly white adults, etc.

Those who prepare appraisals or any statements of valuation, whether they are formal or informal, oral or written (including a competitive market analysis), may consider any factors that affect value. However, race, color, religion, national origin, sex, handicap and familial status are not factors that may be considered.

California Fair Housing Laws

California's fair housing laws include essentially the same prohibitions against discrimination, panic selling, redlining, steering and blockbusting contained in the federal law. Under the **California Government Code, Section 12955**, it is illegal for the owner of any housing accommodation to discriminate against any person because of race, color, religion, sex, marital status, national origin, ancestry, familial status or disability. No advertisement for the sale or rental of housing may indicate a preference, limitation or discrimination based on the protected classes.

It is illegal for any person, bank, mortgage company or other financial institution that provides financial assistance for the purchase, organization or construction of any housing accommodation to discriminate against any person or group of persons because of their race, color, religion, sex, marital status, national origin, ancestry, familial status or disability in the terms, conditions or privileges relating to the obtaining or use of that financial assistance.

Accessibility. Under California law, "discrimination" includes the failure to design and construct a multifamily dwelling of four or more units in a manner that provides access to and use by persons with disabilities. Multifamily dwellings must have at least one accessible building entrance, unless the terrain or other unusual characteristic of the site prohibits accessibility by persons with disabilities. All the doors designed to allow passage into and within all premises must be sufficiently wide to allow passage by persons in wheelchairs. Public and common areas must be accessible, and light switches, electrical outlets, thermostats and other environmental controls must be in accessible locations.

California law requires newly constructed multifamily residential housing units to include reinforced bathroom walls to allow later installation of grab bars around the toilet, tub, shower stall, and shower seat; kitchens and bathrooms must be designed so that an individual in a wheelchair can maneuver about the space.

Barrows v. Jackson. In this 1953 California decision (later affirmed by the U.S. Supreme Court), it was held that a property owner may not recover damages from another for breach of a racially restrictive covenant. The **California Civil Code § 782** (enacted in 1961) subsequently provided that any provision in any deed that purports to restrict the right to sell, lease, rent, use or occupy real property to persons of a particular racial, national or ethnic group is void.

The Rumford Act. The California Fair Employment and Housing Act (Government Code §§ 12900-12996) prohibits discrimination in housing accommodations (sale, rental, lease or financing) on the basis of race, color, religion, sex, marital status, national origin or ancestry. The act prohibits an owner or his or her licensed agent from discriminating, asking prospective buyers or lessees about prohibited discriminatory factors, indicating preference in ads or discriminating against someone who opposed the owner's prior discriminatory practices.

California Civil Rights Act. California Civil Code §§ 51-52, enacted in 1959, prohibits discrimination in California business establishments based on sex, race, color, religion, ancestry and national origin. "Business establishments" includes all professional services of real estate licensees, as well as the "business" of renting or selling property, even if this is not how the owner earns a living.

California law prohibits other types of discrimination, such as discrimination against children in apartment complex rentals and discrimination based on sexual preference.

▦ ENVIRONMENTAL ISSUES

Most states have recognized the need to balance the legitimate commercial use of land with the need to preserve vital resources and protect the quality of the states' air, water and soil. Preservation of a state's environment both enhances the quality of life and helps strengthen property values. The prevention and cleanup of pollutants and toxic wastes not only revitalize the land but create greater opportunities for responsible development.

Hazardous Substances

Pollution and hazardous substances in the environment are important considerations in the real estate economy, because they affect the attractiveness, desirability and market value of cities, industrial, commercial and residential properties. A toxic environment is not a place where anyone would want to live or work.

Hazardous substances include the following:

- **Asbestos.** A mineral that was once used as insulation because it was resistant to fire and contained heat effectively, **asbestos** was banned in 1978. Prior to that year, it was a component of more than 3,000 types of building materials. It was used to cover pipes, ducts, and heating and hot water units. Its fire-resistant properties made it a popular material for use in floor tile, exterior siding and roofing products. The Environmental Protection Agency (EPA) estimates that about 20 percent of the nation's commercial and public buildings contain asbestos.

  Asbestos is highly **friable**: as it ages, its fibers break down easily into tiny filaments and particles. When these particles become airborne, they pose a risk to humans: exposure to microscopic asbestos fibers can result in a variety of respiratory diseases. Airborne asbestos contamination is most prevalent in public and commercial buildings, including schools, although asbestos contamination can also be found in residential properties. If the asbestos fibers in the indoor air of a building reach a dangerous level, the building becomes difficult to lease, finance or insure. No safe level of asbestos exposure has been determined.

  Asbestos is costly to remove because the process requires licensed technicians and specially sealed environments. In addition, removal itself may be dangerous: improper removal procedures may further contaminate the air within the structure. The waste generated must be disposed of at a licensed facility, which further adds to the cost of removal. Encapsulation, or the sealing off of disintegrating asbestos, is an alternate method of asbestos control that may be preferable to removal in certain circumstances.

- **Lead.** For many years, **lead** was used as a pigment and drying agent in alkyd oil-based paint. Lead-based paint may be on any interior or exterior surface, but it is particularly common on doors, windows and other woodwork. The federal government estimates that lead is present in about 75 percent of all private housing built before 1978; that's approximately 57 million homes, ranging from low-income apartments to million-dollar mansions.

  An elevated level of lead in the body can cause serious damage to the brain, kidneys, nervous system and red blood cells. The degree of harm is related to the amount of exposure and the age at which a person is exposed. Lead dust can be ingested, inhaled or consumed in the water supply because of lead pipes or lead solder. Soil and groundwater may be contaminated by everything from lead plumbing in leaking landfills to discarded skeet and bullets from an old shooting range. High levels of lead have been found in the soil near waste-to-energy incinerators. The air may be contaminated by leaded gasoline fumes from gas stations or automobile exhausts.

  The use of lead-based paint was banned in 1978. Licensees who are involved in the sale, management, financing or appraisal of properties constructed before 1978 face potential liability for any personal injury that might be suffered by an occupant. Numerous legislative efforts affect licensees, sellers and landlords. Known lead-based paint hazards must be disclosed to prospective buyers and tenants.

- **Radon.** A radioactive gas, **radon** is produced by the natural decay of other radioactive substances. Although radon can occur anywhere, some areas are known to have abnormally high amounts. The eastern United States is especially rich in radon. When radon enters buildings and is trapped in high concentrations (usually in basements with inadequate ventilation), it can cause health problems. Opinions and scientific evidence differ as to both minimum safe levels and the actual danger posed by exposure. Radon may be the most underestimated cause of lung cancer, particularly for children, individuals who smoke and those who spend considerable time indoors.

Interestingly, the modern practice of creating energy-efficient homes and commercial buildings with practically airtight walls and windows may increase the potential for radon gas accumulation.

- **Urea-Formaldehyde.** Urea-formaldehyde was first used in building materials, particularly insulation, in the 1970s. Gases leak out of the urea-formaldehyde foam insulation (UFFI) as it hardens and become trapped in the interior of a building. In 1982, the Consumer Product Safety Commission banned the use of UFFI. The ban was reduced to a warning after courts determined that there was insufficient evidence to support a ban. Urea-formaldehyde is known to cause cancer in animals, though the evidence of its effect on humans is inconclusive. Formaldehyde does cause some individuals to suffer respiratory problems as well as eye and skin irritations.

- **Carbon Monoxide.** Carbon monoxide (**CO**) is a colorless, odorless gas that occurs as a by-product of burning such fuels as wood, oil and natural gas due to incomplete combustion. Furnaces, water heaters, space heaters, fireplaces and wood stoves all produce CO as a natural result of their combustion of fuel. However, when these appliances function properly and are properly ventilated, their CO emissions are not a problem. When improper ventilation or equipment malfunctions permit large quantities of CO to be released into a residence or commercial structure, it poses a significant health hazard. More than 200 deaths from carbon monoxide poisoning occur each year.

- **Electromagnetic Fields.** One of the most hotly-debated environmental problems today is the issue of **electromagnetic fields (EMFs)**. EMFs are generated by the movement of electrical currents. The use of any electrical appliance creates a small field of electromagnetic radiation: clock radios, blow-driers, televisions and computers all produce EMFs. The major concern regarding electromagnetic fields involves high-tension power lines. The EMFs produced by these high-voltage lines, as well as by secondary distribution lines and transformers, are suspected of causing cancer, hormonal changes and behavioral abnormalities. There is considerable controversy (and much conflicting evidence) about whether EMFs pose a health hazard.

Groundwater Contamination

Groundwater is the water that exists under the earth's surface within the tiny spaces or crevices in geological formations. Groundwater forms the water table, the natural level at which the ground is saturated. This may be near the surface (in areas where the water table is very high) or several hundred feet underground. Surface water can also be absorbed into the groundwater.

Any contamination of the underground water can threaten the supply of pure, clean water for private wells or public water systems. If groundwater is not protected from contamination, the earth's natural filtering systems may be inadequate to ensure the availability of pure water.

Water can be contaminated from a number of sources. Run-off from waste disposal sites, leaking underground storage tanks, uncapped dry wells and use of pesticides and herbicides are some of the main culprits. Because water flows from one place to another, contamination can spread far from its source. Numerous regulations are designed to protect against water contamination. Once contamination has been identified, its source can be eliminated. The water may eventually become clean. However, the process can be time consuming and extremely expensive.

Underground Storage Tanks. Approximately 3 million to 5 million **underground storage tanks** (**UST**s) exist in the United States.

Underground storage tanks are commonly found on sites where petroleum products are used or where gas stations and auto repair shops are located. They also may be found in a number of other commercial and industrial establishments — including printing and chemical plants, wood treatment plants, paper mills, paint manufacturers, dry cleaners and food processing plants — for storing chemical or other process waste. Military bases and airports are also common sites for underground tanks. In residential areas, they are used to store heating oil and propane.

Some tanks are currently in use, but many are long forgotten. It is an unfortunate fact that it was once common to dispose of toxic wastes by simple burial: out of sight, out of mind. Over time, however, neglected tanks may leak hazardous substances into the environment. This permits contaminants to pollute not only the soil around the tank but also adjacent parcels and groundwater.

Some warning signs include the presence of fill pipes, vent lines, stained soil and fumes or odors. Detection, removal and cleanup of surrounding contaminated soil can be an expensive operation.

Recent state and federal laws impose very strict requirements on landowners where underground storage tanks are located to detect and correct leaks in an effort to protect the groundwater. The federal UST program is regulated by the EPA. The regulations apply to tanks that contain hazardous substances or liquid petroleum products and that store at least 10 percent of their volume underground. UST owners are required to register their tanks and adhere to strict technical and administrative requirements. Owners are also required to demonstrate that they have sufficient financial resources to cover any damage that might result from leaks.

Waste Disposal Sites

Americans produce vast quantities of garbage every day. Despite public and private recycling and composting efforts, huge piles of waste materials — from beer cans, junk mail and diapers to food, paint and toxic chemicals — must be disposed of. Old tires are most commonly disposed of in landfill operations, such as abandoned quarries. Landfill operations have become the main receptacles for garbage and refuse. Special hazardous waste disposal sites have been established to contain radioactive waste from nuclear power plants, toxic chemicals and waste materials produced by medical, scientific and industrial processes.

Perhaps the most prevalent method of common waste disposal is simply to bury it. A **landfill** is an enormous hole, either excavated for the purpose of waste disposal or left over from surface mining operations. The hole is lined with clay or a synthetic liner to prevent leakage of waste material into the water supply. A system of underground drainage pipes permits monitoring of leaks and leaching.

Waste is laid on the liner at the bottom of the excavation, and a layer of topsoil is then compacted onto the waste. The layering procedure is repeated again and again until the landfill is full, the layers mounded up sometimes as high as several hundred feet over the surrounding landscape. **Capping** is the process of laying two to four feet of soil over the top of the site and then planting grass or some other vegetation to enhance the landfill's aesthetic value and to prevent erosion. A ventilation pipe runs from the landfill's base through the cap to vent off accumulated natural gases created by the decomposing waste.

Federal, state and local regulations govern the location, construction, content and maintenance of landfill sites. Test wells around landfill operations are installed to constantly monitor the groundwater in the surrounding area, and soil analyses can be used to test for contamination. Completed landfills have been used for such purposes as parks and golf courses. Rapid suburban growth has resulted in many housing developments and office campuses being built on landfill sites.

A Closer Look . . .

A suburban office building constructed on an old landfill site was very profitable until its parking lot began to sink. While the structure itself was supported by pylons driven deep into the ground, the parking lot was unsupported. As the landfill beneath it compacted, the wide concrete lot sank lower and lower around the building. Each year, the building's management had to relandscape to cover the exposed foundations. The sinking parking lot eventually severed underground phone and power lines and water mains. Computers were offline for hours, and flooding was frequent on the ground floor. Finally, leaking gases from the landfill began causing unpleasant odors. The tenants moved out, and the building was left vacant.

Hazardous and radioactive waste disposal sites are subject to strict state and federal regulation to prevent the escape of toxic substances into the surrounding environment. Some materials, such as radioactive waste, are sealed in containers and placed in "tombs" buried deep underground. The tombs are designed to last thousands of years, built according to strict federal and state regulations. These disposal sites are usually limited to extremely remote locations, well away from populated areas or farmland.

Of particular concern in California is the geologic stability of hazardous waste sites. Careful studies must be conducted to ensure that such sites are not built on or near active fault lines.

Environmental issues have a significant impact on the real estate economy. In 1995, a jury awarded $6.7 million to homeowners whose property values had been lowered because of the defendant tire company's negligent operation and maintenance of a hazardous waste dump site. The 1,713 plaintiffs relied on testimony from economists and a real estate appraiser to demonstrate how news stories about the site had lowered the market values of their homes.

CERCLA and Environmental Protection

The majority of legislation dealing with environmental problems has been instituted within the past two decades. Although the EPA was created at the federal level to oversee such problems, several other federal agencies' areas of concern generally overlap.

The **Comprehensive Environmental Response, Compensation, and Liability Act** (**CERCLA**) was created in 1980. It established a fund of $9 billion, called the **Superfund**, to clean up uncontrolled hazardous waste sites and to respond to spills. It created a process for identifying **potential responsible parties** (**PRPs**) and ordering them to take responsibility for the cleanup action. CERCLA is administered and enforced by the federal EPA.

A landowner is liable under CERCLA when a release or a threat of release of a hazardous substance has occurred on his or her property. Regardless of whether the contamination is the result of the landowner's actions or those of others, the owner can be held responsible for the cleanup. This liability includes the cleanup not only of the landowner's property but also of any neighboring property that has been contaminated. A landowner who is not responsible for the contamination can seek recovery reimbursement for the cleanup cost from previous landowners, any other responsible party or the Superfund. However, if other parties are not available, even a landowner who did not cause the problem could be solely responsible for the costs.

Once the EPA determines that hazardous material has been released into the environment, it is authorized to begin remedial action. First, it attempts to identify the potentially responsible parties (PRPs). If the PRPs agree to cooperate in the cleanup, they must agree about how to divide the cost.

If the PRPs do not voluntarily undertake the cleanup, the EPA may hire its own contractors to do the necessary work. The EPA then bills the PRPs for the cost. If the PRPs refuse to pay, the EPA can seek damages in court for up to three times the actual cost of the cleanup.

Liability under the Superfund is considered to be *strict*, *joint and several*, and *retroactive*. **Strict liability** means that the owner is responsible to the injured party without excuse. **Joint and several liability** means that each of the individual owners is personally responsible for the total damages. If only one of the owners is financially able to handle the total damages, that owner must pay the total and collect the proportionate shares from the other owners whenever possible. **Retroactive liability** means that the liability is not limited to the current owner, but includes people who have owned the site in the past.

In 1986, the U.S. Congress reauthorized the Superfund. The amended statute contains stronger cleanup standards for contaminated sites and five times the funding of the original Superfund, which expired in September 1985. The amended act also sought to clarify the obligations of lenders. As mentioned, liability under the Superfund extends to both the present and all previous owners of the contaminated site. Real estate lenders found themselves either as present owners or somewhere in the chain of ownership through foreclosure proceedings.

The amendments created a concept called **innocent landowner immunity**. It was recognized that in certain cases, a landowner in the chain of ownership was completely innocent of all wrongdoing and therefore should not be held liable. The innocent landowner immunity clause established the criteria by which to judge whether a person or business could be exempted from liability. The criteria included the following:

- The pollution was *caused by a third party*.

- The property was *acquired after the fact*.

- The landowner had *no actual or constructive knowledge* of the damage.

- *Due care* was exercised when the property was purchased (the landowner made a reasonable search, called an environmental site assessment) to determine that no damage to the property existed.

- *Reasonable precautions* were taken in the exercise of ownership rights.

California Environmental Regulation

As in many other trends, California has always been in the forefront in environmental protections. While the environmental problems faced in California are the same as in other states, there are some issues that are particularly important. These include

- *air quality* (a problem in urban regions with automobile-based cultures and little public transportation);

- *agricultural toxins* linked to crop-dusting operations and pesticide manufacturers;

- abandoned and operational *mines*;

- abandoned and operational *military installations*;

- *oil* exploration and extraction sites;

- *wood treatment* plants; and

- *scrap metal* operations.

In addition to state versions of the federal laws already discussed, there are *over 750* different California Code sections that regulate the use of land and resources for environmental protection purposes.

CEQA. The **California Environmental Quality Act (CEQA)** was enacted in 1970. It requires local governments and state agencies to conduct environmental reviews on all public and private developments to determine their environmental impact. CEQA's basic goal is to protect California's environment. CEQA accomplishes this by

- taking all actions necessary to protect, rehabilitate and enhance the environmental quality of the state;

- identifying the significant effects of projects on the environment; and

- providing feasible mitigation where possible.

CEQA applies to projects proposed to be undertaken or requiring approval by state and local government agencies. Major projects often require approvals from more than one public agency. In these instances, CEQA requires one of these public agencies to serve as the lead agency in disclosing potential environmental effects.

Under the law, "projects" include the enactment of zoning ordinances, the issuance of conditional use permits and the approval of tentative subdivision maps. A "significant environmental effect" is one that will significantly impact a rare or endangered species of animal or plant or its habitat; the movement of any resident or migratory fish or wildlife species; and the habitat of any fish, wildlife or plants.

The Next Step

This chapter has focussed on the social and regulatory environment in which the real estate economy operates. In the next chapter, we will consider a more "economic" but nonetheless equally "limiting" issue that governs how real estate is owned, transferred and used: financing and taxation.

Chapter 10
REVIEW

- The purpose of STATE AND FEDERAL FAIR HOUSING LAWS is to create a *colorblind marketplace* in which all persons of *similar financial means* have a *similar range of housing choices*.

- The state and federal fair housing laws prohibit DISCRIMINATION IN HOUSING based on *race, color, religion, sex, disability, familial status or national origin*. There are certain exemptions to compliance and strict rules governing the way in which real property is advertised.

- Under the *Fair Housing Act*, persons with disabilities must be permitted to make REASONABLE MODIFICATIONS to rented premises *at their own expense*. The landlord may require that the property be returned to its original condition at the end of the lease period. The AMERICANS WITH DISABILITIES ACT (ADA) applies to *commercial properties* and *employer-employee relationships*.

- Hazardous environmental substances include asbestos, lead, radon, UFFI, CO and (perhaps) EMFs. Owners of existing or former industrial properties must be especially concerned about toxic materials buried in underground storage tanks. Californians must be particularly aware of the geologic stability of hazardous waste disposal sites.

- Under CERCLA, a landowner is liable for toxic pollution cleanup costs if a release or threat of release of a hazardous substance occurred on his or her property. Liability under Superfund is strict, joint and several, and retroactive. Innocent landowner immunity, however, offers a shield for landowners who are completely innocent of any involvement in the conditions giving rise to the hazard.

Chapter 10 QUIZ

1. What is the underlying purpose of the civil rights laws that affect the real estate industry?

   A. To give certain groups an advantage over others in the real estate market place
   B. To ensure that everyone who wants to own a home can do so, regardless of their race or financial means
   C. To create a market place in which all persons of similar financial means have a similar range of housing choices
   D. To require that a homeowner sell his or her property to anyone who offers to buy it

2. The phrase "to achieve a color blind real estate industry" is from which of the following sources?

   A. Title VIII of the Civil Rights Act of 1968
   B. The U.S. Supreme Court in *Plessy v. Ferguson*
   C. California Civil Code § 782
   D. The California Real Estate Commission

3. The federal Fair Housing Act prohibits discrimination in housing on the basis of all of the following, *EXCEPT*:

   A. religion.
   B. disability.
   C. national origin.
   D. sexual preference.

4. A landlord permits a disabled tenant to lower door handles and install bath rails. This is an example of a:

   A. reasonable accommodation.
   B. reasonable modification.
   C. coercive mandate.
   D. taking.

5. Which of the following protects the most classes of persons against discrimination?

   A. ECOA
   B. ADA
   C. Civil Rights Act of 1896
   D. Title VIII

6. All of the following have been proven to be environmental hazards, *EXCEPT*:

   A. lead.
   B. asbestos.
   C. carbon monoxide.
   D. electromagnetic fields.

7. If the EPA identifies a hazardous site but the PRPs refuse to cooperate in the cleanup or reimburse EPA for the cost of doing so, what can the EPA do?

   A. Nothing. One of the primary criticisms of CERCLA is that it fails to provide an enforcement mechanism.
   B. Seek reimbursement, but not punitive damages, in a lawsuit
   C. Seek damages in court for up to three times the actual cost of the cleanup
   D. Arrest the PRPs, who will be subject to up to ten years' imprisonment

8. Liability under Superfund is:

    A. strict only.
    B. strict and several, but not joint.
    C. strict, joint and several, but not retroactive.
    D. strict, joint and several and retroactive.

9. In order to qualify for the innocent landowner immunity offered by CERCLA, a landowner must prove all of the following, *EXCEPT*:

    A. the pollution was caused by a third party.
    B. the property was polluted when he or she bought it.
    C. the landowner did not know that his or her actions would result in the release of toxic materials.
    D. the landowner had no actual or constructive knowledge of the damage.

10. Superfund is administered and enforced by:

    A. CERCLA.
    B. EPA.
    C. PRP.
    D. CEQA.

11   Financing and Taxation

 Objectives:

- Identify the participants in and characteristics of the primary and secondary mortgage markets

- Describe the different types of private and government financing plans available and the advantages and disadvantages of each

- Understand the requirements of the Truth-in-Lending Act, the Equal Credit Opportunity Act, the Community Reinvestment Act and RESPA

- Discuss the types of federal and state taxation relevant to real property, and the effects of taxation on the real estate economy

---

INTRODUCTION TO REAL ESTATE FINANCE

Most real estate transactions require some sort of financing. Few people have the cash in hand necessary to buy a house or another large property. Also, as economic conditions change, the forces of supply and demand reshape the real estate market. Both of these factors have combined to create a complex and rapidly evolving mortgage market. One of the greatest challenges today's real estate licensees face is how to maintain a working knowledge of all the financing techniques available.

Availability of Funds

Money, just like any other resource, is limited in its availability. Availability is affected by the level of savings accumulated by individuals and businesses, which can then be converted into a variety of competing investment alternatives ranging from interest bearing bank accounts and money market instruments to business acquisition and real estate investment.

Allocation. How these limited resources are allocated will generally reflect the level of interest rates available from the various investment alternatives. Decisions to allocate funds to real estate financing are dictated by the three measurements for any investment:

- **Yield.** *Adequate return* based upon the relative risk of the investment.

- **Safety.** Proper protective measures in the form of *sound underwriting* of the credit supported by the real estate value.

- **Liquidity.** This is the principal *disadvantage* of real estate as an investment, due to its heterogeneous nature. Real estate is simply not a highly liquid investment: it takes time to convert a real property asset into a cash asset.

Investor Expectations. Participants in real estate lending will normally demand a higher yield than they would from a high quality corporate bond, which requires much less servicing.

Federal Reserve System

In Chapter 4, we discussed the Federal Reserve System and its role in the U.S. economy. Here, we will review the operation of the Fed, with particular emphasis on its role in real estate financing.

The purpose of the **Federal Reserve System** (the *Fed*) is to maintain sound credit conditions, help counteract inflationary and deflationary trends and create a favorable economic climate.

The Federal Reserve System divides the country into twelve **federal reserve districts**, each served by a federal reserve bank. All nationally chartered banks must join the Fed and purchase stock in its district reserve banks.

The Federal Reserve regulates the flow of money and interest rates in the marketplace indirectly through its member banks by controlling their reserve requirements and discount rates.

Reserve Requirements. The Federal Reserve requires that each member bank keep a certain amount of assets on hand as **reserve funds**. These reserves are unavailable for loans or any other use. This requirement not only protects customer deposits, but also provides a means of manipulating the flow of cash in the money market.

By increasing its reserve requirements, the Federal Reserve in effect limits the amount of money that member banks can use to make loans. When the amount of money available for lending decreases, interest rates (the amount lenders charge for the use of their money) rise. By causing interest rates to rise, the government can slow down an overactive economy by limiting the number of loans that would have been directed toward major purchases of goods and services.

The opposite is also true: by decreasing the reserve requirements, the Fed can encourage more lending. Increased lending causes the amount of money circulated in the marketplace to rise, while simultaneously causing interest rates to drop.

Discount Rates. Federal Reserve member banks are permitted to borrow money from the district reserve banks to expand their lending operations. The interest rate that the district banks charge for the use of this money is called the **discount rate**. This rate is the basis on which the banks determine the percentage rate of interest they will charge their loan customers.

The **prime rate** (the short-term interest rate charged to a bank's largest, most creditworthy customers) is strongly influenced by the Fed's discount rate. In turn, the prime rate is often the basis for determining a bank's interest rate on other loans, including mortgages. In theory, when the Federal Reserve discount rate is high, bank interest rates are high. When bank interest rates are high, fewer loans are made and less money circulates in the marketplace. On the other hand, a lower discount rate results in lower interest rates, more bank loans and more money in circulation.

Primary Mortgage Market

The **primary mortgage market** is made up of the lenders that originate mortgage loans. These lenders make money available directly to borrowers. From a borrower's point of view, a loan is a means of financing an expenditure; from a lender's point of view, a loan is an investment. All investors look for profitable returns on their investments. For a lender, a loan must generate enough income to be attractive as an investment.

Income on the loan is realized from two sources:

1. *Finance charges* collected at closing, such as loan origination fees and discount points

2. *Recurring income* — that is, the interest collected during the term of the loan

An increasing number of lenders look at the income generated from the fees charged in originating loans as their primary investment objective. Once the loans are made, they are sold to investors. By selling loans to investors in the secondary mortgage market, lenders generate funds with which to originate additional loans.

In addition to the income directly related to loans, some lenders derive income from servicing loans for other mortgage lenders or the investors who have purchased the loans.

Servicing involves such activities as:

- collecting payments (including insurance and taxes);

- accounting;

- bookkeeping;

- preparing insurance and tax records;

- processing payments of taxes and insurance; and

- following up on loan payment and delinquency.

The terms of the servicing agreement stipulate the responsibilities and fees for the service.

Participants

Some of the major lenders in the primary market include the following:

- **Thrifts, savings associations and commercial banks.** These institutions are known as fiduciary lenders because of their fiduciary obligations to protect and preserve their depositors' funds. Mortgage loans are perceived as secure investments for generating income and enable these institutions to pay interest to their depositors. Fiduciary lenders are subject to standards and regulations established by government agencies, such as the Federal Deposit Insurance Corporation (FDIC).

The **Financial Institutions Reform, Recovery, and Enforcement Act of 1989 (FIRREA)** created the *Office of Thrift Supervision (OTS)* specifically to govern the practices of fiduciary lenders. The various government regulations (which include reserve fund, reporting and insurance requirements) are intended to protect depositors against the reckless lending that characterized the savings and loan industry in the 1980s.

- **Insurance companies.** Insurance companies accumulate large sums of money from the premiums paid by their policyholders. While part of this money is held in reserve to satisfy claims and cover operating expenses, much of it is free to be invested in profit-earning enterprises, such as long-term real estate loans. Although insurance companies are considered primary lenders, they tend to invest their money in large, long-term loans that finance commercial and industrial properties rather than single-family home mortgages.

- **Credit unions.** Credit unions are cooperative organizations whose members place money in savings accounts. In the past, credit unions made only short-term consumer and home improvement loans. Recently, however, they have branched out to originating longer-term first and second mortgage and deed of trust loans.

- **Pension funds.** Pension funds usually have large amounts of money available for investment. Because of the comparatively high yields and low risks offered by mortgages, pension funds have begun to participate actively in financing real estate projects. Most real estate activity for pension funds is handled through mortgage bankers and mortgage brokers.

- **Endowment funds.** Many commercial banks and mortgage bankers handle investments for endowment funds. The endowments of hospitals, universities, colleges, charitable foundations and other institutions provide a good source of financing for low-risk commercial and industrial properties.

- **Investment group financing.** Large real estate projects, such as high-rise apartment buildings, office complexes and shopping centers, are often financed as joint ventures through group financing arrangements like syndicates, limited partnerships and real estate investment trusts. These forms of group investment strategies are discussed in greater detail in Chapter 12.

- **Mortgage banking companies.** Mortgage banking companies originate mortgage loans with money belonging to insurance companies, pension funds and individuals and with funds of their own. They make real estate loans with the intention of selling them to investors and receiving a fee for servicing the loans. Mortgage banking companies are generally organized as stock companies. As a source of real estate financing, they are subject to fewer lending restrictions than are commercial banks or savings associations. Mortgage banking companies often are involved in all types of real estate loan activities and often serve as intermediaries between investors and borrowers.

- **Mortgage brokers.** Mortgage brokers are not lenders. They are intermediaries who bring borrowers and lenders together. Mortgage brokers locate potential borrowers, process preliminary loan applications and submit the applications to lenders for final approval. Frequently, they work with or for mortgage banking companies. They do not service loans once they are made. Mortgage brokers may also be real estate brokers who offer these financing services in addition to their regular brokerage activities. Many state governments are establishing separate licensure requirements for mortgage brokers to regulate their activities. In California, for instance, mortgage brokers are regulated by the Dept. of Real Estate.

The Secondary Market

In addition to the primary mortgage market, where loans are originated, there is a **secondary mortgage market**. Here, loans are bought and sold only after they have been funded. Lenders routinely sell loans to avoid interest rate risks and to realize profits on the sales. This secondary market activity helps lenders raise capital to continue making mortgage loans. Secondary market activity is especially desirable when money is in short supply; it stimulates both the housing construction market and the mortgage market by expanding the types of loans available.

When a loan is sold, the original lender may continue to collect the payments from the borrower. The lender then passes the payments along to the investor who purchased the loan. The investor is charged a fee for servicing the loan.

Warehousing agencies purchase a number of mortgage loans and assemble them into packages (called **pools**). Securities that represent shares in these pooled mortgages are then sold to investors. Loans are eligible for sale to the secondary market only when the collateral, borrower and documentation meet certain requirements to provide a degree of safety for the investors. The major warehousing agencies are discussed in the following paragraphs.

Fannie Mae. Formerly known as the Federal National Mortgage Association, **Fannie Mae** is a quasi-governmental agency. It is organized as a privately owned corporation that issues its own common stock and provides a secondary market for mortgage loans. Fannie Mae deals in conventional and FHA and VA loans. Fannie Mae buys a block or pool of mortgages from a lender in exchange for mortgage-backed securities, which the lender may keep or sell. Fannie Mae guarantees payment of all interest and principal to the holder of the securities.

Government National Mortgage Association. Unlike Fannie Mae, the **Government National Mortgage Association (GNMA** or **Ginnie Mae)** is entirely a governmental agency. GNMA is a division of the Department of Housing and Urban Development (HUD), organized as a corporation without capital stock. GNMA administers special-assistance programs and works with Fannie Mae in secondary market activities.

In times of tight money and high interest rates, Fannie Mae and Ginnie Mae can join forces through their **tandem plan**. The tandem plan provides that Fannie Mae can purchase high-risk, low-yield (usually FHA) loans at full market rates, with GNMA guaranteeing payment and absorbing the difference between the low yield and current market prices.

Ginnie Mae also guarantees investment securities issued by private offerors (such as banks, mortgage companies and savings and loan associations) and backed by pools of FHA and VA mortgage loans. The Ginnie Mae pass-through certificate is a security interest in a pool of mortgages that provides for a monthly pass-through of principal and interest payments directly to the certificate holder. Such certificates are guaranteed by Ginnie Mae.

Federal Home Loan Mortgage Corporation. The **Federal Home Loan Mortgage Corporation (FHLMC** or **Freddie Mac)** provides a secondary market for mortgage loans, primarily conventional loans. Freddie Mac has the authority to purchase mortgages, pool them and sell bonds in the open market with the mortgages as security. However, FHLMC does not guarantee payment of Freddie Mac mortgages.

Many lenders use the standardized forms and follow the guidelines issued by Fannie Mae and Freddie Mac. In fact, the use of such forms is mandatory for lenders that wish to sell mortgages in the agencies' secondary mortgage market. The standardized documents include loan applications, credit reports and appraisal forms.

Financing Techniques

Now that you understand *where* real estate financing comes from, we'll turn to the *what*: the types of financing available. As mentioned at the beginning of this chapter, real estate financing comes in a wide variety of forms. While the payment plans described in the following sections are commonly referred to as mortgages, they are really loans secured by either a mortgage or a deed of trust.

Straight Loans. A **straight loan** (also known as a **term loan**) essentially divides the loan into two amounts, to be paid off separately. The borrower makes periodic interest payments, followed by the payment of the principal in full at the end of the term. Straight loans were once the only form of mortgage available. Today, they are generally used for home improvements and second mortgages rather than for residential first mortgage loans.

Amortized Loans. The word **amortize** literally means "to kill off slowly, over time." Most mortgage and deed of trust loans are **amortized loans**. That is, they are paid off slowly, over time. Regular periodic payments are made over a term of years, such as 15 or 30 years, although 20-year and 40-year mortgages are also available. Unlike a straight loan payment, an amortized loan payment partially pays off both principal and interest. Each payment is applied first to interest owed; the balance is applied to the principal amount. At the end of the term, the full amount of the principal and all interest due is reduced to zero. Such loans are also called direct reduction loans. Most amortized mortgage and deed of trust loans are paid in monthly installments. However, some are payable *quarterly* (four times a year) or *semiannually* (twice a year).

Different payment plans tend alternately to gain and lose favor with lenders and borrowers as the cost and availability of mortgage money fluctuate. The most frequently used plan is the **fully amortized loan**, or *level-payment loan*. The mortgagor pays a constant amount, usually monthly. The lender credits each payment first to the interest due, then to the principal amount of the loan.

As a result, while each payment remains the same, the portion applied to repayment of the principal grows and the interest due declines as the unpaid balance of the loan is reduced. If the borrower pays additional amounts that are applied directly to the principal, the loan will amortize more quickly. This benefits the borrower because he or she will pay less interest if the loan is paid off before the end of its term. Of course, lenders are aware of this, too, and may guard against unprofitable loans by including penalties for early payment. The amount of the constant payment is determined from a prepared mortgage payment book or a mortgage factor chart.

Adjustable-Rate Mortgages (ARMs). An **adjustable-rate mortgage (ARM)** is generally originated at one rate of interest. That rate then fluctuates up or down during the loan term based on some objective economic indicator. Because the interest rate may change, the mortgagor's loan repayments may also change. Details of how and when the interest rate will change are included in the note.

- The interest rate is tied to the movement of an objective economic indicator called an **index**. Most indexes are tied to U.S. Treasury securities.

- Usually, the interest rate is the index rate plus a premium, called the **margin**. The margin represents the lender's cost of doing business. For example, the loan rate may be 2 percent over the U.S. Treasury bill rate.

A Closer Look . . .

Lenders charge borrowers a certain percentage of the principal as interest for each year a debt is outstanding. The amount of interest due on any one payment date is calculated by computing the total yearly interest (based on unpaid balance) and dividing that figure by the number of payments made each year.

For example, assume the current outstanding balance of a loan is $70,000. The interest rate is 7½ percent per year, and the monthly payment is $489.30. Based on these facts, the interest and principal due on the next payment would be computed as shown:

$70,000 loan balance x .075 annual interest rate = $5,250 annual interest
$5,250 annual interest ÷ 12 months = $437.50 monthly interest
$489.30 monthly payment - 437.50 monthly interest = $51.80 monthly principal
$70,000 loan balance - 51.80 monthly principal = $69,948.20

This process is followed with each payment over the term of the loan. The same calculations are made each month, starting with the declining new balance figure from the previous month.

- **Rate caps** limit the amount the interest rate may change. Most ARMs have two types of rate caps — periodic and aggregate. A **periodic rate cap** limits the amount the rate may increase at any one time. An **aggregate rate cap** limits the amount the rate may increase over the entire life of the loan.

- The mortgagor is protected from unaffordable individual payments by the **payment cap**. The payment cap sets a maximum amount for payments. With a cap, a rate increase could result in negative amortization — that is, an increase in the loan balance.

- The **adjustment period** establishes how often the rate may be changed. For instance, the adjustment period may be monthly, quarterly or annually.

- Lenders may offer a **conversion option**, which permits the mortgagor to convert from an adjustable-rate to a fixed-rate loan at certain intervals during the life of the mortgage. The option is subject to certain terms and conditions for the conversion.

Balloon Loan. When the periodic payments are not enough to fully amortize the loan by the time the final payment is due, the final payment is larger than the others. This is called a **balloon payment**. It is a partially amortized loan because principal is still owed at the end of the term. It is frequently assumed that if payments are made promptly, the lender will extend the balloon payment for another limited term. The lender, however, is not legally obligated to grant this extension and can require payment in full when the note is due.

Growing-Equity Mortgage (GEM). A **growing-equity mortgage (GEM)** is also known as a *rapid-payoff mortgage*. The GEM uses a fixed interest rate, but payments of principal are increased according to an index or a schedule. Thus, the total payment increases, and the loan is paid off more quickly. A GEM is most frequently used when the borrower's income is expected to keep pace with the increasing loan payments.

Reverse-Annuity Mortgage (RAM). A **reverse-annuity mortgage (RAM)** is one in which regular monthly payments are made by the lender to the borrower. The payments are based on the equity the homeowner has invested in the property given as security for the loan. This loan allows senior citizens on fixed incomes to realize the equity they have built up in their homes without having to sell. The borrower is charged a fixed rate of interest, and the loan is eventually repaid from the sale of the property or from the borrower's estate upon his or her death.

▦ LOAN PROGRAMS

Mortgage loans are generally classified based on their **loan-to-value ratios**, or **LTV**s. The LTV is the ratio of debt to value of the property. **Value** is the sale price or the appraisal value, whichever is less. The *lower* the ratio of debt to value, the *higher* the down payment by the borrower. For the lender, the higher down payment means a more secure loan, which minimizes the lender's risk.

Determining LTV. If a property has an appraised value of $100,000, secured by a $90,000 loan, the LTV is 90 percent:

$$\$90,000 \div \$100,000 = 90\%$$

Conventional Loans

Conventional loans are viewed as the most secure loans because their loan-to-value ratios are lowest. Usually, the ratio is 80 percent of the value of the property or less, because the borrower makes a down payment of at least 20 percent. The security for the loan is provided solely by the mortgage; the payment of the debt rests on the borrower's ability to pay. In making such a loan, the lender relies primarily on its appraisal of the security (the real estate). Information from credit reports that indicate the reliability of the prospective borrower is also important. No additional insurance or guarantee on the loan is necessary to protect the lender's interest.

Lenders can set criteria by which a borrower and the collateral are evaluated to qualify for a loan. However, in recent years the secondary mortgage market has had a significant impact on the borrower qualifications, standards for the collateral and documentation procedures followed by lenders.

Loans must meet strict criteria to be sold to the Federal National Mortgage Association and the Federal Home Loan Mortgage Corporation. Lenders can still be flexible in their lending decisions, but they may not be able to sell unusual loans in the secondary market.

Private Mortgage Insurance

One way a borrower can obtain a mortgage loan with a lower down payment is under a **private mortgage insurance (PMI)** program. Because the loan-to-value ratio is higher than for other conventional loans, the lender requires additional security to minimize its risk. The borrower purchases insurance from a private mortgage insurance company as additional security to insure the lender against borrower default. LTVs of up to 95 percent of the appraised value of the property are possible with mortgage insurance.

PMI protects a certain percentage of a loan, usually 25 to 30 percent, against borrower default. Normally, the borrower is charged a fee for the first year's premium at closing. The borrower also pays a monthly fee while the insurance is in force.

Other methods of payment are available, however: the premium may be financed, or the fee at closing may be waived in exchange for slightly higher monthly payments. When a borrower has limited funds for investment, these alternative methods of reducing closing costs are very important. Because only a portion of the loan is insured, once the loan is repaid to a certain level, the lender may agree to allow the borrower to terminate the coverage. Practices for termination vary from lender to lender.

FHA-Insured Loans

The **Federal Housing Administration (FHA)**, which operates under HUD, neither builds homes nor lends money itself. The common term FHA loan refers to a loan that is insured by the agency. These loans must be made by FHA-approved lending institutions. The FHA insurance provides security to the lender in addition to the real estate. As with private mortgage insurance, the FHA insures lenders against loss from borrower default.

The most popular FHA program is Title II, Section 203(b), fixed-interest rate loans for 10 to 30 years on one- to four-family residences. Rates are competitive with other types of loans, even though they are high-LTV loans. Certain technical requirements must be met before the FHA will insure the loans. These requirements include the following:

- The borrower is charged a percentage of the loan as a premium for the FHA insurance. The **up-front premium** is paid at closing by the borrower or some other party. It may also be financed along with the total loan amount. A monthly premium may also be charged. Insurance premiums vary for new loans, refinancing and condominiums.

- FHA regulations set minimum standards for type and construction of buildings, quality of neighborhood and credit requirements for borrowers.

If the purchase price exceeds the FHA-appraised value, the buyer may pay the difference in cash as part of the down payment. In addition, the FHA has set maximum loan amounts for various regions of the country.

The FHA has characterized California as a "High Cost Area." The current county-by-county mortgage limits are:

County Name	1 Living Unit	2 Living Units	3 Living Units	4 Living Units
ALAMEDA	$160,950	$205,912	$248,887	$309,337
ALPINE	$101,250	$114,000	$138,000	$160,500
AMADOR	$123,000	$138,550	$168,350	$194,250
BUTTE	$121,600	$136,950	$166,400	$192,000
CALAVERAS	$125,850	$141,750	$172,200	$198,750
COLUSA	$101,250	$114,000	$138,000	$160,500
CONTRA COSTA	$160,950	$205,912	$248,887	$309,337
DEL NORTE	$101,250	$114,000	$138,000	$160,500
EL DORADO	$151,800	$170,950	$207,700	$239,650
FRESNO	$146,550	$165,050	$200,500	$231,350
GLENN	$101,250	$114,000	$138,000	$160,500
HUMBOLDT	$118,750	$133,750	$162,500	$187,000
IMPERIAL	$101,250	$114,000	$138,000	$160,500
INYO	$147,250	$165,850	$201,500	$232,500
KERN	$140,500	$158,200	$192,250	$221,800
KINGS	$101,250	$114,000	$138,000	$160,500

County Name	1 Living Unit	2 Living Units	3 Living Units	4 Living Units
LAKE	$101,250	$114,000	$138,000	$160,500
LASSEN	$101,250	$114,000	$138,000	$160,500
LOS ANGELES	$160,950	$205,912	$248,837	$309,337
MADERA	$146,550	$165,050	$200,500	$231,350
MARIN	$160,950	$205,912	$248,887	$309,337
MARIPOSA	$108,750	$122,500	$148,850	$171,750
MENDOCINO	$123,500	$139,100	$169,000	$195,000
MERCED	$128,250	$144,450	$175,500	$202,500
MODOC	$101,250	$114,000	$138,000	$160,500
MONO	$119,700	$134,800	$163,800	$189,000
MONTEREY	$160,950	$205,912	$248,887	$309,337
NAPA	$160,950	$205,912	$248,887	$309,337
NEVADA	$152,362	$194,850	$235,550	$292,800
ORANGE	$160,950	$205,912	$248,887	$309,337
PLACER	$151,800	$170,950	$207,700	$239,650
PLUMAS	$101,250	$114,000	$138,000	$160,500
RIVERSIDE	$152,362	$194,850	$235,550	$292,800
SACRAMENTO	$151,800	$170,950	$207,700	$239,650
S. BENITO	$160,950	$205,912	$248,887	$309,337
S. BERNARDINO	$152,362	$194,850	$235,550	$292,800
S. DIEGO	$160,950	$205,912	$248,887	$309,337
S. FRANCISCO	$160,950	$205,912	$248,887	$309,337
S. JOAQUIN	$152,362	$194,850	$235,550	$292,800
S. LUIS OBISPO	$160,950	$205,912	$248,887	$309,337
S. MATEO	$160,950	$205,912	$248,887	$309,337
SA. BARBARA	$160,950	$205,912	$248,887	$309,337
SA. CLARA	$160,950	$205,912	$248,887	$309,337
SA. CRUZ	$160,950	$205,912	$248,887	$309,337
SHASTA	$152,362	$194,850	$235,550	$292,800
SIERRA	$101,250	$114,000	$138,000	$160,500
SISKIYOU	$101,250	$114,000	$138,000	$160,500
SOLANO	$160,950	$205,912	$248,887	$309,337
SONOMA	$160,950	$205,912	$248,887	$309,337
STANISLAUS	$137,150	$154,450	$187,650	$216,550
SUTTER	$101,250	$114,000	$138,000	$160,500
TEHAMA	$101,250	$114,000	$138,000	$160,500
TRINITY	$101,250	$114,000	$138,000	$160,500
TULARE	$117,300	$132,100	$160,550	$185,250
TUOLUMNE	$122,550	$138,000	$167,700	$193,500
VENTURA	$160,950	$205,912	$248,887	$309,337
YOLO	$152,362	$194,850	$235,550	$292,800
YUBA	$101,250	$114,000	$138,000	$160,500

Other types of FHA loans are available, including one-year adjustable-rate mortgages; home improvement and rehabilitation loans; and loans for the purchase of condominiums. The FHA set specific standards for condominium complexes and the ratio of owner-occupants to renters. These standards must be met for a loan on a condominium unit to be financed through the FHA insurance programs.

Prepayment and Assumption. A borrower may repay an FHA-insured loan on a one- to four-family residence without penalty. For loans made before August 2, 1985, the borrower must give the lender written notice of intention to exercise the prepayment privilege at least 30 days before prepayment. If the borrower fails to provide the required notice, the lender has the option of charging up to 30 days' interest. For loans initiated after August 2, 1985, no written notice of prepayment is required.

The assumption rules for FHA-insured loans vary, depending on the dates the loans were originated:

- FHA loans originated before December 1986 generally have no restrictions on their assumptions.

- For an FHA loan originated between December 1, 1986, and December 15, 1989, a creditworthiness review of the prospective assumer is required. If the original loan was for the purchase of a principal residence, this review is required during the first 12 months of the loan's existence. If the original loan was for the purchase of an investment property, the review is required during the first 24 months of the loan.

- For FHA loans originated on December 15, 1989, and later, no assumptions are permitted without complete buyer qualification.

Discount Points. The lender of an FHA-insured loan may charge discount points in addition to a loan origination fee. The payment of points is a matter of negotiation between the seller and the buyer. However, if the seller pays more than 6 percent of the costs normally paid by the buyer (such as discount points, the loan origination fee, the mortgage insurance premium, buydown fees, prepaid items and impound or escrow amounts), the lender will treat the payments as a reduction in sales price and recalculate the mortgage amount accordingly. Points are tax deductible to the buyer regardless of which party pays them.

VA-Guaranteed Loans

The **Department of Veterans Affairs (VA)** is authorized to guarantee loans to purchase or construct homes for eligible veterans and their spouses (including unremarried spouses of veterans whose deaths were service-related). The VA also guarantees loans to purchase manufactured housing (mobile homes) and plots on which to place them. A veteran who meets any of the following time-in-service criteria is eligible for a VA loan:

- 90 days of active service for veterans of World War II, the Korean War, the Viet Nam conflict and the Persian Gulf War

- A minimum of 181 days of active service during interconflict periods between July 26, 1947, and September 6, 1980

- Two full years of service during any peacetime period after September 7, 1980

- Six or more years of continuous duty as a reservist in the Army, Navy, Air Force, Marine Corps or Coast Guard or as a member of the Army or Air National Guard (eligibility expires on October 28, 1999).

The VA assists veterans in financing the purchase of homes with little or no down payments, at comparatively low interest rates. The VA issues rules and regulations that set forth the qualifications, limitations and conditions under which a loan may be guaranteed.

Like the term FHA loan, VA loan is something of a misnomer. The VA does not normally lend money; it guarantees loans made by lending institutions approved by the agency. The term VA loan refers to a loan that is not made by the agency, but is guaranteed by it. There is no VA limit on the amount of the loan a veteran can obtain; this is determined by the lender. The VA limits the amount of the loan it will guarantee.

Prepayment and Assumption. As with an FHA loan, the borrower under a VA loan can prepay the debt at any time without penalty.

VA loans made before March 1, 1988, are freely assumable, although an assumption processing fee of ½ percent of the loan balance will be charged. For loans made on or after March 1, 1988, the VA must approve the buyer and assumption agreement. The original veteran borrower remains personally liable for the repayment of the loan unless the VA approves a release of liability. The release of liability will be issued only if the buyer assumes all of the veteran's liabilities on the loan and the VA or the lender approves both the buyer and the assumption agreement.

Cal-Vet

The popular Cal-Vet program, administered by the California Department of Veterans Affairs, provides low-cost, low-interest loans to qualified veterans for up to $250,000 for single-family homes ($70,000 for housing in mobile home parks and $300,000 for farm properties). Cal-Vet is funded by California general obligation bonds and veterans' revenue bonds; it is not a tax-financed program.

Farm Service Agency

The **Farm Service Agency** (**FSA**), formerly the *Federal Agricultural Mortgage Corporation* (*FAMC*, or *Farmer Mac*), is a federal agency of the Department of Agriculture. The FSA offers programs to help families purchase or operate family farms. Through the *Rural Housing and Community Development Service*, it also provides loans to help families purchase or improve single-family homes in rural areas (generally areas with populations of fewer than 10,000).

FSA loan programs fall into two categories: guaranteed loans, made and serviced by private lenders and guaranteed for a specific percentage by the FSA, and loans made directly by the FSA.

▦ CREATIVE FINANCING TECHNIQUES

Because borrowers often have different needs, a variety of specialized financing techniques have been created. Other techniques apply to various types of collateral. The following pages consider some of the loans that do not fit into the categories previously discussed.

Purchase-Money Mortgages

A **purchase-money mortgage** is a note and mortgage created at the time of purchase. Its purpose is to make the sale possible. The term is used in two ways. First, it may refer to any security instrument that originates at the time of sale. More often, it refers to the instrument given by the purchaser to a seller who takes back a note for part or all of the purchase price. The mortgage may be a first or a junior lien, depending on whether prior mortgage liens exist.

Package Loans

A **package loan** includes not only the real estate but also all personal property and appliances installed on the premises. In recent years, this kind of loan has been used extensively to finance furnished condominium units. Package loans usually include furniture, drapes, carpets and the kitchen range, refrigerator, dishwasher, garbage disposal, washer, dryer, food freezer and other appliances as part of the sales price of the home.

Blanket Loans

A **blanket loan** covers more than one parcel or lot. It is usually used to finance subdivision developments. However, it can finance the purchase of improved properties or consolidate loans as well. A blanket loans usually includes a provision known as a **partial release clause**. This clause permits the borrower to obtain the release of any one lot or parcel from the lien by repaying a certain amount of the loan. The lender issues a partial release for each parcel released from the mortgage lien. The release form includes a provision that the lien will continue to cover all other unreleased lots.

Wraparound Loans

A **wraparound loan** enables a borrower with an existing mortgage or deed of trust loan to obtain additional financing from a second lender without paying off the first loan. The second lender gives the borrower a new, increased loan at a higher interest rate and assumes payment of the existing loan. The total amount of the new loan includes the existing loan as well as the additional funds needed by the borrower. The borrower makes payments to the new lender on the larger loan. The new lender makes payments on the original loan out of the borrower's payments.

A wraparound mortgage can be used to refinance real property or to finance the purchase of real property when an existing mortgage cannot be prepaid. The buyer executes a wraparound mortgage to the seller, who collects payments on the new loan and continues to make payments on the old loan. It also can finance the sale of real estate when the buyer wishes to invest a minimum amount of initial cash. A wraparound loan is possible only if the original loan permits it. For instance, an acceleration and alienation or a due-on-sale clause in the original loan documents may prevent a sale under a wraparound loan.

Open-End Loans

An **open-end loan** secures a note executed by the borrower to the lender. It also secures any future advances of funds made by the lender to the borrower. The interest rate on the initial amount borrowed is fixed, but interest on future advances may be charged at the market rate in effect. An open-end loan is often a less costly alternative to a home improvement loan. It allows the borrower to "open" the mortgage or deed of trust to increase the debt to its original amount, or the amount stated in the note, after the debt has been reduced by payments over a period of time. The mortgage usually states the maximum amount that can be secured, the terms and conditions under which the loan can be opened and the provisions for repayment.

Construction Loans

A **construction loan** is made to finance the construction of improvements on real estate such as homes, apartments and office buildings. The lender commits to the full amount of the loan, but disburses the funds in payments during construction. These payments are also known as **draws**. Draws are made to the general contractor or the owner for that part of the construction work that has been completed since the previous payment. Before each payment, the lender inspects the work. The general contractor must provide the lender with adequate waivers that release all mechanic's lien rights for the work covered by the payment.

This kind of loan generally bears a higher-than-market interest rate because of the risks involved for the lender. These include the inadequate release of mechanics' liens, delays in construction or the financial failure of the contractor or subcontractors.

Construction loans are generally short-term or interim financing. The borrower pays interest only on the monies that have actually been disbursed. The borrower is expected to arrange for a permanent loan, also known as an *end loan* or **take-out loan**, that will repay or "take out" the construction financing lender when the work is completed. Some lenders now offer construction-to-permanent loans that become fixed mortgages upon completion. Participation financing is when a lender demands an equity position in the project as a requirement for the loan.

Sale-and-Leaseback

Sale-and-leaseback arrangements are generally used to finance large commercial or industrial properties. The land and building, usually used by the seller for business purposes, are sold to an investor. The real estate is then leased back by the investor to the seller, who continues to conduct business on the property as a tenant. The buyer becomes the lessor, and the original owner becomes the lessee. This enables a business to free money tied up in real estate to be used as working capital.

Sale-and-leasebacks involve complicated legal procedures, and their success is usually related to the effects the transaction has on the firm's tax situation. Legal and tax experts should always be involved in this type of transaction.

Buydowns

A **buydown** is a way to temporarily lower the initial interest rate on a mortgage or deed of trust loan. Perhaps a homebuilder wishes to stimulate sales by offering a lower-than-market rate. A lump sum is paid in cash to the lender at the closing. The payment offsets (and so reduces) the interest rate and monthly payments during the mortgage's first few years. Typical buydown arrangements reduce the interest rate by 1 to 3 percent over the first one to three years of the loan term. After that, the rate rises. The assumption is that the borrower's income will also increase and that the borrower will be more able to absorb the increased monthly payments.

Home Equity Loans

Using the **equity** buildup in a home to finance purchases is an alternative to refinancing. **Home equity loans** are a source of funds for homeowners to use for a variety of financial needs, many of which have wide-ranging economic impact beyond the residence involved:

- To finance the purchase of expensive items

- To consolidate existing installment loans on credit card debt

- To pay medical, education, home improvement or other expenses

The original mortgage loan remains in place; the home equity loan is junior to the original lien. If the homeowner refinances, the original mortgage loan is paid off and replaced by a new loan. (This is an alternative way to borrow the equity; it's not really a home equity loan.)

A home equity loan can be taken out as a fixed loan amount or as an equity line of credit. With the home equity line of credit, the lender extends a line of credit that the borrower can use whenever he or she wants. The borrower receives his or her money by a check sent to them, deposits made in a checking or savings account, or a book of drafts the borrower can use up to his or her credit limit.

The homeowner must consider a number of factors before deciding on a home equity loan. The costs involved in obtaining a new mortgage loan or a home equity loan, current interest rates, total monthly payments, and income tax consequences are all important issues to be examined.

▦ FINANCING LEGISLATION

The federal government regulates the lending practices of mortgage lenders through the Truth-in-Lending Act, the Equal Credit Opportunity Act, the Community Reinvestment Act of 1977 and the Real Estate Settlement Procedures Act. This type of regulation of the marketplace represents the government's efforts to ensure free and fair behavior by participants.

Truth-in-Lending Act and Regulation Z

Regulation Z, promulgated pursuant to the **Truth-in-Lending Act**, requires credit institutions to inform borrowers of the true cost of obtaining credit. Its purpose is to permit borrowers to compare the costs of various lenders and avoid the uninformed use of credit.

Regulation Z applies when credit is extended to individuals for personal, family or household uses. The amount of credit sought must be $25,000 or less. Regardless of the amount, however, Regulation Z always applies when a credit transaction is secured by a residence. The regulation does not apply to business or commercial loans or to agricultural loans of more than $25,000.

Under Regulation Z, a consumer must be fully informed of all finance charges and the true interest rate before a transaction is completed. The finance charge disclosure must include any loan fees, finder's fees, service charges and points, as well as interest. In the case of a mortgage loan made to finance the purchase of a dwelling, the lender must compute and disclose the annual percentage rate (APR). However, the lender does not have to indicate the total interest payable during the term of the loan. Also, the lender does not have to include actual costs such as title fees, legal fees, appraisal fees, credit reports, survey fees and closing expenses as part of the finance charge.

Creditor. A **creditor**, for purposes of Regulation Z, is any person who extends consumer credit more than 25 times each year or more than 5 times each year if the transactions involve dwellings as security. The credit must be subject to a finance charge or payable in more than four installments by written agreement.

Three-Day Right of Rescission. In the case of most consumer credit transactions covered by Regulation Z, the borrower has three days in which to rescind the transaction by merely notifying the lender. This right of rescission does not apply to residential purchase-money or first mortgage or deed of trust loans. In an emergency, the right to rescind may be waived in writing to prevent a delay in funding.

Advertising. Regulation Z provides strict regulation of real estate advertisements that include mortgage financing terms. General phrases like "liberal terms available" may be used, but if details are given, they must comply with the act. The annual percentage rate (APR) — which is calculated based on all charges rather than the interest rate alone must be stated.

Advertisements for buydowns or reduced-interest rate mortgages must show both the limited term to which the interest rate applies and the annual percentage rate. An advertisement for a variable-rate mortgage must include

- the number and timing of payments;

- the amount of the largest and smallest payments; and

- a statement of the fact that the actual payments will vary between these two extremes.

Specific credit terms, such as down payment, monthly payment, dollar amount of the finance charge or term of the loan, may not be advertised unless the advertisement includes the following information:

- Cash price

- Required down payment

- Number, amounts and due dates of all payments

- Annual percentage rate

- Total of all payments to be made over the term of the mortgage (unless the advertised credit refers to a first mortgage or deed of trust to finance the acquisition of a dwelling)

Penalties. Regulation Z provides penalties for noncompliance. The penalty for violation of an administrative order enforcing Regulation Z is $10,000 for each day the violation continues. A fine of up to $10,000 may be imposed for engaging in an unfair or a deceptive practice. In addition, a creditor may be liable to a consumer for twice the amount of the finance charge, for a minimum of $100 and a maximum of $1,000, plus court costs, attorney's fees and any actual damages. Willful violation is a misdemeanor punishable by a fine of up to $5,000, one year's imprisonment or both.

Equal Credit Opportunity Act

The federal **Equal Credit Opportunity Act (ECOA)**, mentioned in Chapter 10, prohibits lenders and others who grant or arrange credit to consumers from discriminating against credit applicants on the basis of any of the following factors:

- Race

- Color

- Religion

- National origin

- Sex

- Marital status

- Age (provided the applicant is of legal age)

- Dependence on public assistance

In addition, lenders and other creditors must inform all rejected credit applicants of the principal reasons for the denial or termination of credit. The notice must be provided in writing, within 30 days. The federal Equal Credit Opportunity Act also provides that a borrower is entitled to a copy of the appraisal report if the borrower paid for the appraisal.

Community Reinvestment Act

Community reinvestment refers to the responsibility of financial institutions to help meet their communities' needs for low- and moderate-income housing. In 1977, Congress passed the **Community Reinvestment Act of 1977 (CRA)**. Under the CRA, financial institutions are expected to meet the deposit and credit needs of their communities, participate and invest in local community development and rehabilitation projects, and participate in loan programs for housing, small businesses and small farms.

The law requires any federally supervised financial institution to prepare a statement containing

- a *definition* of the geographical boundaries of its community;

- an *identification* of the types of community reinvestment credit offered (such as residential housing, housing rehabilitation, small-business, commercial and consumer loans); and

- *comments* from the public about the institution's performance in meeting its community's needs.

Financial institutions are periodically reviewed by one of four federal financial supervisory agencies: the Comptroller of the Currency, the Federal Reserve's Board of Governors, the Federal Deposit Insurance Corporation, and the Office of Thrift Supervision. The institutions must post a public notice that their community reinvestment activities are subject to federal review, and must make the reviews public.

Real Estate Settlement Procedures Act

The federal **Real Estate Settlement Procedures Act (RESPA)** applies to any residential real estate transaction involving a new first mortgage loan. RESPA is designed to ensure that buyer and seller are both fully informed of all settlement costs.

Computerized Loan Origination (CLO) and Automated Underwriting. A computerized loan origination (CLO) system is an electronic network for handling loan applications through remote computer terminals linked to several lenders' computers. With a CLO system, a real estate broker or salesperson can call up a menu of mortgage lenders, interest rates and loan terms, then help a buyer select a lender and apply for a loan right from the brokerage office.

The licensee may assist the applicant in answering the on-screen questions and in understanding the services offered. The broker in whose office the terminal is located may earn fees of up to one half point of the loan amount. The borrower, not the mortgage broker or lender, must pay the fee. The fee amount may be financed, however. While multiple lenders may be represented on an office's CLO computer, consumers must be informed that other lenders are available. An applicant's ability to comparison shop for a loan may be enhanced by a CLO system; the range of options may not be limited.

On the lenders' side, new automated underwriting procedures can shorten loan approvals from weeks to minutes. Automated underwriting also tends to lower the cost of loan application and approval by reducing lenders' time spent on the approval process by as much as 60 percent. The Federal Home Loan Mortgage Corporation uses a system called Loan Prospector. Fannie Mae uses a system called Desktop Underwriter that reduces approval time to minutes, based on the borrower's credit report, a paycheck stub and a drive-by appraisal of the property. Complex or difficult mortgages can be processed in less than 72 hours. Through automated underwriting, one of a borrower's biggest headaches in buying a home — waiting for loan approval — is eliminated. In addition, a prospective buyer can strengthen his or her purchase offer by including proof of loan approval.

▦ TAXATION

In order to provide services to citizens, governments take on many roles: welfare, police and fire protection, community planning and environmental concerns, employer to an increasingly large percentage of the population, utility provider in some cases, ombudsman and other roles. To support this vast array of duties, government generates revenue from various sources.

Types of Taxes

Income, excise, and property taxes, bonds and assessments are all forms of taxation. Taxes are classified by economists into three distinct categories:

1. **Progressive tax.** In a **progressive tax system**, the tax rate increases in direct relation to income. Federal income tax, for example, is paid on the basis of taxable income. As the income rises from one tax bracket to another, the percentage of taxation increases accordingly.

2. **Proportional tax.** In a **proportional tax system**, the tax rate remains the same regardless of the value of the item or amount of income. From time to time, proprosals are made by politicians to change the U.S. income tax system from a progressive to a proportional system, or "flat tax." Sales tax is an example of how a proportional tax system works. Whether one purchases a $50 radio or a $5,000 big-screen television, the percentage sales tax levied on the item remains the same. In an income tax context, the result is identical: a person who earns $50,000 in one year would pay the same tax rate as a person who earned $50 million in one year. Of course, the dollar amounts paid by each person would be significantly different.

3. **Regressive tax.** A **regressive tax system** is one in which the tax rate declines as the value of the taxable item or income increases. To some extent real property under California's famous Proposition 13 (discussed below) falls in this category, since value for assessment purposes does not necessarily increase at the same rate as the market, which reduces the real tax obligation. Income tax might be considered regressive in practice, because those with more income often have the ability to shelter more of it. Federal Social Security and self-employment taxes are prime examples of

regressive taxes, because they do not apply to income above a certain level.

User Fees and Other Charges

Governments derive some income by charging fees for services. In the area of real estate, these include documentary tax stamps, recording charges, map filing and processing fees, building permit fees, annual levies based upon revenues generated by properties, license fees and property registration for rent control.

Parking fines, legal judgments, overdue book fines and late charges of any nature are also revenue sources. The federal government derives substantial revenue from seigniorage, the difference between minting cost and the face value of the coin. Federal, state and local agencies also generate revenue from various pamphlets, publications and Internet services that are sold to the public.

Ad Valorem Property Taxation

Ad valorem taxation means that tax levies are imposed by government in proportion to the value of the asset taxed (proportional tax). In the case of real property, tax assessors determine property value to establish the property tax base, which is then used to determine the tax rate to be imposed upon property owners in the county where the property is located.

Proposition 13

In California, **Proposition 13** (sometimes referred to as the "taxpayers' revolt initiative") passed in 1978. In the twenty years since then, Proposition 13 has limited the ability of governing bodies to increase the tax base by increased valuation except when the property is sold. Despite cuts in services and facilities (such as education, health care and public assistance) that resulted from its passage, Proposition 13 retained popularity primarily by delivering on its promise of limiting the tax rate.

Inequalities in Real Property Taxation. Ad valorem tax assessments are based upon the tax collector's secured rolls (real property) and the unsecured roll (personal property). The owner of real property acquired prior to Proposition 13 has a definite advantage over persons who have recently purchased property in California. As long as property remains in the same hands, taxation is limited to a 2 percent annual increase in valuation without regard to the percentage increase in market value of the property. This produces considerable inequality of assessment between new and long-time owners.

Reassessment Procedure. Any purchaser of property is assessed for the actual market price. Upon closing of the sale, the details of the transfer are made available to the assessor's office from the transfer statement provided by the purchaser. The property is then reassessed and a supplemental tax bill is issued covering the period from the closing date until the next taxing period in order to avoid escaped revenues on the lower base. This reassessment also occurs when improvements are added between taxation periods and as a result of building permits.

Effect on Tax Structure. To some extent, Proposition 13 means that California property tax is not strictly an ad valorem tax. To further complicate this issue, homeowners' and senior citizens' exemptions are available to certain taxpayers and not to the population as a whole. An appeals process is available to challenge assessor's valuations, but few citizens avail themselves of the opportunity because they don't understand the process or do not expect to benefit from it.

Reallocation of Resources

Some parties at both ends of the taxation spectrum provide minimal sources of tax revenue. These are individuals at the poverty level and the very rich, who have the ability to shelter large amounts of income. This places a larger proportion of the tax burden upon the large middle class to provide the revenues required to operate government at all levels, effectively subsidizing the benefits enjoyed by non-payers at both ends. The net result is a reallocation of resources in directions determined by government policy.

Poverty Level. Income is redistributed to individuals who fall below the federally mandated poverty level group by the government through various welfare and public assistance programs, which are funded by taxes. Current "welfare reform" legislation at both the state and federal levels is designed to remove people from welfare dependence through job training programs and assistance.

The 1997 federal poverty guidelines are

Size of Family Unit	48 Contiguous States and D.C.	Alaska	Hawaii
1	$ 7,890	$ 9,870	$ 9,070
2	10,610	13,270	12,200
3	13,330	16,670	15,330
4	16,050	20,070	18,460
5	18,770	23,470	21,590
6	21,490	26,870	24,720
7	24,210	30,270	27,850
8	26,930	33,670	30,980

Working Poor. Between those dependent on government assistance for their day-to-day living and the financially self-sufficient middle class are those employed individuals who, while earning incomes above the federally mandated poverty levels, are nonetheless compelled to seek some assistance in order to survive.

Middle Class. Proportionally higher taxes mean that this group has less disposable income available to generate savings and provide investment dollars for increasing capital. The term "middle class" is used broadly, and popularly includes both social and economic characteristics. (Hard work and sound values, for instance, are the positive characteristics ascribed to the middle class; there are negative ones as well.) It may, however, be generally defined as the lower 60 percent of the population living above poverty level.

The productive segment of the economy, particularly the middle class, shifts a sizable segment of its income to government functions and to those who need assistance. While this is generally considered a socially beneficial purpose, it contributes to the problem of housing affordability for the middle class, where many households are unable to save enough for a downpayment.

Upper Class. Despite taxes, this group — generally considered those in the upper 20 percent of the U.S. income range — retains the highest degree of disposable personal income which in turn generates faster percentage increases in personal net worth and future earning capacity.

The Next Step

In Chapter 12, we will expand on our basic discussion of finance and taxation and look at the economics of real estate investment.

Chapter 11
REVIEW

- The purpose of the **FEDERAL RESERVE SYSTEM** is to maintain *sound credit conditions*, help *counteract inflationary and deflationary trends* and create a *favorable economic climate*. It accomplishes this goal by regulating the flow of money and interest rates in the economy indirectly through member banks by controlling their *reserve requirements* and the *discount rate*.

- The **PRIMARY MORTGAGE MARKET** is made up of lenders that *originate mortgage loans* as a means of generating profit. Some of the lenders in the primary mortgage market include thrifts, savings associations and commercial banks; insurance companies; credit unions; pension funds; endowment funds; investment groups; and mortgage banking companies.

- The **SECONDARY MORTGAGE MARKET** is where loans are *bought and sold by investors* after they have been funded. Participants in the secondary market include warehousing agencies, Fannie Mae, GNMA and FHLMC.

- A variety of **MORTGAGE LOAN STRUCTURES** are available to borrowers. These include straight loans, amortized loans, adjustable-rate loans, balloon loans, growing-equity mortgages and reverse-annuity mortgages.

- Mortgage loans are usually classified based on their **LOAN-TO-VALUE RATIO (LTV)**, the *ratio of debt to the property's value*.

- **CONVENTIONAL LOANS** are considered the most secure, because they have the lowest LTV ratios. Other types of loans are **FHA-INSURED** and **VA-GUARANTEED**, both of which have specific qualification requirements.

■ Because borrowers often have different needs, a variety of **SPECIALIZED FINANCE TECHNIQUES** are available: purchase-money mortgages, package loans, blanket loans and wraparound loans, for instance. Open-end loans, construction loans, sale-and-leaseback loans, buydowns and home equity loans are other popular alternatives.

■ The federal government **REGULATES** the practices of mortgage lenders through the *Truth-in-Lending Act (Regulation Z)*; the *Equal Credit Opportunity Act*, the *Community Reinvestment Act of 1977* and the *Real Estate Settlement Procedures Act*.

■ In order to provide services to citizens, governments take on many roles: welfare, police and fire protection, community planning and environmental protection among others. To support this vast array of duties, government generates income through **TAXATION**, fees and penalties.

■ Individuals at both ends of the income spectrum tend to provide minimal tax revenues; a larger proportion of the tax burden is placed on the **MIDDLE CLASS**. Reallocation of income and resources is a result of government policy-making decisions.

Chapter 11
QUIZ

1. All of the following would be likely to result from the Fed decreasing its reserve requirements, *EXCEPT*:

   A. increased lending activity.
   B. increased circulation of money in the economy.
   C. decreased saving.
   D. decreased interest rates.

2. The prime rate is:

   A. the rate lenders charge for a mortgage loan.
   B. a long-term interest rate charged to banks by the Fed.
   C. the short-term interest rate charged to a bank's most creditworthy customers.
   D. the rate paid by banks on the average passbook savings account.

3. All of the following are included in a lender's servicing of a loan, *EXCEPT*:

   A. bookkeeping.
   B. credit approval.
   C. processing payments.
   D. pursuing delinquent payments.

4. All of the following are lenders in the primary mortgage market, *EXCEPT*:

   A. pension funds.
   B. insurance companies.
   C. mortgage banking companies.
   D. mortgage brokers.

5. A mortgage loan in which the borrower makes periodic interest payments, followed by the payment of principal in full at the end of the loan term is what kind of mortgage?

   A. Straight
   B. Amortized
   C. Balloon
   D. Growing-equity

6. In an adjustable-rate mortgage, a limit on the amount the interest rate may increase at any one time is called a(n):

   A. payment cap.
   B. periodic rate cap.
   C. adjustment period.
   D. aggregate periodic cap.

7. A property has a sales price of $280,000 and is appraised at $250,000. The buyer has obtained a loan for $210,000. What is the LTV?

   A. 72 percent
   B. 77 percent
   C. 84 percent
   D. 86 percent

8. Funds for Federal Housing Administration loans are usually provided by:

   A. the Federal Housing Administration.
   B. the Federal Reserve.
   C. mortgage lenders.
   D. the seller.

9. A loan secures a note executed by a borrower to the lender. The loan also secures any future advances of funds made by the lender to the borrower. The interest rate on the original loan amount is fixed, but the future advances will be made at the market rate then in effect. This is what type of loan?

   A. Buydown
   B. Wraparound
   C. Package
   D. Open-end

10. Which of the following statements correctly describes a proportional tax system?

   A. The tax rate increases in proportion to income.
   B. The tax rate declines proportionate to the increase in value of the taxable item or income.
   C. The tax rate remains the same regardless of the value of the item or the amount of income.
   D. It is the opposite of a so-called flat tax.

12   The Economics of Real Estate Investment

 Objectives:

- Explain the reasons why real estate may — or may not — be a good investment for a particular investor

- Understand the concepts of appreciation, income, leverage, equity, pyramiding and depreciation

- Identify the various forms of investment ventures: syndicates, REITs and REMICs

---

▦ INVESTING IN REAL ESTATE

Even though changes in the economy have increased risk or lowered returns, the investment market continues to devise innovative and attractive investment strategies, particularly for a popular investment such as real estate.

Advantages of Real Estate Investment

In recent years, real estate values have fluctuated widely in various regions of the country. This results in some investments failing to produce returns greater than the rate of inflation (that is, serving as inflation hedges). Yet many real estate investments have shown above-average rates of return, generally greater than the prevailing interest rates charged by mortgage lenders. In theory, this means an investor can use the leverage of borrowed money to finance a real estate purchase and feel relatively sure that, if held long enough, the asset will yield more money than it cost to finance the purchase.

Real estate offers investors greater control over their investments than do other options, such as stocks, bonds or other securities. Real estate investors also receive certain tax benefits. Both leveraging and taxes are discussed in full later in this chapter.

Disadvantages of Real Estate Investment

Unlike stocks and bonds, real estate is not highly liquid over a short period of time. **Liquidity** refers to how quickly an asset may be converted into cash. For instance, an investor in listed stocks has only to call a stockbroker when funds are needed. The stockbroker sells the stock, and the investor receives the cash. In contrast, a real estate investor may have to sell the property at a substantially lower price than desired to ensure a quick sale. Of course, a real estate investor may be able to raise a limited amount of cash by refinancing the property.

Real estate investment is expensive. Large amounts of capital are usually required.

It is difficult to invest in real estate without expert advice. Investment decisions must be based on careful studies of all the facts, reinforced by a thorough knowledge of real estate and the manner in which it is affected by the marketplace.

Real estate requires active management. A real estate investor can rarely sit idly by and watch his or her money grow. Management decisions must be made. How much rent should be charged? How should repairs and tenant grievances be handled? The investor may want to manage the property personally. On the other hand, it may be preferable to hire a professional property manager. Sweat equity (physical improvements accomplished by the investor personally) may be required to make the asset profitable. Many good investments fail because of poor management.

Finally, despite its popularity, real estate investment is far from a sure thing. In fact, it involves a high degree of risk. The possibility always exists that an investor's property will decrease in value during the period it is held or that it will not generate enough income to make it profitable.

The Investment

Real estate investors hope to achieve various investment objectives. Their goals can be reached more effectively depending on the type of property and manner of ownership chosen. The most prevalent form of real estate investment is direct ownership. Both individuals and corporations may own real estate directly and manage it for appreciation or cash flow (income). Property held for **appreciation** is generally expected to increase in value while it's owned and to show a profit when it's sold. Income property is just that: property held for current income as well as a potential profit upon its sale.

Appreciation

Real estate is an avenue of investment open to those interested in holding property primarily for appreciation. Two main factors affect appreciation: inflation and intrinsic value.

- **Inflation** is the increase in the amount of money in circulation. When more money is available, its value declines. When the value of money declines, wholesale and retail prices rise. This is essentially an operation of supply and demand, as discussed in Chapter 2.

- The **intrinsic value** of real estate is the result of a person's individual choices and preferences for a given geographical area. As a rule, the greater the intrinsic value, the more money a property commands upon its sale.

Unimproved Land. Quite often, investors speculate in purchases of either agricultural land or undeveloped land located in what is expected to be a major path of growth. In these cases, however, the property's intrinsic value and potential for appreciation are not easy to determine. This type of investment carries with it many inherent risks. How fast will the area develop? Will it grow sufficiently for the investor to make a good profit? Will the expected growth occur? More important, will the profits eventually realized from the property be great enough to offset the costs of holding it, such as property taxes? Because these questions often cannot be answered with any degree of certainty, lending institutions may be reluctant to lend money for the purchase of raw land.

Income tax laws do not allow the **depreciation** (cost recovery) of land. Also, such land may not be liquid (salable) at certain times under certain circumstances because few people will purchase raw or agricultural land on short notice. Despite all the risks, however, land has historically been a good inflation hedge if held long term. It can also be a source of income to offset some of the holding costs. For example, agricultural land can be leased out for crops, timber production or grazing.

A Closer Look . . .

A few years ago, a real estate investor learned from her friends in the state capital that the governor was about to announce that a major new international airport would be built at a rural site currently occupied by an abandoned industrial site. The investor immediately bought several large tracts near the proposed airport location. Once the airport was in place, she planned to sell the land to developers for the hotels, restaurants and office buildings that would be in demand. The governor announced the airport, and the value of the investment soared. In an election before construction began, however, the governor was defeated. The newly elected governor decided that the proposed airport would be a waste of taxpayer money, and the project died for lack of political support, leaving the investor holding largely worthless land around a potentially toxic site.

Income Property

The wisest initial investment for a person who wishes to buy and personally manage real estate may be rental income property.

Cash Flow. The object of directing funds into income property is to generate spendable income, usually called cash flow. **Cash flow** is the total amount of money remaining after all expenditures have been paid. These expenses include taxes, operating costs and mortgage payments. The cash flow produced by any given parcel of real estate is determined by at least three factors: amount of rent received, operating expenses and method of debt repayment.

Generally, the amount of rent (income) that a property may command depends on a number of factors, including the property's location, physical appearance and amenities. If the cash flow from rents is not enough to cover all expenses, negative cash flow will result.

To keep cash flow high, an investor should attempt to keep operating expenses reasonably low. Such operating expenses include general maintenance of the building, repairs, utilities, taxes and tenant services (switchboard facilities, security systems and so forth).

An investor often stands to make more money by investing with borrowed money, usually obtained through a mortgage loan or deed of trust loan. Low mortgage payments spread over a long period of time result in a higher cash flow because they allow the investor to retain more income each month; conversely, high mortgage payments contribute to a lower cash flow.

Investment Opportunities. Traditional income-producing property includes apartment and office buildings, hotels, motels, shopping centers and industrial properties. In the past, investors have found well-located, one- to four-family dwellings to be among the most favorable investments. However, in recent years many communities have seen severe overbuilding of office space and shopping centers. The result has been high vacancy rates.

Leverage

Leverage is the use of borrowed money to finance an investment. As a rule, an investor can receive a maximum return from the initial investment (the down payment and closing and other costs) by making a small down payment, paying a low interest rate and spreading mortgage payments over as long a period as possible.

The effect of leveraging is to provide a return that reflects the result of market forces on the entire original purchase price, but that is measured against only the actual cash invested. For example, if an investor spends $100,000 for rental property and makes a $20,000 down payment, then sells the property five years later for $125,000, the return over five years is $25,000. Disregarding ownership expenses, the return is not 25 percent ($25,000 compared with $100,000), but 125 percent of the original amount invested ($25,000 compared to $20,000).

Risks are directly proportionate to leverage. A high degree of leverage translates into greater risk for the investor and lender because of the high ratio of borrowed money to the value of the real estate. Lower leverage results in less risk. When values drop in an area or vacancy rates rise, the highly leveraged investor may be unable to pay even the financing costs of the property.

Equity Buildup

Equity buildup is that portion of the loan payment directed toward the principal rather than the interest, plus any gain in property value due to appreciation. In a sense, equity buildup is like money in the investor's bank account. This accumulated equity is not realized as cash unless the property is sold or refinanced. However, the equity interest may be sold, exchanged or mortgaged (refinanced) to be used as leverage for other investments.

Pyramiding

An effective method for a real estate investor to increase his or her holdings without investing additional capital is through **pyramiding**. Pyramiding is simply the process of using one property to drive the acquisition of additional properties. Two methods of pyramiding can be used: pyramiding through sale and pyramiding through refinance.

In *pyramiding through selling*, an investor first acquires a property. He or she then improves the property for resale at a substantially higher price. The profit from the sale of the first property is used to purchase additional properties. Thus, the proceeds from a single investment (the point of the pyramid) provide the means for acquiring other properties. These properties are also improved and sold, and the proceeds are reinvested, until the investor is satisfied with his or her return. Of course, the disadvantage is that the proceeds from each sale are subject to capital gains taxation, as discussed below.

The goal of *pyramiding through refinancing*, on the other hand, is to use the value of the original property to drive the acquisition of additional properties while retaining all the properties acquired. The investor refinances the original property and uses the proceeds of the refinance to purchase additional properties. These properties are refinanced in turn to enable the investor to acquire further properties, and so on. By holding on to the properties, the investor increases his or her income-producing property holdings while simultaneously delaying the capital gains taxes that would result from a sale.

▦ TAX BENEFITS

One of the main reasons real estate investments were popular and profitable in the past is that tax laws allowed investors to use losses generated by such investments to shelter income from other sources. Although laws have changed and some tax advantages of owning investment real estate are altered periodically, with professional tax advice, an investor can still make a wise real estate purchase.

Exchanges

Real estate investors can defer taxation of capital gains by making property **exchanges**. Even if property has appreciated greatly since its initial purchase, it may be exchanged for other property. A property owner will incur tax liability on a sale only if additional capital or property is also received. Note, however, that the tax is deferred, not eliminated. Whenever the investor sells the property, the capital gain will be taxed.

To qualify as a tax-deferred exchange under § 1031 of the Internal Revenue Code, the properties involved must be of *like kind* — that is, real estate for real estate of equal value. The fact that the real estate is improved or unimproved is immaterial. Any additional capital or personal property included with the transaction to even out the value of the exchange is called **boot**.

The IRS requires tax on the boot to be paid at the time of the exchange by the party who receives it. The value of the boot is added to the basis of the property for which it is given. Tax-deferred exchanges are governed by strict federal requirements, and competent guidance from a tax professional is essential.

Depreciation

Depreciation, or *cost recovery*, allows an investor to recover the cost of an income-producing asset through tax deductions over the asset's useful life. While investors rarely purchase property without expecting it to appreciate over time, the tax laws maintain that all physical structures deteriorate (and lose value) over time. Cost recovery deductions may be taken only on personal property and improvements to land. Furthermore, they can be taken only if the property is used in a trade or business or for the production of income. Thus, a cost recovery deduction cannot be claimed on an individual's personal residence, and land cannot be depreciated. Technically, land never wears out or becomes obsolete.

Depreciation taken periodically in equal amounts over an asset's useful life is called **straight-line depreciation**.

Deductions

In addition to tax deductions for depreciation, investors may be able to **deduct** losses from their real estate investments. The tax laws are very complex. The amount of loss that may be deducted depends on whether an investor actively participates in the regular, day-to-day management of the rental property or makes management decisions. Other factors are the amount of the loss and the source of the income against which the loss is to be deducted. Investors who do not actively participate in the management or operation of the real estate are considered passive investors. Passive investors may not use losses to offset active income derived from active participation in real estate management, wages or income from stocks, bonds and the like. The tax code cites specific rules for active and passive income and losses and may be subject to changes.

Certain tax credits are allowed for renovation of older buildings, low-income housing projects and historic property. A tax credit is a direct reduction in the tax due rather than a deduction from income before tax is computed. Tax credits encourage the revitalization of older properties and the creation of low-income housing. The tax laws governing these issues are also complex.

Real estate must be analyzed in conjunction with an investor's other investments and overall financial goals and objectives. Income tax consequences also have a significant bearing on an investor's decisions. Competent tax advice should be sought to help an investor carefully evaluate the ramifications of an investment decision.

Installment Sales

A taxpayer who sells real property and receives payment on an installment basis pays tax only on the profit portion of each payment received. Interest received is taxable as ordinary income. Many complex laws apply to installment sales, and a competent tax adviser should be consulted.

▦ INVESTING WITH OTHERS

Because of the expense and complexity of real estate investments, it is often desirable for investors to enter into co-venturing agreements with others. This pooling of resources permits investment in larger, more lucrative projects, as well as a degree of risk-sharing. These arrangements may take many forms, but some of the most popular are real estate investment syndicates, real estate investment trusts and real estate mortgage investment conduits.

Real Estate Investment Syndicates

A **real estate investment syndicate** is a business venture in which people pool their resources to own or develop a particular piece of property. This structure permits people with only modest capital to invest in large-scale operations. Typical syndicate projects include high-rise apartment buildings and shopping centers. Syndicate members realize some profit from rents collected on the investment. The main return usually comes when the syndicate sells the property.

Syndicate participation can take many legal forms. For instance, syndicate members may hold property as tenants in common or joint tenants. Various kinds of partnership, corporate and trust ownership options are possible. Private syndication generally involves a small group of closely associated or experienced investors. Public syndication, on the other hand, involves a much larger group of investors who may or may not be knowledgeable about real estate as an investment. Any pooling of individuals' funds raises questions of securities registration under federal and state securities laws. These are commonly referred to as blue-sky laws.

To protect members of the public who are not sophisticated investors, but who may still be solicited to participate in syndicates, securities laws govern the offer and sale of securities. Real estate securities that fall under the definition of a public offering must be registered with state officials and the federal Securities and Exchange Commission (SEC). Pertinent factors include the number of prospects solicited, the total number of investors, the financial background and sophistication of the investors and the value or price per unit of investment.

Forms of Syndicates. A **general partnership** is organized so that all members of the group share equally in the managerial decisions, profits and losses involved with the investment. A certain member (or members) of the syndicate is designated to act as trustee for the group. The trustee holds title to the property and maintains it in the syndicate's name.

Under a **limited partnership** agreement, one party (or parties), usually a developer or real estate broker, organizes, operates and holds responsibility for the entire syndicate. This person is called the general partner. The other members of the partnership are merely investors; they have no voice in the organization and direction of the operation. These passive investors are called limited partners.

The limited partners share in the profits, and the general partner is compensated out of the profits. The limited partners stand to lose only as much as they invest — nothing more. Like their level of participation, their risk of loss is limited. The general partner is totally responsible for any excess losses incurred by the investment.

The sale of a limited partnership interest involves the sale of an investment security as defined by the SEC. As a result, the sale is subject to state and federal laws concerning the sale of securities. Unless exempt, the securities must be registered with the SEC and the appropriate state authorities.

Real Estate Investment Trusts

By directing their funds into **real estate investment trusts (REITs)**, real estate investors take advantage of the same tax benefits as do mutual fund investors. A real estate investment trust does not have to pay corporate income tax as long as 95 percent of its income is distributed to its shareholders. Certain other conditions must also be met. To qualify as a REIT, at least 75 percent of the trust's income must come from real estate. Investors purchase certificates in the trust, which in turn invests in real estate or mortgages (or both). Profits are distributed to investors.

REITs are subject to complex restrictions and regulations. A competent attorney should be involved at all stages of a REIT's development.

Real Estate Mortgage Investment Conduits

A **real estate mortgage investment conduit (REMIC)** has complex qualification, transfer and liquidation rules. For instance, the REMIC must satisfy the asset test. The asset test requires that after a start-up period, almost all assets must be qualified mortgages and permitted investments. Furthermore, investors' interests may consist of only one or more classes of regular interests and a single class of residual interests. Holders of regular interests receive interest or similar payments based on either a fixed rate or a variable rate. Holders of residual interests receive distributions (if any) on a pro rata basis.

The Next Step

Lending, financing, investing and taxation are all based on the value of a property. As we've seen, it is the operation of the marketplace that is the ultimate determiner of value. But the price a willing buyer pays for a property may be influenced by subjective factors unrelated to the marketplace, and the sales price may be inflated or understated in relation to market value. How do those lenders, financiers, investors and taxing bodies make an accurate determination of value? The appraisal process is the method, and its economic impact is significant. In the next chapter, we'll look at how appraisal affects the real estate economy.

Chapter 12
REVIEW

- Investing in real estate has several distinct **ADVANTAGES**: *above-average rates of return* (compared with other types of investment opportunities), *greater investor control* and *tax benefits*.

- Investing in real estate has some **DISADVANTAGES**, too: *low liquidity, high capital requirements, complexity, intense management* and *risk*.

- Real estate is an avenue of investment especially attractive to those who are interested in holding property for **APPRECIATION**. *Income tax laws do not allow the depreciation of land*, however.

- **CASH FLOW** is *the total amount of money remaining after all expenditures have been paid*. Traditional income-producing properties include apartment and office buildings, hotels, shopping centers and industrial properties.

- *The use of borrowed money to finance an investment* is called **LEVERAGE**. Leverage permits an investor to receive a maximum return from the initial investment by making a small down payment, paying a low interest rate on the loan and spreading mortgage payments over a long period.

- **PYRAMIDING** is *the process of using one property to drive the acquisition of additional properties*.

- Real estate investors can defer taxation of **CAPITAL GAINS** by making **PROPERTY EXCHANGES**. Investors can **DEPRECIATE** *improvements on land*, but not the land itself or a personal residence. *Losses* incurred in real estate investments may be **DEDUCTED** from the investor's *income taxes*.

- Investors may choose to enter into co-venturing agreements with others, including real estate investment syndicates, REITs and REMICs.

Chapter 12 QUIZ

1. All of the following are advantages to real estate investment, *EXCEPT*:

    A. liquidity.
    B. rate of return.
    C. investor control.
    D. tax benefits.

2. The increase in the amount of money available in circulation is referred to as:

    A. liquidity.
    B. inflation.
    C. cash flow.
    D. leverage.

3. The use of borrowed money to finance an investment is called:

    A. equity buildup.
    B. pyramiding.
    C. boot.
    D. leverage.

4. *H* is a real estate investor. *H* refinances one of her office buildings, and uses the proceeds of the refinance to purchase a small shopping center. *H* then refinances the shopping center and uses the additional money to buy two office buildings and a vacant lot. What is *H* doing?

   A.   Pyramiding through selling
   B.   Leveraging
   C.   Pyramiding through refinancing
   D.   Investing through equity buildup

5. Two investors exchange unimproved properties. Because one property is worth more than the other, one of the investors also receives $50,000 in cash. What is the cash called?

   A.   Cost recovery
   B.   Like kind property
   C.   Boot
   D.   Leverage

6. Depreciation taken periodically in equal amounts over the useful life of an asset is referred to as:

   A.   equity buildup depreciation.
   B.   pyramiding through depreciation.
   C.   straight-line depreciation.
   D.   appreciation.

7. *X*, *Y* and *Z* enter into a business relationship in which all three will share equally in decision making, profits and losses. What type of arrangement is this?

   A.   Limited partnership
   B.   Shared cooperation agreement
   C.   Limited venture
   D.   General partnership

8. *X* and *Y* enter into a real estate investment partnership in which *X* will make all day-to-day decisions and *Y* will merely contribute capital and take a wholly passive role. What type of syndicate is this?

   A. General partnership
   B. Limited partnership
   C. Passive partnership
   D. It is not any form of partnership

9. A real estate investment trust does not have to pay corporate income tax as long as what percentage of its income is distributed to its shareholders?

   A. 75 percent
   B. 87 percent
   C. 95 percent
   D. 100 percent

10. How is a REMIC different from a REIT?

   A. At least 50 percent of a REIT's income must be derived from real estate; REMICs are not subject to any controls over the type of investments held.
   B. Almost all of a REMIC's assets must be qualified mortgages.
   C. A REIT invests in real estate loans; a REMIC invests in income properties.
   D. REITs are subject to an asset test; REMICs are not.

13 The Economics of Appraisal

Objectives:

- Understand how the need for appraisal services evolved and how the modern appraisal industry is regulated

- Compare and contrast the three approaches to appraisal: what their distinguishing features are and when each one is used

- Describe the appraisal process from beginning to end

THE EVOLUTION OF PROPERTY VALUATION

At one time, people were nomadic and land was not owned or considered in terms of wealth. Western European colonists, for instance, laughed at the "simplistic" Native Americans who accepted beads and trinkets in exchange for land ownership. The Native Americans, on the other hand, were astonished that the Western Europeans were willing to pay valuable trade items for something the Native Americans did not think of as being ownable by anyone. This illustrates a clear clash in land valuation concepts.

When domestication of animals and crops began to emerge, land served as the basis for agricultural technologies. Still, its value as a commodity in its own right was not readily apparent, since there was a seemingly infinite abundance available for use.

There is a widely recognized economic theory that all wealth is ultimately derived from land. Under this theory, ownership of land evolved as the main form of measuring wealth even in strictly agricultural economies. The sale of land became the sale of the basic means for the production of wealth.

With the industrial revolution in the 19th century, land took on new meaning in the economic and social system. Factories needed fixed locations, and workers moved to where the jobs were. Mobility has important effects on real estate value. Value rises when properties sell more frequently. In other words, the shorter the turnover time, the more rapid the escalation of value. This partially explains why in the northeast and southern states where homes frequently pass from generation to generation, the relative rise in real estate value is not as dramatic as in the more mobile Sun Belt states. One might say that mobility is a key factor in the enhancement of value.

The Need for Appraisal

As the nation became more mobile and property turned over more rapidly, the property valuation process gained in importance. Appraisal has evolved from mere personal observations and oral opinions of value to an orderly, formalized process of investigation and reporting.

Estimates of value have come to be required for

- *lending* on real estate to provide a margin of safety for lenders

- establishing *replacement value* of improvements for insurance purposes

- apportioning *taxation* of an individual property in relation to the total valuation of properties eligible for taxation on the assessment rolls

- *taking* of property for a public purpose (condemnation or eminent domain proceedings)

- *partition* of property in settlement of disputes over division of assets

- *inheritance tax*

- *benchmark of value* in the resolution of what a seller is willing to sell for and what a buyer is willing to pay

- *confirmation of asset value* for a variety of other purposes, both personal and business

▦ THE APPRAISAL INDUSTRY

An **appraisal** is an opinion of value based on supportable evidence and approved methods. An **appraiser** is an independent person trained to provide an unbiased estimate of value. Appraising is a professional service performed for a fee.

The role of an appraiser is to determine market value. An appraiser develops a supportable and objective report about the value of the subject property, relying on experience and expertise in valuation theories to evaluate market data. The appraiser does not establish the property's worth; instead, he or she verifies what the market indicates.

Regulation of Appraisal Activities

Title XI of the Financial Institutions Reform, Recovery, and Enforcement Act of 1989 (FIRREA) requires that any appraisal used in connection with a federally related transaction must be performed by a competent individual whose professional conduct is subject to supervision and regulation. Appraisers must be licensed or certified according to state law.

Each state adopts its own appraiser regulations, which must conform to federal requirements that follow criteria established by the Appraisal Foundation. The Appraisal Foundation is a national body composed of representatives of major appraisal organizations. Appraisers are required to follow the Uniform Standards of Professional Appraisal Practice (USPAP).

A **federally related transaction** is any real estate-related financial transaction in which a federal financial institution or regulatory agency engages. This includes transactions involving the sale, lease, purchase, investment or exchange of real property. It also includes the financing, refinancing or use of real property as security for a loan or an investment, including mortgage-backed securities.

In California, appraisers are licensed and regulated through the Office of Real Estate Appraisers (OREA). *Appraisal* is defined by the California Business and Professions Code (§11302) as

> a written statement independently and impartially prepared by a qualified appraiser setting forth an opinion in a federally related transaction as to the market value of an adequately described property as of a specific date, supported by the presentation and analysis of relevant market information.

California appraisers may be licensed in one of three classifications. Licensed Appraisers may appraise only noncomplex residential properties up to $1 million in value; Certified Residential Appraisers may appraise any residential property regardless of value; and General Certification Appraisers may appraise residential or commercial properties.

▦ ESSENTIAL ELEMENTS OF VALUE

Like professionals in any industry, appraisers use certain terms that have specific meanings. *Value* is one of these. To understand appraisal, we must understand what is meant by value.

Value

To have **value** in the real estate market — that is, to have monetary worth based on desirability — a property must have the following characteristics:

- **Demand.** The need or desire for possession or ownership backed by the financial means to satisfy that need

- **Utility.** The property's usefulness for its intended purposes

- **Scarcity.** A finite supply

- **Transferability.** The relative ease with which ownership rights are transferred from one person to another

Market Value

Generally, the goal of an appraiser is to estimate **market value**. The market value of real estate is the most probable price that a property should bring in a fair sale. This definition makes three assumptions:

1. A competitive and open market exists.

2. The buyer and seller are assumed to be acting prudently and knowledgeably.

3. The price not affected by unusual economic circumstances.

The following are essential to determining market value:

- The *most probable price* is **not** the average or highest price.

- The buyer and seller must be *unrelated* and *acting without undue pressure*.

- Both buyer and seller must be *well informed* about the property's use and potential, including *defects* and *advantages*.

- A *reasonable time* must be allowed for exposure in the open market.

- Payment must be made *in cash or its equivalent*.

- The price must represent a *normal consideration* for the property sold, unaffected by special financing amounts or terms, services, fees, costs or credits incurred in the market transaction.

Market Value and Market Price

Market value is an opinion of value based on an analysis of data. The data may include not only an analysis of comparable sales, but also an analysis of potential income, expenses and replacement costs (less any depreciation). **Market price**, on the other hand, is what a property actually sells for: its sales price. In theory, market price should be the same as market value. Market price can be taken as accurate evidence of current market value, however, only if the conditions essential to market value exist. Sometimes, property may be sold below market value; for instance, when the seller is forced to sell quickly or when a sale is arranged between relatives.

Market Value and Cost

An important distinction can be made between market value and cost. One of the most common misconceptions about valuing property is that cost represents market value. Cost and market value may be the same. In fact, when the improvements on a property are new, cost and value are likely to be equal. But more often, cost does not equal market value. "Cost" refers to labor and materials. For example, a homeowner may install a swimming pool for $15,000; however, the cost of the improvement may not add $15,000 to the value of the property.

Basic Principles of Value

A number of economic principles can affect the value of real estate. The most important are defined in the text that follows.

- **Anticipation.** According to the principle of **anticipation**, value is created by the expectation that certain events will occur. Value can increase or decrease in anticipation of some future benefit or detriment. For instance, the value of a house may be affected if rumors circulate that an adjacent property may be converted to commercial use in the near future. If the property has been a vacant eyesore, it is possible that the neighboring home's value will increase. On the other hand, if the vacant property is perceived as a park or playlot that added to the neighborhood's quiet atmosphere, the news might cause the house's value to decline.

- **Change.** No physical or economic condition remains constant. This is the principle of **change**. Real estate is subject to natural phenomena such as tornadoes, fires and routine wear and tear. The real estate business is subject to market demands, like any other business. An appraiser must be knowledgeable about both the past and perhaps about the predictable effects of natural phenomena and the behavior of the marketplace.

- **Competition.** The interaction of supply and demand creates **competition**. Excess profits tend to attract competition. For example, the success of a retail store may cause investors to open similar stores in the area. This tends to mean less profit for all stores concerned unless the purchasing power in the area increases substantially.

- **Conformity.** The principle of **conformity** says that value is created when a property is in harmony with its surroundings. Maximum value is realized if the use of land conforms to existing neighborhood standards. In single-family residential neighborhoods, for instance, buildings should be similar in design, construction, size and age.

- **Contribution.** Under the principle of **contribution**, the value of any part of a property is measured by its effect on the value of the whole. Installing a swimming pool, greenhouse or private bowling alley may not add value to the property equal to the cost. On the other hand, remodeling an outdated kitchen or bathroom probably would.

- **Highest and best use.** The most profitable single use to which a property may be put, or the use that is most likely to be in demand in the near future, is the property's **highest and best use**. The use must be

  — physically *possible*,

  — legally *permitted*,

  — financially *feasible*, and

  — maximally *productive*.

  The highest and best use of a site can change with social, political and economic forces. For instance, a parking lot in a busy downtown area may not maximize the land's profitability to the same extent an office building might. Highest and best use of the land is noted in every appraisal.

- **Increasing and diminishing returns.** The addition of more improvements to land and structures increases value only to the assets' maximum value. Beyond that point, additional improvements no longer affect a property's value. As long as money spent on improvements produces an increase in income or value, the law of increasing returns applies. At the point where additional improvements do not increase income or value, the law of diminishing returns applies. No matter how much money is spent on the property, the property's value does not keep pace with the expenditures.

- **Plottage.** The principle of **plottage** holds that merging or consolidating adjacent lots into a single larger one produces a greater total land value than the sum of the two sites valued separately. For example, two adjacent lots valued at $35,000 each might have a combined value of $90,000 if consolidated. The process of merging two separately owned lots under one owner is known as assemblage.

- **Regression and progression.** In general, the worth of a better-quality property is adversely affected by the presence of a lesser-quality property. This is known as the principle of **regression**. Thus, in a neighborhood of modest homes, a structure that is larger, better maintained or more luxurious would tend to be valued in the same range as the less lavish homes. Conversely, under the principle of **progression**, the value of a modest home would be higher if it were located among larger, fancier properties. The larger property might be termed *overimproved*; the small one *underimproved*. Both would be detrimental conditions.

- **Substitution.** The principle of **substitution** says that the maximum value of a property tends to be set by how much it would cost to purchase an equally desirable and valuable substitute property.

- **Supply and demand.** As we learned in Chapter 2, the principle of *supply and demand* says that the value of a property depends on the number of properties available in the marketplace — the supply of the product. Other factors include the prices of other properties, the number of prospective purchasers and the price buyers will pay.

▦ THE THREE APPROACHES TO VALUE

To arrive at an accurate estimate of value, appraisers traditionally use three basic valuation techniques: the sales comparison approach, the cost approach and the income approach. The three methods serve as checks against each other. Using them narrows the range within which the final estimate of value falls. Each method is generally considered most reliable for specific types of property.

The Sales Comparison Approach

In the **sales comparison approach**, an estimate of value is obtained by comparing the property being appraised (the subject property) with recently sold comparable properties (properties similar to the subject). Because no two parcels of real estate are exactly alike, each comparable property must be analyzed for differences and similarities between it and the subject property. This approach is a good example of the principle of substitution, discussed above. The sales prices of the comparables must be adjusted to the subject property to account for any dissimilarities. The principal factors for which adjustments must be made include the following:

- **Property rights.** An adjustment must be made when less than fee simple, the full legal bundle of rights, is involved. This includes land leases, ground rents, life estates, easements, deed restrictions and encroachments.

- **Financing concessions.** The financing terms must be considered, including adjustments for differences such as mortgage loan terms and owner financing.

- **Conditions of sale.** Adjustments must be made for motivational factors that would affect the sale, such as foreclosure, a sale between family members or some nonmonetary incentive.

- **Date of sale.** An adjustment must be made if economic changes occur between the date of sale of the comparable property and the date of the appraisal.

- **Location.** Similar properties might differ in price from neighborhood to neighborhood or even between locations within the same neighborhood.

- **Physical features and amenities.** Physical features, such as age, size and condition, may require adjustments.

The sales comparison approach is essential in almost every appraisal of real estate. It is considered the most reliable of the three approaches in appraising single-family homes, where the intangible benefits may be difficult to measure otherwise. Most appraisals include a minimum of three comparable sales reflective of the subject property.

The Cost Approach

The **cost approach** to value is also based on the principle of substitution. The cost approach consists of five steps:

1. Estimate the *value of the land as if it were vacant* and available to be put to its highest and best use.

2. Estimate the *current cost of constructing buildings and improvements*.

3. Estimate the *amount of accrued depreciation* resulting from the property's physical deterioration, functional obsolescence and external depreciation.

4. Deduct the *accrued depreciation* (Step 3) from the *construction cost* (Step 2).

5. Add the *estimated land value* (Step 1) to the *depreciated cost* of the building and site improvements (Step 4) to arrive at the total property value.

There are two ways to look at the construction cost of a building for appraisal purposes: reproduction cost and replacement cost new.

Reproduction cost is the construction cost at current prices of an exact duplicate of the subject improvement, including both the benefits and the drawbacks of the property. **Replacement cost new** is the cost to construct an improvement similar to the subject property using current construction methods and materials, but not necessarily an exact duplicate. Replacement cost new is more frequently used in appraising older structures because it eliminates obsolete features and takes advantage of current construction materials and techniques.

Determining Reproduction or Replacement Cost New. An appraiser using the cost approach computes the reproduction or replacement cost of a building using one of the following methods:

- **Square-foot method.** The cost per square foot of a recently built comparable structure is multiplied by the number of square feet (using exterior dimensions) in the subject building. This is the most common and easiest method of cost estimation.

- **Unit-in-place method.** In the unit-in-place method, the replacement cost of a structure is estimated based on the construction cost per unit of measure of individual building components, including material, labor, overhead and builder's profit. Most components are measured in square feet, although items such as plumbing fixtures are estimated by cost. The sum of the components is the cost of the new structure.

- **Quantity-survey method.** The quantity and quality of all materials (such as lumber, brick and plaster) and the labor are estimated on a unit cost basis. These factors are added to indirect costs (for example, building permit, survey, payroll, taxes and builder's profit) to arrive at the total cost of the structure. Because it is so detailed and time consuming, this method is usually used only in appraising historical properties. It is, however, the most accurate method of appraising new construction.

- **Index method.** A factor representing the percentage increase of construction costs up to the present time is applied to the original cost of the subject property. Because it fails to take into account individual property variables, this method is useful only as a check of the estimate reached by one of the other methods.

Depreciation. In a real estate appraisal, depreciation is a loss in value due to any cause. It refers to a condition that adversely affects the value of an improvement to real property. Land does not depreciate — it retains its value indefinitely, except in such rare cases as downzoned urban parcels, improperly developed land or misused farmland.

Depreciation is considered to be curable or incurable, depending on the contribution of the expenditure to the value of the property. For appraisal purposes, depreciation is divided into three classes, according to its cause:

1. **Physical deterioration**

   — *Curable:* an item in need of repair, such as painting (deferred maintenance), that is economically feasible and would result in an increase in value equal to or exceeding the cost.

   — *Incurable:* a defect caused by physical wear and tear if its correction would not be economically feasible or contribute a comparable value to the building. The cost of a major repair may not warrant the financial investment.

2. **Functional obsolescence**

   — *Curable:* outmoded or unacceptable physical or design features that are no longer considered desirable by purchasers. Such features, however, could be replaced or redesigned at a cost that would be offset by the anticipated increase in ultimate value. Outmoded plumbing, for instance, is usually easily replaced. Room function may be redefined at no cost if the basic room layout allows for it. A bedroom adjacent to a kitchen, for example, may be converted to a family room.

   — *Incurable:* currently undesirable physical or design features that could not be easily remedied because the cost of cure would be greater than its resulting increase in value. An office building that could not be economically air-conditioned, for example, would suffer from incurable functional obsolescence if the cost of adding air conditioning were greater than its contribution to the building's value.

3. **External obsolescence**

— *Incurable:* This type of depreciation, caused by negative factors not on the subject property (such as environmental, social or economic forces) is always incurable. The loss in value cannot be reversed by spending money on the property. For example, proximity to a nuisance, such as a polluting factory or a deteriorating neighborhood, is one factor that could not be cured by the owner of the subject property.

Straight-Line Depreciation. The easiest but least precise way to determine depreciation is the **straight-line method**, also called the economic age-life method. Depreciation is assumed to occur at an even rate over a structure's economic life, the period during which it is expected to remain useful for its original intended purpose. The property's cost is divided by the number of years of its expected economic life to derive the amount of annual depreciation.

The cost approach is most helpful in the appraisal of newer or special-purpose buildings such as schools, churches and public buildings. Such properties are difficult to appraise using other methods because there are seldom enough local sales to use as comparables and because the properties do not ordinarily generate income.

The Income Approach

The **income approach** to value is based on the *present value of the rights to future income*. It assumes that the income generated by a property will determine the property's value. The income approach is used for valuation of income-producing properties such as apartment buildings, office buildings and shopping centers. In estimating value using the income approach, an appraiser must take five steps:

1. *Estimate* annual potential gross income. An estimate of economic rental income must be made based on market studies. Current rental income may not reflect the current market rental rates, especially in the case of short-term leases or leases about to terminate. Potential income includes other income to the property from such sources as vending machines, parking fees and laundry machines.

2. *Deduct* an allowance for vacancy and rent loss, based on published vacancy and rent loss rates (obtainable from management companies), to determine effective gross income.

3. *Deduct* the annual operating expenses from the effective gross income to arrive at the annual net operating income (NOI). Management costs are always included, even if the current owner manages the property. Mortgage payments (principal and interest) are debt service and not considered operating expenses.

4. *Estimate* the price a typical investor would pay for the income produced by this particular type and class of property. This is done by estimating the rate of return (or yield) that an investor will demand for the investment of capital in this type of building. This rate of return is called the capitalization (or "cap") rate and is determined by comparing the relationship of net operating income to the sales prices of similar properties that have sold in the current market. For example, a comparable property that is producing an annual net income of $15,000 is sold for $187,500. The capitalization rate is $15,000 divided by $187,500, or 8 percent. If other comparable properties sold at prices that yielded substantially the same rate, it may be concluded that 8 percent is the rate that the appraiser should apply to the subject property.

5. *Apply* the capitalization rate to the property's annual net operating income to arrive at the estimate of the property's value.

With the appropriate capitalization rate and the projected annual net operating income, the appraiser can obtain an indication of value by the income approach.

Gross Rent or Gross Income Multipliers. Certain properties, such as single-family homes and two-unit buildings, are not purchased primarily for income. As a substitute for a more elaborate income capitalization analysis, the gross rent multiplier (GRM) and gross income multiplier (GIM) are often used in the appraisal process. Each relates the sales price of a property to its rental income.

Because single-family residences usually produce only rental incomes, the gross rent multiplier is used. This relates a sales price to monthly rental income. However, commercial and industrial properties generate income from many other sources (rent, concessions, escalator clause income and so forth), and they are valued using their annual income from all sources.

The formulas are:

- For five or more residential units, commercial or industrial property:

  Sales price ÷ Gross income = GIM

- For one to four residential units:

  Sales price ÷ Gross rent = GRM

For example, if a home recently sold for $82,000 and its monthly rental income was $650, the GRM for the property would be computed as

$82,000 ÷ $650 = 126.2 GRM

To establish an accurate GRM, an appraiser must have recent sales and rental data from at least four properties that are similar to the subject property. The resulting GRM can then be applied to the estimated fair market rental of the subject property to arrive at its market value. The formula would be

Rental income x GRM = Estimated market value

Reconciliation

When the three approaches to value are applied to the same property, they normally produce three separate indications of value. **Reconciliation** is the art of analyzing and effectively weighing the findings from the three approaches.

The process of reconciliation is more complicated than simply taking the average of the three estimates of value. An average implies that the data and logic applied in each of the approaches are equally valid and reliable and should therefore be given equal weight. In fact, however, certain approaches are more valid and reliable with some kinds of properties than with others.

For example, in appraising a home, the income approach is rarely valid, and the cost approach is of limited value unless the home is relatively new. Therefore, the sales comparison approach is usually given greatest weight in valuing single-family residences. In the appraisal of income or investment property, the income approach normally is given the greatest weight. In the appraisal of churches, libraries, museums, schools and other special-use properties where little or no income or sales revenue is generated, the cost approach usually is assigned the greatest weight. From this analysis, or reconciliation, a single estimate of market value is produced.

▦ THE APPRAISAL PROCESS

Although appraising is not an exact or a precise science, the key to an accurate appraisal lies in the methodical collection and analysis of data. The appraisal process is an orderly set of procedures used to collect and analyze data to arrive at an ultimate value conclusion. The data are divided into two basic classes:

1. **General data:** covers the nation, region, city and neighborhood. Of particular importance is the neighborhood, where an appraiser finds the physical, economic, social and political influences that directly affect the value and potential of the subject property.

2. **Specific data:** covers details of the subject property as well as comparative data relating to costs, sales, and income and expenses of properties similar to and competitive with the subject property.

The Appraisal Report

Once the approaches have been reconciled and an opinion of value has been reached, the appraiser prepares a report for the client. The report should

- identify the real estate and real property interest;

- state the purpose and intended use of the appraisal;

- define the value to be estimated;

- state the effective date of the value and the date of the report;

- state the extent of the process of collecting, confirming and reporting the data;

- list all assumptions and limiting conditions that affect the analysis, opinion and conclusions of value;

- describe the information considered, the appraisal procedures followed and the reasoning that supports the report's conclusions: if an approach was excluded, the report should explain why;

- describe (if necessary or appropriate) the appraiser's opinion of the highest and best use of the real estate;

- describe any additional information that may be appropriate to show compliance with the specific guidelines established in the Uniform Standards of Professional Appraisal Practice (USPAP) or to clearly identify and explain any departures from these guidelines; and

- include a signed certification, as required by the Uniform Standards.

Unacceptable Appraisal Practices

The following are examples of appraisal practices that Fannie Mae considers unacceptable:

- Inclusion of inaccurate factual data about the subject neighborhood, site, improvements, or comparable sales.

- Failure to comment on negative factors with respect to the subject neighborhood, subject property, or proximity of the subject property to adverse influences.

- Use of comparables which the appraiser has not personally inspected by at least driving by them.

- Selection and use of inappropriate comparable sales or the failure to use comparables that are locationally and physically the most similar to the subject property.

- Use of data — particularly comparable sales data — provided by parties who have a financial interest in the transaction, without verifying the information from a disinterested source.

  For example, it would be inappropriate to use comparable sales provided by the broker who is handling the sale unless the appraiser verifies the data with another source and makes an independent investigation to determine that the comparables are the best ones available.

- Use of adjustments to the comparable sales that do not reflect the market's reaction to the differences between the subject property and the comparables, or failure to make adjustments when they are clearly indicated.

- Valuation that is based — either partially or completely — on the race, color or national origin of either the prospective owners or occupants of the property or of the present owners or occupants in the vicinity of the subject property.

- Development of a valuation conclusion that is not supported by available market data.

The Next Step

The next chapter continues our focus on the economic analysis of real estate. In "Analyzing Residential Income Property," we'll consider the tools used in performing a structured economic analysis of a particular segment of the market.

Chapter 13
REVIEW

▬ An **APPRAISAL** is an *opinion of value based on supportable evidence and approved methods*. An **APPRAISER** is *an independent person trained to provide an unbiased estimate of value for a fee*. FIRREA requires states to establish appraiser licensing procedures and industry regulations for appraisers who participate in **FEDERALLY RELATED TRANSACTIONS**.

▬ To have **VALUE** in the real estate market, a property must have certain characteristics: *demand, utility, scarcity* and *transferability*.

▬ The appraiser's goal is to estimate **MARKET VALUE**. Market value is *an opinion of value based on an analysis of collected data*. **MARKET PRICE** is what a property actually sells for.

▬ A number of **ECONOMIC PRINCIPLES** can affect the value of real estate. These include *anticipation, change, competition, conformity, contribution, highest and best use, increasing and diminishing returns, plottage, regression and progression, substitution* and *supply and demand*.

▬ The three approaches to value are the **SALES COMPARISON APPROACH**, the **COST APPROACH** and the **INCOME APPROACH**. The art of analyzing and effectively weighing the findings from the three approaches is called **RECONCILIATION**.

▬ The **APPRAISAL PROCESS** is an orderly set of procedures used to collect and analyze data to arrive at an ultimate value conclusion. The data are divided into two classes: *general* and *specific*. Once the approaches have been reconciled and an opinion of value has been reached, the appraiser prepares a detailed **APPRAISAL REPORT** for the client.

Chapter 13
QUIZ

1. An appraisal is a(n):

    A. determination of a property's worth.
    B. professional's educated opinion of value.
    C. opinion of market price.
    D. "ballpark guesstimate" of worth.

2. Which of the following most completely defines a federally related transaction?

    A. Any real estate transaction in the United States
    B. Any real estate-related financial transaction in which federal property is bought or sold
    C. Any real estate-related financial transaction in which a federal financial institution or regulatory agency engages
    D. Any real estate-related transaction in which the federal government is the purchaser

3. *J* bought his house for $150,000. When *J* put the house up for sale, he asked $175,000. The house eventually sold for $162,500. An appraiser valued the house at $165,000. Based on these facts, what is the market value of *J*'s house?

    A. $150,000
    B. $162,500
    C. $165,000
    D. $175,000

4. In the previous question, what is the market price of *J*'s house?

    A. Cannot tell from these facts
    B. $162,500
    C. $165,000
    D. $175,000

5. "Value is created by the expectation that certain events will occur." This statement defines which economic principle?

    A. Conformity
    B. Highest and best use
    C. Anticipation
    D. Supply and demand

6. *Q* builds an eight-bedroom brick house with a tennis court, greenhouse and indoor pool in a neighborhood of modest two-bedroom aluminum-sided houses on narrow lots. The value of *Q*'s house is likely to be affected by what economic principle?

    A. Conformity
    B. Assemblage
    C. Regression
    D. Change

7. In the previous question, the owners of the more modest homes in *Q*'s neighborhood may find that the value of their homes is affected by what economic principle?

    A. Contribution
    B. Increasing returns
    C. Substitution
    D. Progression

8. Location, physical features and conditions of sale would be primary considerations in which of the approaches to value?

    A. Cost approach only
    B. Sales comparison approach only
    C. Income and cost approach only
    D. Income approach only

9. To air-condition an old 20-story office building would require removing all the stone from the building's facade, cutting large holes through its three-foot-thick interior walls and rewiring the entire structure. When the job was completed, the building would not only lack historical charm, but would be structurally unsafe for tenants. This is an example of which type of depreciation?

    A. Curable physical deterioration
    B. Curable functional deterioration
    C. External obsolescence
    D. Incurable functional obsolescence

10. A three-apartment building recently sold for $380,000. Its monthly income was $2,400. What is the GRM for this property?

    A. .0063
    B. 9.12
    C. 13.19
    D. 158.3

Analyzing Residential Income Property

 Objectives:

- Describe and explain the four-step process of analyzing residential income property

- Demonstrate how investment performance may be analyzed using simple formulas

- Define net present value and internal rate of return as measures of investment performance and profitability

---

ANALYZING RESIDENTIAL INCOME PROPERTY: A PROCESS APPROACH

The decision to buy a personal residence is usually highly subjective. The economic benefits of equity buildup and appreciation are secondary to its utility and amenity value. Investment in residential income property, on the other hand, is an economic decision — as we discussed in Chapter 12. In order to reach any conclusion on the purchase of a residential site in a given situation, it is important to establish the basic objective of the project.

Once the objective has been defined, a scientific approach to problem solving can be applied. The scientific method formulates a question, gathers data, analyzes it, forms a hypothesis and tests it. In a real estate project, a modified version of this scientific process can be used to analyze the economic benefits of a particular project.

▦ STEP ONE: CLARIFYING THE ISSUE

Before we can begin gathering data and developing an answer, we need to know what the question is. Formulating the question is based on five evaluations: location, financial goals, taxes, ownership structure and development issues.

Location

Has careful consideration gone into the choice of neighborhood, before any further investigation takes place? Is this location compatible with management objectives? It is important to remember when developing residential property that this will be someone's home. The importance of providing an appropriate residential environment appealing to the consumer is absolutely paramount.

Financial Goals

Is this property to be acquired for development and sale or held as an investment? What is an acceptable return on investment? If the property is to be held as an investment, will it be a long-term or short-term holding? What form of project financing is to be used? The objectives may vary depending on whether the project is new construction or an existing residential property.

Tax Considerations

Is this property designed to attain "dealer" status for tax purposes by selling as a subdivision, or will it be subject to less harsh tax treatment as an "investor" with landlord status, to be resold later?

Structuring of Ownership

Will the ownership be corporate, limited partnership, trust, general partnership or in the names of individuals? If some form of joint entity is chosen, are the combined objectives of the owners compatible?

Development Considerations

In the case of a project to be developed or in the rehabilitation of an existing property, is the construction done by the developers or are the services of a general contractor to be used? This decision has a marked impact on the total project budget and scheduling.

▦ STEP TWO: COLLECTING THE DATA

The scope of the study is dependent upon the size of the project and the developer's financial commitment to the undertaking. With this in mind, here are some of the sources of data that might be utilized in formulating an investment decision involving residential real estate.

Finding Current Economic Data

The most current economic data indicating potential growth patterns or clouds on the national or local economic horizon can be obtained free from the following sources (including their Internet addresses on the World Wide Web [www]):

- U.S. Census Bureau: `census.gov`

- White House Economic Statistics: `whitehouse.gov`

- Bureau of Economic Analysis: `bea.doc.gov/bea`

- Federal Reserve: `stls.frb.org/fred`

- Federal Reserve Statistics: `bog.frb.fed.us/releases`

- USDA Economics and Statistics: `econ.ag.gov`

- California Trade & Commerce Agency: `commerce.ca.gov`

- California Economic Diversification and Revitalization (CEDAR): `cedar.ca.gov`

- California Department of Labor: `calmis.cahwnet.gov`

- California Department of Commerce Demographic Research Unit — `dof.ca.gov/html/Demograp/druhpar.htm`

Other excellent sources of timely residential housing data include the National Association of REALTORS® (`www.realtors.com`) and the National Association of Home Builders (`www.nahb.com`).

Traditional Sources

Direct and indirect information about the area can be gleaned from newspapers of all types from the *Wall Street Journal* to neighborhood publications, promotional pieces for local developments, sales studies conducted by local economic groups, economically oriented publications of local firms such as banks or public utilities, and other publicity brochures.

Local television also serves to provide a feel for the character of the area and price levels in general. Local chambers of commerce have a wealth of information about local economies, amenities, attractions and resources. Local tastes and price levels of residential real estate can be learned from licensees and appraisers who are active in the area.

Along with print and visual media, local radio stations, business owners, newspaper archives, libraries and museums can all add to the investigator's knowledge of the area.

Local Government. Local government bodies such as housing authorities, redevelopment agencies and planning departments can provide good, strong information about the community's commitment to housing development and rehabilitation, as well as clarify land-use, zoning and infrastructure issues.

Other useful local authorities include road departments (for information about present access and future planned transportation developments) and local school administrations.

Other Local Sources. The developer cannot afford to overlook any local source that might have a bearing on the project. For example, if one company is the major employer in the area, its future plans for expansion or contraction would bear heavily on the decision to go ahead or abandon plans. Influential political or environmental groups should also be sounded out at this stage. This is also the point at which to consult with neighborhood and community associations, both to create a cooperative atmosphere and to identify potential areas of contention.

Market Surveys

The developer may decide to conduct a custom-tailored survey to determine local housing preference, especially if a specialized market is being targeted. For example, in certain recreational areas manufactured and modular housing may be more popular than conventional "stick built" housing. Are the probable customers looking for garden kitchens, spacious yards, spas, swimming pools, air-conditioning, solar applications, golf courses, tennis and other recreational facilities?

Research Design. Studies will vary depending on whether the project is multiunit, such as apartments, cooperatives or condominiums, traditional detached single family homes or something in between. The nature of the project has a definite bearing on the type of data which will influence the decision of purchase or pass.

▦ STEP THREE: INTERPRETING THE DATA

A developer can collect mountains of facts, figures and opinions, but unless all those elements can be assimilated and arranged in a meaningful pattern, they are worthless. One of the principal concerns is the site under study itself. If the objective of the study is to determine the most suitable site, the factors outlined below will prove useful in making the selection. If there is just one site under study, reducing the data down to this level will help determine whether to proceed, abandon or modify the project.

Analysis would normally consist of a feasibility study including:

- Project Description

- Area Description

- Competition

- Cost Analysis

Project Description

Improvements. A physical description of the existing or proposed improvements is a basic requirement of the analysis. This can vary from a simple purchase of an existing home to the development of hundreds of new homes or apartments.

Prices. The local market as well as development costs will determine price ranges or rent levels. The study may cease at this point if it is determined that the costs of production are not adequately rewarded due to unattractive prevailing price levels.

Amenities. This analysis will be based on a study of average amenities for the area. If every housing project has built-in appliances, a fireplace and two or three bedrooms, then product differentiation will probably be in the area of additional amenities or design features within these parameters.

Lot Size, Unit and Room Size. If the surrounding area features half-acre house lots and the developer seeks to create postage stamp lots, demand will be questionable. If local zoning requires a certain lot size, of course, that creates the minimum legal boundaries. Developers should be aware that room-size expectations are different in urban and suburban markets.

Area Description

Economic Trends. This is an extremely broad topic that includes employment, median income, tax rates, ethnic mix, lifestyle, absorption rates of new projects, retail sales, future trends and essentially any other issues the developer can think of.

Infrastructure, Transportation and Services. Not only availability but capacity of utilities and services should be emphasized in the analysis. All aspects of transportation and access need to be assimilated and discussed in logical order. Not only are public utilities and appropriately lighted and signed street arterials essential, police and fire protection and other public services must be adequate to present and future needs.

Shopping. Commercial centers from regional malls right down to the local grocery or minimall should be noted. If the project involves a sizable investment, this should be analyzed for a seven- to ten-mile radius from the project. Remember that in our culture, grocery stores and shopping centers are the "hunting grounds" for the local population. Just as a herd of predatory animals will establish a territory where there is plentiful prey and accessible water, modern urbanites and suburbanites require access to their sources of food and clothing.

Schools and Houses of Worship. The entire spectrum of educational facilities should be listed in detail, including day care centers and preschools, public and private elementary and high schools, and local community colleges, business schools and universities.

The proximity of churches, temples, mosques and other religious institutions is often a competitive advantage: whether or not the consumers are spiritually oriented, the presence of religious institutions is often interpreted as a positive sign of stability and tradition.

Other Community Amenities. These include recreational and athletic facilities (such as parks, health clubs and public playgrounds), health care (hospitals and clinics) and special features such as cultural institutions and events (museums, orchestras, theaters and fairs). There must be a good match between amenities and the project's intended customers. For instance, if the target group is composed of older or retired persons, the proximity of playgrounds may be of less relevance than the quality of local health care facilities. On the other hand, the absence of places to take the grandchildren may be off-putting to potential buyers.

Competition

Just as when one is seeking a personal residence and wants to compare prices, obviously the best approach is to look at price levels of similar housing in the same area. Of particular concern in a development project is the financing available on competitive merchandise and its availability for the project in question. If, for example, government funds are available for a competing project and not for the project in question, it might affect the price that must be charged to the consumer.

Cost Analysis

Budgetary concerns are not necessarily the last item addressed, since failure to pass the test of affordability may kill the project at once. Affordability applies to both the consumer and the developer. It is important to examine realistically the amount of capital available as compared with the total capital outlay required for acquisition, development, marketing, and all other costs attributable to the objective of the investment.

▦ STEP FOUR: MAKING THE DECISION

Before the ultimate decision of whether or not to buy, the accumulated data must be put to the test. Once arranged in orderly fashion, do the facts support the decision to purchase? The answer to this question is how we test our "hypothesis" that a particular investment decision is a sound one. If the facts support the purchase, then interim methods of land holding may be pursued for a proposed project while the balance of the due diligence process takes place. In the case of a home or condominium purchase, it may be time for an acceptable offer and entry into escrow.

If the answer to our hypothetical question supports going the final step, decision making involves two elements — factual conclusions and recommended strategies for action. Over the coming days, months and years, the project can be monitored by repeating these steps in a continuing cycle of assessment and follow-up.

Conclusions

It is important to have a clear and logical summary of the results of the study leading to the decision to buy or pass. As with other types of income properties, an appropriate return on investment and appreciation of invested capital must be ensured. In order to maximize these items, proven approaches to investment analysis must be undertaken.

Strategies

Following from the conclusions are a series of strategies for carrying out the decision in the most profitable manner. Specific choices at this point include the number of units to be produced and, if in phases, how many units to each phase. There may be recommendations as to unit and room sizes, amenities and community facilities that affect the marketability of the product. There will also be recommendations about the type of financing and terms to be made available to buyers, such as buydowns, graduated payments and adjustable rates.

The decision making process for individual unit purchase for investment or personal consumption is along the same lines, with additional attention to possible remodeling or additional amenities.

Assessment and Follow-Up

Nothing in life remains static. To assume that conditions will remain as they are is dangerously naive on the part of any developer. Once the property has been brought under the developer's preliminary control (through a lease-option, option to purchase or escrow with contingencies) there may still be discoveries in the due diligence process (such as unavailability of water, downzoning or local "slow growth" initiatives) that might affect the project. In the case of an existing property, inspection might uncover serious structural flaws or environmental hazards that affect value. The prudent developer will remain flexible, and not stubbornly stick to a project that proves unfeasible at this stage.

▦ MEASURES OF INVESTMENT PERFORMANCE

There are several commonly used calculations that an investor may use to evaluate a property or project. For the purchase of an existing property, real figures should be available based on past performance. For proposed construction, or a purchase where significant changes will be made, the same approaches are used, with projected figures in a pro forma analysis.

Direct Capitalization

As a measure of economic productivity, direct capitalization is expressed in this formula:

$$R = \frac{i}{V}$$

where **R** = *overall Rate of Return*
     i = *projected annual net operating Income*
    V = *Value*

For example, a property purchased for $300,000 (**V**) that produces an annual net operating income of $36,000 (**i**) may be said to produce an overall rate of return of 12 percent (**R**):

$$\$36,000 \div \$300,000 = .12 \text{ or } 12\%$$

This overall rate is a device used in valuation of a property in the income approach, assuming that normal financing is available, and such rates are established in the market through the interaction of buyers and sellers. This rate would tend to evaluate the investment only with 100 percent equity investment, a rare occurrence, and reversion (future sale) is not considered.

Cash-on-Cash Return

The same technique that is used in direct capitalization can be applied to the evaluation of equity investments by using cash-on-cash returns. The cash-on-cash return method gives a prospective investor a much better evaluation of the investment than an estimate of value based on direct capitalization alone.

This analysis uses the same formula as direct capitalization:

$$R = \frac{i}{V}$$

where R = *Rate of Return on cash invested*
i = *cash flow after debt service*
V = *equity investment*

For example, a property purchased for $300,000 with $75,000 cash down payment, and producing a net annual operating income of $36,000, would require a debt service of $23,700 on a $225,000 mortgage at 10%, leaving a cash flow of $12,300.

$12,300 ÷ $75,000 = .164 or 16.4%

While this technique presents a better analysis of the investment, it still fails to take into consideration the fact that debt service includes some equity build-up through amortization and that there is a possibility of reversion in the property. The reversion will come from the sale of the property at some predicted time in the future.

Band of Investment Analysis

If the purchase of the property is financed, each component of financing represents a band of investment. By analyzing the proportion of an overall capitalization rate that is allocated to each band of investment, an equity yield rate can be established.

For example, assume that an investment property can be purchased at an overall capitalization rate of 12 percent. If a first trust deed loan of 80 percent of the purchase price can be obtained for 30 years at an annual interest rate of 10 percent, this represents the first band of investment. The equity band is the remaining 20 percent of the purchase price.

Assume the first loan has a mortgage constant of .105309 (the annual debt service divided by the original principal amount of the loan). By multiplying the percentage of the total purchase price that this band of investment represents (80 percent) by the mortgage constant for this available financing (.105309), a capitalization rate is derived for this band of investment.

This capitalization rate is then subtracted from the overall capitalization rate to determine what portion of the overall rate is available to apply to the next band of investment, the equity band.

80% x .105309 = .0842

(or 8.42% of the capitalization rate to apply to the first band of investment)

12.00% (overall capitalization rate)
– 8.42% (applied to the first band)
= 3.58% (to apply to the equity band)

.0358 ÷ .20 = .179, or 17.9% (equity yield)

This greatly increased equity yield, significantly higher than the overall capitalization rate, reflects the advantage of leverage and shows clearly that a capitalization rate alone does not analyze a leveraged investment. It also becomes clear that an overall capitalization rate alone is not an adequate tool for a direct comparison between a real estate investment and other types of investments that will compete for the investor's funds.

Pay-Back Period

The pay-back period is the length of time required for the stream of cash flows produced by the investment to equal the original cash outlay. By measuring this period, the investor determines how long the investment funds are at risk. The cash outlay is divided by the annual cash flow. For example,

$75,000 ÷ $12,300 = 6.10 years

Pay-back periods are used to compare investment opportunities. A different investment might have higher returns in early years and nothing thereafter. In general, the shorter the pay-back period, the more attractive the investment. However, the total return may be more significant to some investors.

Proceeds per Dollar Invested

An investment may be evaluated according to the total anticipated proceeds from income and reversion upon sale of the property. The problem with this technique is that each dollar received is treated the same, regardless of when received, even though it is generally recognized that a dollar to be received one year from now is worth less than a dollar received today.

Discounted Cash Flows

Based on the theory that a dollar to be received in the future is worth less than a dollar in hand today (compound interest theory), a discounted cash flow analysis can be used to evaluate a series of negative and positive cash flows over the anticipated ownership of a property. The cash flows used can be either before-tax or after-tax calculations, but the more complete investment analysis for the client would require the use of after-tax cash flows. The mathematics of this procedure is relatively simple but lengthy. It is accomplished by the following formula:

$$PV = \frac{CF_1}{(1 + i)} + \frac{CF_2}{(1 + i)^2} + \ldots + \frac{CF_n}{(1 + i)^n}$$

where **PV** = *Present Value of the discounted cash flows*
CF = *Cash Flow*
i = *discount rate used to reflect the time value of money*

But don't worry: this laborious arithmetic is accomplished quickly and easily with a few keystrokes on a basic financial calculator!

Net Present Value

An evaluation of the investment is frequently accomplished by determining the **net present value (NPV)** of a series of negative and positive discounted cash flows, where the first cash flow is the initial cash outlay, subsequent cash flows are the after-tax cash flows projected for the property and the final cash flow is the anticipated value of the reversion from the sale of the property in five, ten or fifteen years.

Interpretation. A positive NPV indicates that the financial value of the investor's assets would be increased by this investment. An NPV of exactly zero means that the future cash flows have been discounted exactly to present value. NPV for one investment can be compared with NPV for another investment, and these comparisons can provide useful data in investment decision making. The greater the NPV, the greater would be the increase in the value of the investor's assets.

Internal Rate of Return

Internal rate of return (IRR) is the annual rate of return on capital generated by an investment over the entire period of its ownership.

Calculation. A series of discount rates is applied to a projected series of negative and positive cash flows to determine the net present value (NPV) of the cash flows at each discount rate. First a high discount rate is used, then a low discount rate. Next a slightly lower high rate is used, then a slightly higher low rate, and so on. These calculations continue in a reiterative process until a certain discount rate produces a NPV of approximately zero. This discount rate is the internal rate of return (IRR). *The calculation of IRR, being a reiterative process, is accomplished quickly and easily with a financial calculator.*

Application. The procedure enables a prospective investor in real estate to make direct comparisons of the real estate investment with other investments, such as bonds, notes and other securities.

The Next Step

In the next chapter (which is also the last one), we'll focus on analyzing commercial investment property, and compare the various types of analysis appropriate for different kinds of properties.

Chapter 14
REVIEW

■ The **FIRST STEP** in analyzing a potential residential income property is to make five preliminary evaluations: location, financial goals, tax considerations, ownership structure and development considerations.

■ The **SECOND STEP** in analyzing a potential residential income property is to collect the data necessary for making a sound financial decision.

■ The **THIRD STEP** in analyzing a potential residential income property is to interpret the data, based on the nature of the project, the area under consideration, the actual and potential competition and a cost analysis.

■ The **FINAL STEP** in analyzing a potential residential income property is to determine whether the accumulated and interpreted data support a decision to purchase.

■ There are several commonly used **CALCULATIONS** that an investor may use to evaluate a property or project. These include direct capitalization, cash-on-cash return, band of investment analysis, pay-back period, proceeds per dollar invested and discounted cash flows. An evaluation of the investment is frequently accomplished by determining its net present value and internal rate of return.

Chapter 14
QUIZ

1. In the first step of analyzing a residential income property, all of the following are considerations, *EXCEPT*:

    A. location.
    B. financial goals.
    C. ownership structure.
    D. cost analysis.

2. Which of the following sources of information would be likely to have the *least* current economic data about a particular location?

    A. www.census.gov
    B. Local chamber of commerce
    C. State housing authority
    D. Encyclopedia yearbook

3. In a feasibility study performed during step three of a residential income property analysis, which of the following items would normally be first?

    A. Competition
    B. Cost Analysis
    C. Project Description
    D. Area Description

4. Which of the following correctly expresses the formula for measuring direct capitalization?

   A. R = i x V
   B. V ÷ R = i
   C. C = R x i
   D. R = i ÷ V

5. If a property is purchased for $250,000 that produces an annual net operating income of $28,000, what is the property's overall rate of return?

   A. 8.9 percent
   B. 11 percent
   C. 70 percent
   D. $222,000

6. Which of the following correctly expresses the formula used to evaluate equity investments using the cash-on-cash return method?

   A. R = i x V
   B. V ÷ R = i
   C. C = R x i
   D. R = i ÷ V

7. What is the pay-back period?

    A. The time during which a borrower is permitted to repay a mortgage loan

    B. A term that refers to the practice of leveraging one project to finance another at a more acceptable rate of interest

    C. The length of time required for the stream of cash flows produced by an investment to equal the original cash outlay

    D. The contractual length of time demanded by a buyer during which he or she is permitted to a full refund of any downpayment

8. A dollar to be received in the future is worth:

    A. less than a dollar in hand today.

    B. more than a dollar in hand today.

    C. the same as a dollar in hand today.

    D. the value of today's dollar, minus the difference between its value and the value of the future dollar $(PV - (F - P) = FV)$.

9. What does a positive NPV mean?

    A. The future cash flows have been discounted to exactly present value.

    B. The investor's assets will be unlikely to increase in value.

    C. The financial value of the investor's assets will be increased by the investment.

    D. The greater the NPV, the less the investor's assets will grow.

10. The annual rate of return on capital generated by an investment over the entire period of its ownership is referred to as its:

   A. total rate of return (TRR).
   B. internal rate of return (IRR).
   C. net present value (NPV).
   D. annualized net return (ANR).

15 Analyzing Commercial Investment Property

 Objectives:

- Describe the characteristics of various classes of commercial property: office, retail, industrial and special purpose

- Apply a process approach to commercial property analysis

- Explain the different issues arising in new construction versus existing structures

---

FUNDAMENTAL PRINCIPLES

Investment or income-producing property is designed to do just that — produce income. The degree to which income-producing property achieves this goal is measured by whether it provides a satisfactory return relative to risk for the investor. Rapid changes in the real estate investment arena today, ranging from tax law changes to overseas investment, make adherence to basic proven investment principles more important than ever.

Many of the analytical principles outlined for residential property in the previous chapter also apply to commercial and industrial invest-

336

ment properties as well. The flowchart below reviews the systematic investigative approach described in Chapter 14.

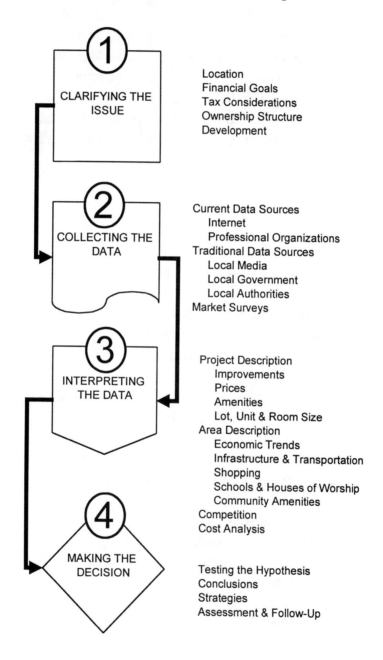

①

CLARIFYING THE ISSUE

Location
Financial Goals
Tax Considerations
Ownership Structure
Development

②

COLLECTING THE DATA

Current Data Sources
   Internet
     Professional Organizations
Traditional Data Sources
   Local Media
   Local Government
   Local Authorities
Market Surveys

③

INTERPRETING THE DATA

Project Description
   Improvements
   Prices
   Amenities
   Lot, Unit & Room Size
Area Description
   Economic Trends
   Infrastructure & Transportation
   Shopping
   Schools & Houses of Worship
   Community Amenities
Competition
Cost Analysis

④

MAKING THE DECISION

Testing the Hypothesis
Conclusions
Strategies
Assessment & Follow-Up

▦ TYPES OF PROPERTY

The scientific approach outlined above should be applied at the outset in selecting the type of investment. There is a wide range of choices for investment property, each with its own highly specialized characteristics. Investors in this area have formed many specific professional groups, which can be valuable sources of information. The array of investment property types can be grouped under four major headings: office, retail, industrial and special purpose.

Office Property

This type of property is composed of several distinct classifications:

General Purpose. The generic office building is for general offering to business, professional and financial occupants. Typically, a large tenant, such as a bank or retailer, will occupy most of the ground floor space. The upper floors are typically leased as office space to professional and medical service providers.

Special Purpose. Some office buildings are designed to accommodate the specific space, electrical or other needs of a particular type of tenant: physicians or communications companies, for example. They may have special construction, utility and permit requirements that add to project costs in new developments.

Community-of-Interest Facilities. In some buildings, common tenant goals are involved. Garment or jewelry wholesalers, interior decorators, art galleries or furniture wholesalers may cluster in a single structure.

"Parasite" Structures. Firms that do business with a common large company, or whose noncompetitive businesses appeal to the large company's customers, may locate on the same parcel or in the same building as the "host" company.

Retail Property

From the traditional central business districts and commercial strips that dotted the landscape after World War II, retailing has gone through a variety of changes that have introduced the minimall, "big box" retailer and the super-regional center with a variety of intermediate categories. These were described in detail in Chapter 8. Of course, many retail properties are free-standing buildings, too.

Minimall. This usually represents the conversion of a corner service station site into a row of stores. The size of the site may be from less than an acre to two or three acres. The building(s) may be configured in a variety of ways: parking in front and stores in back, L shapes, U shapes, subterranean parking and rooftop parking, single story and multistory — all with the objective of maximizing the available space. Because of limited available space, many of these facilities lack adequate parking: as a result, they have difficulty maintaining a stable tenancy and experience comparatively high turnover rates.

Neighborhood Shopping Center. These are usually four to ten acres in size with a single large store (typically a supermarket or drugstore) as the principal (anchor) tenant, supporting a variety of smaller stores and services.

Community Shopping Center. Stepping up from groceries to consumer goods, this is a ten- to thirty-acre site with a moderate-sized department store or factory outlet as the principal tenant.

Regional and Superregional Centers. Often enclosed, these are large malls containing two or more major department stores. These anchors serve as drawing power for the smaller mall shops, which are referred to as "satellites."

"Big Box" Power Centers. This type of mall focuses on a new class of discount stores, such as Wal-Mart, that deal in volume sales at bargain prices. It is usually on a site about the size of a community center. A variation of this concept is the upscale manufacturer's outlet, for those with elegant tastes and limited means.

Industrial Property

The classification *industrial property* includes such properties as manufacturers, assemblers, distributors, warehouses and research-and-development facilities. The construction of an industrial facility is usually very closely linked to its intended use. Most of them, however, include the following features:

- Floors and foundations that are capable of bearing higher than normal weight loads (such as those involving heavy machinery)

- High ceilings (to accommodate large equipment, catwalks and overhead conveyors)

- Independent power generators, or higher than normal utility service, as well as specialized plumbing, electrical or other power systems

- Loading docks, shipping and receiving bays

- Multimode accessibility — that is, the site is accessible by various forms of transportation; a site may include its own rail spur, for instance, in addition to roadways and proximity to air- or seaports

Incubator Buildings. Often, small or start-up manufacturing businesses do not have the financial strength of larger companies, although they still have specific needs for industrial space. Incubator facilities are typically existing large industrial properties that are subdivided into multiple smaller units. The tenants cluster in the "incubator" and are able to establish themselves commercially and financially before they leave the nest. The shorter term leases (offered at higher rates) give the investor in incubator projects an increased rate of return — along with the greater risk of vacancy and tenant default.

Industrial Parks. Industrial parks are collections of industrial buildings, often covering very large campuses. The parks are sometimes based on a common theme, such as technology industries or warehousing and distribution. Some associated office space is included.

Office Parks. These are mixed-use facilities that are conglomerate in nature. There may be light manufacturing, office space, related service businesses (such as stationery and fast printing), warehousing and restaurants, all within the same facility.

Special Purpose Properties

Management is the key element in the success of any income-producing property. In the case of special purpose properties, however, it is doubly critical. Most of the categories described below are businesses as well as buildings, and the decisions that management makes with respect to the conduct of the business represent the difference between success and failure. Some of the properties in this category include

- hotels and motels,

- parking structures,

- service stations,

- multiscreen motion picture theaters,

- bowling alleys,

- sports and other recreational facilities and

- private airplane hangars.

Other Specialized Uses. These vary from food freezer operations in the fields to amusement parks like Great America, Marine World, SeaWorld and, of course, Disneyland. Some uses — like the trampoline parks, skate parks and drive-in theaters of the past and ministorage of today — might be classified as transitory, a way of deriving revenue from temporarily underdeveloped land while some more permanent form of income production is considered.

▦ COMMERCIAL PROPERTY INVESTMENT: AN ANALYTICAL APPROACH

Before any specific project can be properly analyzed economically, the factors of value that affect the investment decision must be identified and weighed. The basic economic strengths and weaknesses of the area under study are of particular importance in the decision to commit investment dollars. To make sure the purchase meets the investment objectives of the acquiring entity, a number of pertinent factors of value must be considered.

Economic Base of the Area

Land, labor and capital are the key tools that any entrepreneur needs to derive a profit from an investment of assets and ingenuity. Adequate acreage in a configuration suitable to the planned development (or to service existing improvements) is essential. So is a sufficient labor pool with suitable skills. In some developments, labor may have to be imported if the area does not have built-in appeal, and compensatory measures must be taken.

Finally, adequate capital (that is, the financial resources to see the entire investment reach fruition) is a prime consideration.

Infrastructure Availability

The availability of adequate infrastructure is essential. Transportation is especially critical in the case of industrial properties, which require considerable capacity for electrical generation, water supply, road access, natural gas and waste disposal. Communications, fire and police protection, transportation facilities and a variety of other factors all play a part in selection of a suitable property.

Attitude of Government

Companies are dissuaded from locating in many areas because of government attitudes. In other areas, local governments actively welcome newcomers. Some states, particularly in New England, have undertaken aggressive programs to attract business. California has been able to function as a magnet due to the appeal of the state's economy, culture, resources and environment.

"NIMBY"

Like their local governments, citizens sometimes welcome new companies into their neighborhoods and other times actively oppose the move-in. This is a particular issue for companies that are politically controversial, socially unpopular or associated with the generation of unpleasant or toxic side-effects. The tendency of citizens to oppose disagreeable neighbors — which can include a wide array of entities, from small businesses such as funeral parlors, fast-food restaurants, bars and dry cleaners to nuclear power plants, waste incinerators and airports — is known among planners as the "**NIMBY** phenomenon." NIMBY is an acronym that stands for "*Not In My Back Yard.*"

Environmental Matters

The environmental and worker safety concerns that have been raised since the mid-seventies have altered the attitude of commercial and industrial investors, due to the considerable liability that ownership of such property might entail. Hidden problems may arise from contaminated ground, water or air from prior activity on the property. These issues were discussed at length in Chapter 10.

Competitive Factors

Office and retail space in many locations is in a state of oversupply. In others, new construction goes on almost daily. This local condition plays a key role in any investment decision. In general, a glut of office or commercial space affects value negatively, through the simple operation of supply and demand: if there are many vacant spaces from which to choose, the competition rate is high, and the result is lower rents and lower rates of return for investors.

SAMPLE ECONOMIC ANALYSIS: NEW CONSTRUCTION

The Back Story: A developer proposes to build a fifteen story steel and concrete office building containing 300,000 total square feet roughly 85 percent of which will be rentable. The project will include three levels of underground parking containing 60,000 square feet. An office building development site has been selected containing 50,000 square feet.

Project Cost. The cost of the development is as follows:

Land	50,000 sq. ft. @ $125 / sq. ft.	=	$ 6,250,000
Improvements			
Shell (15 stories)	300,000 sq. ft. @ $150.00 / sq. ft.	=	$45,000,000
Underground garage	60,000 sq. ft. @ $70.00 / sq. ft.	=	$ 4,200,000
Net rentable space	255,000 sq. ft. x $25.00 / sq. ft.	=	$ 6,375,000
Total Cost of Improvements		=	$55,575,000
TOTAL PROJECT COST	(land plus improvements)	=	**$61,825,000**

Income Potential. The costs outlined above are then compared with the potential economic productivity of the building, based upon comparable rentals and vacancy rates in the area, to derive the following data:

255,000 rentable sq. ft. x $2.50 / sq. ft.		
x 12 months		$7,650,000
– Vacancy Allowance		($ 700,000)
Effective Income	=	$6,950,000
+ Net Parking Revenue		$ 900,000
Net Before Expenses	=	$7,850,000
– Expenses	=	($1,850,000)
Net Income Before Debt Service	=	**$6,000,000**

Cap Rate Analysis for Value. Assuming that a capitalization rate of 9.5 percent is acceptable, use the following formula to derive an economic value for the property:

$$\text{Value} = \frac{\text{Income}}{\text{Rate}}$$

So, in this example, the value of the property is

$6,000,000 ÷ .95 = $6,315,789

Financing Terms. The property qualifies for a $43,370,000 permanent loan. Based upon the cost figures above, this would require an equity investment by the developer of $18,455,000. A permanent loan is available, with a fixed rate based on a thirty-year amortization, with annual principal and interest installments of approximately $4,260,000.

Return On Investment. The costs, income and terms outlined above leave a net spendable income after debt service of $557,400, a rather pale 3 percent return on investment. Each developer or investor must decide, on a case-by-case basis, whether the projected return is acceptable given his or her goals.

SAMPLE ECONOMIC ANALYSIS: EXISTING PROPERTY

The Back Story: This investment opportunity is a 15-story steel and concrete office structure containing 300,000 square feet of gross space, total net rentable space consisting of 255,000 square feet leased at an average of $1.85 per square foot per month. In addition, the structure contains an underground parking garage that can accommodate 615 vehicles. Approximately 60 percent of the parking is used by tenants for an additional monthly fee of $60 per space. Half the remaining parking adds revenue of $150 per space per month, and the remaining spaces are used by the general public at an average of $250 per space per month. Expenses for the building, after allowing 7½ percent for depreciation and maintenance, amount to 35 percent of the effective income of the structure. A cap rate of 9.5 is acceptable.

Cash Flow Analysis. The first step is to convert the raw data to a cash flow analysis. This is done by taking income from all sources and measuring it against incurred expenses to derive net operating income.

Net Rentable Space	255,000 sq. ft. x $1.85	=	$471,750 x 12	=	$5,661,000
Parking Revenue	369 spaces @ $60	=	$ 22,140		
	123 spaces @ $150	=	$ 18,450		
	123 spaces @ $250	=	$ 30,750		
			$ 71,340 x 12	=	$ 856,080
Total Monthly Revenue					$6,517,080
Vacancy and Maintenance (7½ percent)				-	($ 488,781)
Effective Income					**$6,028,299**
Expense Allowance	Parking: 60%	=	$ 513,648		
	Building: 35%	=	$1,981,350		
Total Expense			$2,494,998		($2,494,998)
Net Operating Income (NOI)				=	**$3,533,301**

Valuation. The net operating income figure obtained from the historical data would tend to support an economic valuation of:

$3,533,301 ÷ .95 = $3,719,264

This figure would represent the investor's "bottom line" offer. It would be probably be difficult for a seller to justify an asking price significantly higher than $3,800,000 or so for this property.

Financing. A loan is available for financing this project in the amount of $27,900,000 with a 30-year term and fixed interest at the current rate. Annual mortgage payments on this debt would be $2,790,719, the majority of which would be interest.

Return on Investment. Assuming that the $9,300,000 difference between the loan and the indicated value would be provided in cash, the return on the cash flow after debt service would be approximately 8 percent (representing the difference between the NOI and the mortgage payments divided by the $9,300,000 investment).

Tax Considerations. The investment should be considered from the standpoint of the investor's tax exposure. If the replacement value of the improvements is estimated to be $19,000,000, the annual straight line depreciation (based on the building's remaining useful life of 27½ years) would be reported as $51,463. This represents the difference between net income after debt service and the depreciation amount. Since the figure of reportable income is still positive and passive, other projects that the investor has that may be reporting negative cash flow figures after depreciation could be offset against this positive after-tax figure.

The Last Step

That concludes our discussion of commercial real estate, and our general introduction to real estate economics. Congratulations on making it all the way to the end! In the final pages, let's turn our attention from the real estate economy as it is today, and do a little forward-thinking, toward the coming century.

▦ TRENDS FOR THE 21ST CENTURY

Finally, let's take a look toward the future and the economic challenges that lie ahead for real estate professionals. We won't worry here about the challenge of selling time-share properties on Mars or how many people will fit in your hover-car. Rather we'll consider how the real estate market is likely to change over the next thirty years or so and ask what those changes may mean for the industry and for you. Those with foresight and imagination can respond creatively to the constant changes in the economic environment.

Population

Here are some projections from the U.S. Census Bureau about the changing population of the nation, the region and California itself between now and the year 2025:

- Over the next thirty years the West is projected to grow at nearly twice the national average, while the Northeast and Midwest grow at one-half the U.S. total rate.

- International migration is expected to play a dominant role in the population growth of the West, while both international and domestic migration will be important contributors to growth of the South.

- The South will continue to be the most populous region of the U.S. during the next thirty years. The Midwest, the second most populated region in the Nation in 1995, will switch places with the third most populated region, the West, by 2005.

- California, currently the most populous state, was home to 12 percent of the U.S. population in 1995. By 2025, more that 15 percent of Americans will live in California, which will add 17.7 million people — almost as if the entire population of the state of New York packed up and switched coasts! California's population in 2025 will be somewhere between 41 and 46 million people.

• California is projected to add the largest number of international migrants (8 million) — more than one-third of the total population of immigrants to the U.S. between the mid-1990s and 2025.

• After 2015, Florida is projected to replace New York as the third most populous state, with Texas ranked second.

• Racially, the white population is projected to be the slowest-growing ethnic group between now and 2025. The African-American population is projected to be the second slowest-growing in all regions, except the South where it will rank third. The Asian population is the fastest-growing group in all regions. The Asian population is projected to have the greatest gains in the West with an increase of 7 million persons. Of the total added to the U.S. Asian population by 2025, 56 percent will be in the Western states. California will be home to 41 percent of the Asian population, the largest concentration in the country.

• The Hispanic origin population of the U.S. will increase rapidly by 2025, accounting for 44 percent of total U.S. population growth. The Hispanic origin population is the second fastest-growing population. In 1995, California had the largest share of the nation's Hispanic population (9 million) followed by Texas, New York, Florida and Illinois. California's Hispanic population will more than double over the projection period, to 21 million.

• In 2025, Alaska will be the state with the highest proportion of its population under 20 years of age (34 percent), followed closely by California (33 percent).

Note: An official Census Bureau report detailing these and other projected population changes (as well as details explaining how the information was gathered, compiled and adjusted) is included in **Appendix II**. While the real estate industry's product is land, its market is people, and that market is changing rapidly.

Land Supply

Land is becoming a scarce commodity, reduced in supply by a variety of influences at the same time that it must be allocated among an ever larger number of people. Land scarcity, combined with increased population pressure, will cause increased emphasis on density and siting.

The growing acceptance of home offices and the technological feasibility of telecommuting for many in the work force will have a definite effect on housing design, dictating consideration for work as well as living space.

Land acquisition and development in the Sun Belt states will continue, but the nation's older northern and eastern urban areas may enjoy a renaissance as flexibility of residential location is afforded through the magic of electronics. Consumers will be attracted to these places by the generally lower housing prices, resulting from population shifts, and the unusual varieties of housing available.

Transportation

Mobility has become a serious problem, particularly in urban areas, during the last decade of the 20th century. National, state and local governments maintain streets and arterial systems; governments control land, sea and air transport and space exploration. Billions of dollars have been spent on studies of different ways to link where people live and where they work. Today, with some people living literally thousands of miles from their work stations, transportation needs take on an entirely new dimension. Transportation is also closely linked to the issue of environmental quality, which, as we've seen, is an economic issue directly related to property values. Similarly, transportation issues may make or break residential, commercial, retail and industrial developments. Rising fuel costs may eventually force people who currently live in suburbs far from their work to move closer to city centers — or alternatively, city-based jobs could move out to where the "stranded" employees live, further crippling the nation's urban centers.

Employment

By the end of the first quarter of the 21st century, the workforce may be far different from today's. Electronics and high-tech service industries will continue to experience the phenomenal growth we see currently, while heavy industries such as steel and automobile manufacturing will continue to be dominated by overseas expansion. With an explosion of the service economy, more and more American workers will require retraining, and the typical office-based nine-to-five job of today is likely to be a thing of the past. Mobile offices, home offices, satellite offices and shared facilities are likely to replace more individual and localized workplaces. The number of part-time and temporary employees will grow rapidly, as companies bring in outside expertise to perform individual tasks on projects, rather than retraining existing workers. What will this mean for the real estate economy and for people's ability to afford housing? Will the scattering of once-centralized work sites lead to a more mobile population, one less linked to a specific geographic location? If so, what will that mean for the housing industry?

▦ A FINAL WORD . . .

The future can be projected with statistics and models, but we will only know what the nation's economy will look like in thirty years when we get there. No matter what direction the economy takes, however, the fundamental principles you've learned here, combined with old-fashioned entrepreneurial savvy, foresight and a willingness to take risks and act ahead of the curve will help ensure your success in the real estate marketplace of the 21st century.

Chapter 15
REVIEW

■ **OFFICE BUILDINGS** include a variety of classifications: *general purpose, special purpose, community of interest facilities* and *parasite structures.*

■ **RETAIL PROPERTY** includes *free-standing facilities* as well as such developments as *minimalls, neighborhood shopping centers, community shopping centers, regional centers* and *"big box" power centers.*

■ **INDUSTRIAL PROPERTY** includes traditional *factory and R&D facilities* as well as *incubator buildings, industrial parks* and *office parks.* Industrial real estate is characterized by *load-bearing floors and foundations, high ceilings, independent power generators, loading docks, shipping bays,* and *multimodal accessibility.*

■ **SPECIAL PURPOSE PROPERTIES** are businesses as well as buildings: *hotels and motels, parking structures, service stations* and *bowling alleys,* for example.

■ Before any specific property can be analyzed, the **FACTORS OF VALUE** that affect the investment decision must be identified and weighed: the area's *economic base,* available *infrastructure, government and neighborhood attitudes, environmental issues* and *competitive factors.*

■ Different **ANALYTICAL EXPECTATIONS** apply to *existing properties* and *new construction.*

■ The big trend for the **21ST CENTURY** is *growth*: growing populations, growing ethnic diversity, a growing service economy and growing transportation headaches. Land is becoming a scarce commodity, and the growth of telecommuting may change consumers' expectations for their homes.

Chapter 15
QUIZ

1. General purpose, special purpose and "parasite" structures are all classifications of which type of property?

   A. Retail
   B. Industrial
   C. Office
   D. Special purpose

2. Several importers agree to rent separate space in the same building in order to reduce their costs. What kind of building is this?

   A. General purpose
   B. Special purpose
   C. Community of interest
   D. Parasite

3. Garland Towne Centre is on a twenty-five acre site. It has a dozen stores and a mid-size factory outlet as an anchor tenant. What type of retail property is this?

   A. Neighborhood shopping center
   B. Community shopping center
   C. Regional center
   D. Power center

4. An industrial development in which new manufacturers are able to establish their businesses is known as a(n):

   A. industrial park.
   B. special purpose building.
   C. start-up center.
   D. incubator.

5. Someone interested in purchasing or investing in an industrial property would be looking for all of the characteristics below, *EXCEPT*:

   A. weight-bearing floors and foundations.
   B. high ceilings.
   C. independent power generator.
   D. site isolation from transportation systems.

6. The tendency of neighboring property owners to oppose any development or industry that is perceived to threaten their property values or quality of life is a phenomenon known by what acronym?

   A. BYOB
   B. NIMBY
   C. NIDDI
   D. NOMYB

7. In the town of San Salmon, there were 100 potential tenants looking for office space and 380 available vacant units. In Bryrwood Clyffs, there were 20 potential tenants in search of office space and 12 available vacant units. Based on these facts, which of the following statements is true?

   A. Rents will be higher in San Salmon than in Bryrwood Clyffs.
   B. Rents will be higher in Bryrwood Clyffs than in San Salmon.
   C. Because San Salmon has more potential tenants than Bryrwood Clyffs, it has a stronger office property market.
   D. If a developer adds 60 more office units to the Bryrwood Clyffs market, rental rates will probably increase.

8. Total Project Cost =

   A. Revenue + Income
   B. Land + Improvements
   C. Improvements + Net Income before Debt Service
   D. Land + Expense Allowance

9. An existing small office building has a total monthly revenue of $380,000. Vacancy and maintenance expenses are $97,500. Other expenses total $104,000. Assuming a capitalization rate of .93 is acceptable to the investor, what is the net operating income of this property?

   A. $166,005
   B. $178,500
   C. $276,000
   D. $353,400

10. According to the U.S. Census Bureau, what percentage of the U.S. population will live in California in the year 2025?

   A. 8 percent
   B. 12 percent
   C. 15 percent
   D. 17.7 percent

Comprehensive Glossary of Real Estate Economics

Acceleration Clause

The clause in a mortgage or deed of trust that can be enforced to make the entire debt due immediately if the borrower defaults on an installment payment or other covenant.

Accession Rate

The number of employees added to the payroll during a given period; an important leading indicator of future business conditions.

Ad Valorem

A Latin term meaning "to value" or "in proportion to the value." Used to describe taxes where the amount of tax is based on the value of the thing taxed.

Adjusted Cost Basis

The value on the books of a taxpayer, which is original cost plus improvements less depreciation.

Affordability

As applied to housing, a rent or price that does not severely strain the personal budget. Measures include (1) rent-to-income ratios, (2) percentage of households able to afford a median-price home and (3) percentage of necessary income (what percentage of income necessary to qualify for a median-price house does a median-income family have?).

Affordability Index

Measurement of the percentage of potential buyers who can afford a median-priced home.

Agent

One who acts or has the power to act for another. A fiduciary relationship is created under the law of agency when a property owner, as the principal, executes a listing agreement or management contract authorizing a real estate broker to be his or her agent. Similarly, a buyer may be the principal in an agency relationship.

Agribusiness

The sector of the economy concerned with the production, processing and distributing of agricultural products.

Amortization

The liquidation of a financial obligation on an installment basis. Recovery of cost or value over a period of time. An amortized loan is one in which the principal as well as interest is payable in monthly or other periodic installments over the term of the loan.

Amplitude

The measure of highness and lowness of comparative points in the business cycle: the difference between a trough and a peak.

Annual Percentage Rate (APR)

A term used in the Truth-in-Lending Act. It represents the relationship of the total finance charge (interest, discount points, origination fees, loan broker commission) to the amount financed.

Anticipation

The principle of appraisal that value can increase or decrease based on the expectation of some future benefit or detriment.

Appraisal

An estimate of the quantity, quality or value of something. The process through which conclusions of property value are obtained; also refers to the report that sets forth the appraiser's process of estimation and conclusion of value.

Appreciation

An increase in the worth or value of a property due to economic or related causes, which may prove to be either temporary or permanent. Appreciation is the opposite of depreciation.

Assessed Value

Value placed on property for the purpose of computing real property taxes.

Assessment

The imposition of a tax, levy or charge, usually according to established rates.

Balance of Trade

The difference between a nation's exports and imports of merchandise to and from all other countries, usually covering a specific period.

Balance Sheet

A financial statement showing assets, liabilities and net worth as of a specific date.

Balloon Frame

Method of home construction in which the structure is built on a shell of light lumber, without heavy support posts.

Balloon Payment

Any payment on a note which is significantly greater than the other installment payments. California's Real Estate Law considers any payment that is twice the smallest installment payment as a balloon payment.

Barter

A form of exchange in which goods or services are traded for goods or services. Before the invention of money, barter was the only basis for exchange. Money-based economies, however, have not eliminated the use of barter.

Basis

The financial interest that the Internal Revenue Service attributes to an owner of an investment property for the purpose of determining annual depreciation and gain or loss on the sale of the asset. If a property was acquired by purchase, the owner's basis is the cost of the property plus the value of any capital expenditures for improvements to the property, minus any depreciation allowable or actually taken. The result of this calculation is the owner's "adjusted basis."

Benchmark

A statistical term for comprehensive data used as a basis for developing and adjusting interim estimates made from sample information.

Blanket Loan

A mortgage that covers more than one parcel of real estate, providing for each parcel's partial release from the mortgage lien upon repayment of a definite portion of the total debt.

Blighted Area

A declining area in which real property values are seriously affected by destructive economic forces, such as encroaching inharmonious property uses, poverty and/or rapidly depreciating buildings.

Blockbusting

The illegal act of inducing the sale, lease or listing of residential property on the grounds of loss to value, increase of crime or decline in quality of schools due to entry into the neighborhood of persons of another race, religion, ancestry or national origin.

Boom

A period of extraordinarily strong demand for goods and services and rapidly rising prices. Employment and use of productive capacity exceed normal levels.

Boot

Money or property given to make up any difference in value or equity between two properties in an exchange.

Building Code

An ordinance that specifies minimum standards of construction for buildings to protect public safety and health.

Building Permit

Written governmental permission for the construction, alteration or demolition of an improvement, showing compliance with building codes and zoning ordinances.

Bundle of Legal Rights

The concept, originating in feudalism, that land ownership includes ownership of all legal rights to the land. Traditionally, the bundle includes possession, control, enjoyment, exclusion and disposition.

Business Cycle

A type of fluctuation characterized by expansions occurring at about the same time in many economic activities, followed by similarly general contractions and then revivals. The sequence is recurrent but not of consistent length.

Buydown

A financing technique used to reduce the monthly payments for the first few years of a loan. Funds in the form of discount points are given to the lender by the builder or seller to buy down or lower the effective interest rate paid by the buyer. This reduces the monthly payments for a set time.

Buyer's Market

Many properties for sale with few buyers; a supply and demand situation in which the buyer has the advantage in price negotiations, due to a surplus of properties on the market at the same time.

Capital

One of the factors of production. Goods used for production of goods and services. Usually but not always refers to man-made goods such as machinery and structures. (Live animals would be part of the capital of a riding stable.)

Capital Expenditures

Investments of cash or liability incurred for additions or betterments; usually land, buildings, machinery and equipment.

Capital Formation

Spending on fixed capital such as machinery and buildings. Public and private spending on capital formation is a measure of the extent to which an economy is socialized.

Capital Gain

The gain received on the sale of real or personal property, other than property sold as stock-in-trade.

Capitalism

An economic system that emphasizes private ownership of the means of production and distribution, individual enterprise, profit as incentive, unfettered competition, and limited regulation of markets.

Capitalization

A mathematical process for estimating the value of a property using an acceptable rate of return on the investment and the annual net operating income expected to be produced by the property. The formula is expressed as Income ÷ Rate = Value.

Capitalization Rate

The rate of return a property will produce on the owner's investment.

Cash Flow

The net spendable income from an investment, determined by deducting all operating and fixed expenses from the gross income. When expenses exceed income, negative cash flow results.

Caveat Emptor

Latin term meaning *Let the buyer beware*. The buyer must examine the purchase and buy at his or her own risk. In most cases, no longer applicable to real estate transactions.

Census

A count of population or some other characteristic, such as housing, and the statistical information derived from it. Every ten years, the U.S. Bureau of the Census conducts a nationwide census of population and housing.

CERCLA

The Comprehensive Environmental Response, Compensation, and Liability Act is a federal law that establishes a process for identifying parties responsible for creating hazardous waste sites, forcing liable parties to clean up toxic sites, bringing legal action against responsible parties and funding the abatement of toxic sites. *See* Superfund.

Change

The economic (and appraisal) principle that no physical or economic condition remains constant.

Civil Rights Act of 1866

Federal law that prohibits racial discrimination in the sale and rental of housing.

Clustering

The grouping of home sites within a subdivision on smaller lots than normal, with the remaining land used as common areas.

Coincident Indicator

An indicator that experiences the peaks and troughs of the business cycle at approximately the same time as general economic activity.

Collateral

A tangible security, usually readily convertible into cash, deposited with a creditor to guarantee repayment of a loan.

Command Economies

Economies that are largely government controlled. In general, the countries that are socialist are command-oriented, but with some market activity permitted or even encouraged.

Commission

A fee paid to an agent or broker for negotiating a sale; usually based on a percentage of the selling price.

Commodity

Any physical good or product, whether manufactured, agricultural or mineral.

Comparables

Properties used in an appraisal report that are substantially equivalent to the subject property.

Comparative Analysis

A method of appraisal in which selling prices of similar properties are used as the basis for arriving at the value estimate. Also called market data approach.

Condemnation

A judicial or administrative proceeding to exercise the power of eminent domain, through which a government body or municipality takes private property for public use and compensates the owner.

Conformity

The appraisal principle that holds that the greater the similarity among properties in an area, the better they will hold their value.

Consumer

An individual who buys goods and services for personal use rather than for resale, processing, or manufacture.

Consumer Price Index (CPI)

Published by the Bureau of Labor Statistics, the CPI measures change in prices for a carefully defined market basket of goods and services, including food, rent, maintenance costs, medical and dental services, transportation, entertainment, clothing and other items commonly purchased. The average prices of a base year are defined as 100, so an index of 200 means prices have doubled since that base year.

Contraction

The segment of the business cycle curve that reflects a falling off of economic activity.

Contribution

The principle that the value of a particular component is measured in terms of its contribution to the value of the whole property or as the amount that its absence would detract from the value of the whole.

Conventional Loan

A loan that is not underwritten by a government agency, and that requires no insurance or guarantee.

Corporation

An entity or organization, created by operation of state law, whose rights of doing business are essentially the same as those of an actual individual. An "artificial person" under the law. A corporation has continuous existence until it is dissolved according to legally established procedures.

Cost

As it applies to real estate, the amount expended (labor, material and/or money) in acquiring or producing the commodity; the sum of money necessary to bring a property into existence.

Cost Approach

The process of estimating the value of a property by adding to the estimated land value the appraiser's estimate of the reproduction or replacement cost of the building, less depreciation.

Cost of Living

The money cost of maintaining a particular standard of living in terms of purchased goods and services.

Credit Rating

An evaluation of the financial trustworthiness of a company or individual, particularly with regard to meeting financial obligations.

Cyclical Industry

An industry whose sales and profits reflect to a great extent the ups and downs of the business cycle.

Deed Restrictions

Clauses in a deed that restrict future uses of the property: a private land use control that may impose a vast variety of limitations and conditions on the size of buildings, types of structures permitted or uses allowed.

Deflation

A decrease in the general price level due to a decrease in total spending relative to the supply of goods on the market. The immediate effect is to increase purchasing power.

Demand

The amount of goods people are willing and able to buy at a given price. *See* Supply.

Demand Curve

A graphic display of demand for a particular product or service. The curve's slope is affected by the degree to which price affects demand. When price has a relatively small effect on demand, the line or curve will be close to the vertical. When price has a strong effect on demand, the line or curve will be closer to horizontal.

Demographics

The study and description of a population.

Density Zoning

Zoning ordinances that restrict the maximum average number of houses or other structures per acre (or other measurement) that may be built within a particular area.

Depreciation

(1) In appraisal, loss in value due to any cause, including physical deterioration, functional obsolescence and external obsolescence. (2) In real estate investment, an expense deduction for tax purposes taken over the period of ownership of an income property.

Depression

A period of very low use of productive capacity and very high unemployment.

Discount Points

A loan fee charged by a lender to increase the lender's yield or effective interest rate. One discount point equals 1 percent of the amount of the loan.

Discount Rate

The interest rate set by the Federal Reserve Board that institutions must pay to borrow money from it.

Dow-Jones Industrial Average

An economic indicator that measures prices paid for thirty representative companies in the stock market.

Duration

In a business cycle, the length of a contraction, an expansion or the period from trough to trough or from peak to peak.

Economic Base

The sector of an economy that sells products and services to customers from outside the community, bringing external dollars into the community. Customers need not literally be outside the community at the time of the transaction; they may be business visitors or tourists. The important thing is that their money is outside money.

Economic Indicators

Measures of the economy's performance. The Commerce Department's Bureau of Economic Analysis (BEA) uses 300 indicators, classified as leading, coinciding, or lagging. Leading indicators warn in advance of changes in business activity. Coinciding indicators reflect the present state of the economy. Lagging indicators trail the business cycle, rising for several months after a downturn has started.

Economic Life

The period during which an improvement earns enough profit to justify maintaining it. The period during which an improvement adds value to the land.

Economics

The social science that studies, describes and analyzes an economy.

Economy
Any system designed for the production, distribution and consumption of necessary and desired goods and services.

Elasticity of Demand
The responsiveness of demand to price. Demand is defined as elastic if a 1 percent price reduction results in a 1 percent (or more) increase in demand. It is defined as inelastic if a 1 percent price reduction results in less than a 1 percent increase in demand.

Elasticity of Supply
The responsiveness of quantity supplied to price. If a 1 percent increase in price prompts at least a 1 percent increase in offerings on the market, then supply is said to be elastic.

Eminent Domain
The right of a government or municipal body to acquire property for public use through a court action called condemnation, in which the court decides that the proposed use is a public use and determines the just compensation to be paid to the owner.

Employee
Someone who works as a direct employee of an employer and has employee status. The employer is obligated to withhold income taxes and Social Security taxes from the compensation of employees.

Enabling Act
State legislation that confers zoning powers on municipal governments.

Encapsulation
A method of controlling environmental contamination by sealing off a dangerous substance.

Encumbrance

Anything — such as a mortgage, tax or judgment lien, an easement, restriction of the use of land or an outstanding marital right — that may diminish the value or use and enjoyment of a property.

Entrepreneur

Someone who personally starts a business and undertakes its risks.

Equal Credit Opportunity Act (ECOA)

The federal law that prohibits discrimination in the extension of credit. ECOA protects credit applicants against discrimination on the basis of race, color, religion, national origin, sex, age or marital status.

Equalization

The raising or lowering of assessed values for tax purposes in a particular county or taxing district to make them equal to assessments in other counties or districts.

Equalization Factor

A factor (number) by which the assessed value of a property is multiplied to arrive at a value for the property that is in line with other tax assessments.

Equilibrium Point

The middle stage of the life cycle of property value; the static point at the peak of its value; the point at which supply and demand are in harmonious balance.

Equilibrium Price

The price at which supply and demand are in balance. The price on the vertical axis opposite the point of intersection of demand and supply curves.

Equity

The interest or value that an owner has in property over and above any indebtedness.

Escalator Clause

A clause in a lease providing for an increase or decrease in rent to cover specific contingencies. Some leases have escalator clauses based upon the cost of living index, and are referred to as index-leases.

Exchange

A transaction in which all or part of the consideration is the transfer of like-kind property (such as real estate for real estate).

Expansion

The segment of the business cycle curve that reflects a rise in economic activity.

Externalities

The principle that economic or noneconomic factors outside a property may have positive or negative effects on its value.

Fair Housing Act

The federal law prohibiting discrimination in housing based on race, color, religion, sex, handicap, familial status or national origin.

Fair Market Value

The most probable price a willing, fully informed buyer will pay to a willing, fully informed seller in an arm's-length transaction.

Fannie Mae

A quasi-governmental agency established to purchase any kind of mortgage loans in the secondary mortgage market from the primary lenders. (Previously known as the Federal National Mortgage Insurance Agency, or FNMA.)

Federal Open Market Committee (FOMC)

U.S. government body responsible for making monetary policy, composed of the governors and directors of the Federal Reserve banks.

Federal Reserve System

The country's central banking system, which is responsible for the nation's monetary policy by regulating the supply of money and interest rates.

Feudal System

An economic system of ownership usually associated with precolonial England, in which the king or other sovereign is the source of all rights. The right to possess real property was granted by the sovereign to an individual as a life estate only. Upon the death of the individual, title passed back to the sovereign, not the descendant's heirs.

FHA Loan

A mortgage loan insured by the Federal Housing Administration and made by an approved lender in accordance with the FHA's regulations.

FIRREA

The Financial Institutions Reform, Recovery and Enforcement Act, enacted in response to the savings and loan crisis of the 1980s, restructured the savings and loan association regulatory system and established standards for property appraisal.

Forecast

An estimate of future events, stated as probabilities. A forecast may be implicit or explicit.

Forecasting

In appraisal, taking the past as a guide to the future together with present conditions and tempering this with the appraiser's judgment for the projection of the future.

Free Market

A market uncontrolled by government, free of regulations. Producers in such a market are free to produce what they want in quantities and at prices that they choose. Production restraints or incentives come from responses of potential buyers.

Friedman, Milton

Nobel Prize-winning economist and proponent of monetarist and free-market economics.

Functional Obsolescence

A loss of value to an improvement to real estate arising from functional problems, often caused by age or poor design.

Gantt Chart

A bar-style chart commonly used in scheduling construction projects, in which project activities are shown on a horizontal time scale.

Gold Standard

A system of valuing a nation's currency based on the amount of gold in the national treasury (the "gold standard").

Goods

Material things perceived to have monetary or exchange value.

Government National Mortgage Association

Ginnie Mae (or GNMA) is a government agency that plays an important role in the secondary mortgage market. It sells mortgage-backed securities that are backed by pools of FHA and VA loans.

Gross Annual Multiplier

Appraises an income property based on a multiple of the gross annual income.

Gross Income Multiplier

"Rule of thumb" method of appraising income-producing (commercial or industrial) property. Price ÷ Gross annual income.

Gross Monthly Multiplier

Appraises a rental residence based upon a multiple of the gross monthly income.

Gross National Product (GNP)

The dollar value of all goods and services produced by a nation's economy in a year. Technically, this means the market value of newly produced final goods and services. The value of intermediate goods and services is assumed to be incorporated in the final value.

Gross Rent Multiplier

The figure used as a multiplier of the gross monthly income of a property to produce an estimate of the property's value.

Ground Rent

Earnings of improved property credited to earnings of the ground itself after allowance is made for earnings of improvements.

Growth Cycles

A cyclic pattern in rates of economic growth, rather than in the general level of economic activity reflected in business cycles.

Highest and Best Use

The possible use of a property (land plus improvements) that would produce the greatest net income to its owner and thereby develop the highest value.

Home Equity Loan

A loan (sometimes referred to as a line of credit) under which a property owner uses his or her residence as collateral and can then draw funds up to a prearranged amount against the property's value.

Household

All the persons who live in a housing unit.

Housing

A cluster of rights to the occupancy of permanent structures built for long-term occupation and designed to support personal living, not the production of goods or services. When we buy or rent housing, we are purchasing those rights. Housing refers to the physical stock of dwelling units in a community, state or nation.

Housing Starts

Beginning construction of new housing. Housing starts are an index of construction activity and thus an important economic indicator.

Housing Stock

The total dwelling units in a community or state or the nation as a whole.

Housing Unit

A physical structure with a full range of living facilities in one or more rooms, within which an individual, group or family may live privately, separated from people in other units.

Improvement

Any structure erected on a site to enhance the value of the property.

Income Approach

The process of estimating the value of an income-producing property through capitalization of the annual net income expected to be produced by the property during its remaining useful life.

Index Method

The appraisal method of estimating building costs by multiplying the original cost of the property by a percentage factor to adjust for current construction costs.

Indicators

Certain characteristics or facets of an economy relied on by economists as symptoms of the relative health of the whole. Indicators may be coincident (reflecting the economy's present state), lagging (trailing the business cycle) or leading (providing advance notice of change).

Industrial Park

An area laid out with streets and plots to provide a landscaped setting for light industry, warehouses and other businesses. Today these are often called business parks, reflecting the shift to service firms.

Industrial Revolution

The profound transformation of the means of production that first occurred in England between 1750 and 1850. In that century, England changed from a country of farming villages and cottage industries to a country of factory towns. New machinery, new energy sources and new ways of organizing labor were at the core of this revolution: the steam engine, improved textile machines, the use of coal rather than wood as fuel and the rise of the factory system.

Inflation

The gradual reduction of the purchasing power of the dollar, usually related directly to the increases in the money supply by the federal government.

Infrastructure

Basic physical and social facilities: roads, dredged harbors, airports, bridges, electrical power generation and transmission, schools and universities, mail and telephone systems, radio, television and newspapers, water supply and waste disposal, etc.

Institutional Lender

A financial intermediary or depository, such as a savings and loan association, commercial bank or life insurance company, which pools money of its depositors and then invests funds in various ways, including real estate loans.

Interest

A charge made by a lender for the use of money.

Interest Rate

A rate of return on capital. The percentage of a sum of money charged for its use.

Interim Financing

A short-term, temporary loan used until permanent financing is available, such as a construction loan.

Internal Rate of Return

A measurement of the rate at which the present worth of future cash flows equals an investor's initial capital investment.

Interstate Land Sales Full Disclosure Act

A federal law that regulates the sale of certain real estate in interstate commerce.

Intrinsic Value

An appraisal term referring to the value created by a person's personal preferences for a particular type of property.

Investment

Money directed toward the purchase, improvement and development of an asset in expectation of income or profits.

Joint Venture

The joining of two or more people to conduct a specific business enterprise. A joint venture is similar to a partnership in that it must be created by agreement between the parties to share in the losses and profits of the venture. It is unlike a partnership in that the venture is for one specific project only, rather than a continuing business relationship.

Just Compensation

Payment due to a land owner when the government seizes his or her property in exercising its police power.

Keynes, John Maynard

Author of the *General Theory of Employment, Interest and Money* (1936). Argued in favor of government intervention in the free market in order to stimulate full employment.

Land

The earth's surface, extending downward to the center of the earth and upward indefinitely into space, including things permanently attached by nature, such as trees and water.

Legal Tender

A form of money that by law must be accepted in payment for all debts. Currency and coins are legal tender, checks are not.

Leverage

The use of borrowed money to purchase an investment that realizes enough income to cover the expense of the financing with the excess accruing to the purchaser.

Liabilities

Claims of creditors; debts.

Lien

A right given by law to certain creditors to have their debts paid out of the property of a defaulting debtor, usually by means of a court sale.

Limited Partnership

A business arrangement in which the operation is administered by one or more general partners and funded, by and large, by limited or silent partners, who are by law responsible for losses only to the extent of their investments.

Liquidity

The ease with which investments can be immediately converted into cash.

Loan-to-Value Ratio (LTV)

The relationship between the amount of the mortgage loan and the value of the real estate being pledged as collateral.

M1

The Federal Reserve's basic measure of the nation's money supply.

Manufactured Home

A structure transportable in one or more sections, designed for dwelling. Includes mobile homes, but is not the same as factory-built (prefabricated or modular) housing.

Market

A particular arena of economic exchange (a local community, a state, the nation) in which buyers and sellers arrange transactions, influenced by levels of supply and demand. A place where goods can be bought and sold and a price established.

Market Price

The price actually paid for property.

Market Rent
The rental income that a property would probably bring in the open market, based on market data.

Market Value
The price for which property can be sold on the open market given a willing seller, a willing buyer and a reasonable time to make the sale. The most probable price property would bring in an arm's length transaction under normal conditions on the open market.

Marketing
All the activities that contribute to the sale of a product or service.

Marx, Karl
Author of the *Communist Manifesto* (1848) and *Das Kapital* (1867). Exponent of worker control of the means of production and the historical inevitability of a socialist revolution to attain economic equality.

Master Plan
A comprehensive plan to guide the long-term physical development of a particular area. Also referred to as a *general plan*.

Median
The middle number in a series. If there are five numbers ranging from low to high, the third number is the median: 126 128 *130* 145 158. The median is not the same as the average: here, the average is 137.4.

Mercantilism

An economic policy of European trading states during the 16th, 17th and 18th centuries when, through exploration and colonization, they extended European power to other parts of the globe. The policy emphasized strong state control over imports and exports with a view to importing only raw materials, exporting finished goods and accumulating precious metals that could be used to pay mercenary armies.

Mixed Economies

Contemporary economies in which economic decisions and actions are undertaken in both private and public spheres.

Monetarist

Monetarists are economists who believe that control of the economy is best accomplished through control of the money supply. A monetarist policy is one that uses control of the money supply to accomplish particular goals. Noted monetarists include Nobel Prize-winning economist Milton Friedman.

Monetary Policy

Governmental regulation of the amount of money in circulation through such institutions as the Federal Reserve Board.

Money

Any object or commodity that people in a given society or group commonly accept and use in payment for goods or services.

Mortgage

A conditional transfer or pledge of real estate as security for the payment of a debt. Also, the document creating a mortgage lien.

Mortgage Banker

Mortgage loan company that originates, services and sells loans to investors.

Mortgage Broker

An agent of a lender who brings the lender and borrower together. The broker receives a fee for this service.

Mortgagee

A lender in a mortgage loan transaction.

Mortgage Lien

A lien or charge on the property of a mortgagor that secures the underlying debt obligations.

Mortgagor

A borrower in a mortgage loan transaction.

Nasdaq 100 Index

A common stock market indicator representing the 100 largest nonfinancial domestic companies on the Nasdaq market.

National Association of REALTORS® (NAR)

The largest professional interest organization of real estate licensees in the world, whose members are entitled to the title *REALTOR*®.

Natural Increase

In a population, excess of births over deaths.

Needs

Certain resources are absolutely needed for biological survival, e.g., water, food and protection from the elements. For the most part, "needs" are defined by the group within which one lives, and the group's definitions of need are influenced by capability. An unattainable condition will seldom be defined as a need.

Negotiable Instrument

A promissory note or check that meets certain legal requirements, allowing it to be traded freely in commerce. A written promise or order to pay a specific sum of money that may be transferred by endorsement or delivery. The transferee then has the original payee's right to payment.

Neighborhood

An identifiable grouping of individuals, buildings or business enterprises within, or as part of, a larger community. An area within a town or city that may or may not have formal boundaries. Inside the neighborhood, residents and/or merchants often have a sense of common identity or at the very least shared locality.

Net Lease

A lease requiring the tenant to pay not only rent but also costs incurred in maintaining the property, including taxes, insurance, utilities and repairs.

Net Migration

Characteristic of a population study in which the number of people coming into an area is divided by the number of people who leave during the same period.

Net Operating Income (NOI)

The income projected for an income-producing property after deducting losses for vacancy and collection and operating expenses.

Nonconforming Use

A use of a property that is permitted to continue after a zoning ordinance prohibiting it has been established for the area.

Nonhomogeneity

A lack of uniformity; dissimilarity. Because no two parcels of land are exactly alike, real estate is said to be nonhomogeneous.

Obsolescence

The loss of value due to factors that are outmoded or less useful. Obsolescence may be functional or economic.

Open-End Loan

A mortgage loan that is expandable by increments up to a maximum dollar amount, the full loan being secured by the same original mortgage.

Option

An agreement to keep open for a set period an offer to sell or purchase property.

Package Loan

A real estate loan used to finance the purchase of both real property and personal property, such as in the purchase of a new home that includes carpeting, window coverings and major appliances.

Participation Loan

As a concession for making a loan on commercial property the lender is given a portion of ownership, which allows him to participate in the profits.

Partnership

An association of two or more individuals who carry on a continuing business for profit as co-owners. Unlike a corporation, a partnership is legally regarded as a group of individuals rather than as a single entity. A partnership may be general or limited.

Passive Activity Income

Income from real estate or other business in which an owner does not actively participate in management. An IRS classification.

Payment Cap

The limit on the amount the monthly payment can be increased on an adjustable-rate mortgage when the interest rate is periodically adjusted.

Peak

The top segment of the business cycle curve, a period during which productivity and employment are higher than in the preceding and succeeding periods.

Percentage Lease

A lease, commonly used for commercial property, in which rental is based on the tenant's gross sales at the premises; it usually stipulates a base monthly rental plus a percentage of gross sales above a certain amount.

Physical Deterioration

A reduction in a property's value resulting from a decline in physical condition; can be caused by action of the elements or by ordinary wear.

Planned Unit Development (PUD)

A planned combination of diverse land uses, such as housing, recreation and shopping, in one high-density contained development or subdivision.

Planning Commission

A local government body that plans the physical growth of a community and recommends zoning ordinances and other laws for that purpose.

Points

A point is 1 percent of the amount of the loan, paid to the lender at the time the loan is made.

Police Power

The right of the state to regulate the use of private property for the protection of the health, safety, morals or general welfare of the public.

Poverty

Government agencies use a technical definition based entirely on money income. It changes every year to reflect the Consumer Price Index.

Primary Mortgage Market

The mortgage market in which loans are originated, consisting of lenders such as commercial banks.

Principal

(1) A sum loaned or employed as a fund or an investment, as distinguished from its income or profits. (2) The original amount (as in a loan) of the total due and payable at a certain date. (3) A main party to a transaction; the person for whom an agent works.

Private Enterprise

In economics, the term "private" is used to identify an activity that is not owned or operated by government. A private enterprise is a business not owned or operated by government.

Profit

The excess of return on an investment less expenditures.

Progression

In appraisal, the opposite of the principle of regression. An appraisal principle that states that the value of a lesser-quality property is favorably affected by the presence of a better-quality property.

Prosperity

In the business cycle, the ideal state of a healthy economy: high employment, productivity and income combining to create a general sense of stability.

Purchase-Money Mortgage

A note secured by a mortgage or deed of trust given by a buyer, as borrower, to a seller, as lender, as part of the purchase price of the real estate.

Pyramiding

The process of acquiring additional properties by refinancing properties already owned and investing the loan proceeds in additional properties.

Quantity-Survey Method

The appraisal method of estimating building costs by calculating the cost of all the physical components in the improvements, adding the cost to assemble them and then including the indirect costs associated with such construction.

Radon

A naturally occurring gas suspected of causing lung cancer.

Rate Cap

The limit on the amount the interest rate can be increased at each adjustment period in an adjustable-rate loan. The cap may also set the maximum interest rate that can be charged during the life of the loan.

Real Estate

Land; a portion of the earth's surface extending downward to the center of the earth and upward infinitely into space, including all things permanently attached to it, whether naturally or artificially.

Real Estate Investment Trust (REIT)

Trust ownership of real estate by a group of individuals who purchase certificates of ownership in the trust, which in turn invests the money in real property and distributes the profits back to the investors free of corporate income tax.

Real Estate Market

Consists of properties for sale and buyers in search of properties. The market is most often local, but modern information systems facilitate national offerings and searching, and the market for very expensive properties is often international.

Real Estate Mortgage Investment Conduit (REMIC)

A tax entity that issues multiple classes of investor interests (securities) backed by a pool of mortgages.

Real Estate Settlement Procedures Act (RESPA)

A federal law requiring certain disclosures to consumers about mortgage loan settlements and prohibiting the payment or receipt of kickbacks and certain kinds of referral fees.

Real Property

Land, things fixed to the land (buildings, roads, walls, natural and planted vegetation) and appurtenances including incidental rights such as easements. The interests, benefits and rights inherent in the ownership of real estate.

Recession

At least two successive quarters of economic contraction.

Reclamation

Any method for bringing waste natural resources into productive use.

Reconciliation

The final step in the appraisal process, in which the appraiser combines the estimates of value received from the sales comparison approach, cost approach and income approach to arrive at a final estimate of market value for the subject property.

Recovery

In the business cycle, the process of an economy recovering from a depression.

Redevelopment

Rehabilitation of a blighted area, such as clearing slum housing and erecting new buildings.

Redlining

The illegal practice of a lending institution denying loans or restricting their number for certain areas of a community.

Regional Analysis

Examination of a region's population and economy.

Regression

An appraisal principle that states that the value of a better-quality property is affected adversely by the presence of a lesser-quality property. The opposite of progression.

Regulation Z

Implements the Truth-in-Lending Act, requiring credit institutions to inform borrowers of the true cost of obtaining credit.

Replacement Cost

In appraisal, the construction cost at current prices of a property that is not necessarily an exact duplicate of the subject property, but serves the same purpose or function as the original.

Reproduction Cost

In appraisal, the construction cost at current prices of an exact duplicate of the subject property.

Restrictive Covenant

A clause in a deed that limits the way real estate ownership may be used. A private land-use restriction.

Reverse-Annuity Mortgage

A loan under which the home owner receives monthly payments based on his or her accumulated equity rather than a lump sum. The loan must be repaid at a prearranged date or upon the death of the owner or the sale of the property.

Sales Comparison Approach

In appraisal, the process of estimating the value of a property by examining and comparing actual sales of comparable properties.

Secondary Mortgage Market

A market for the purchase and sale of existing mortgages, designed to provide greater liquidity for mortgages originated in the primary mortgage market. Federally sponsored, quasi-private institutions that buy mortgages from primary lenders.

Sector

Specialized area of economic activity, as the agricultural sector, manufacturing sector or trade sector.

Seigniorage

The difference between the cost of minting coins and a coin's face value.

Service-Producing Sector

A major category of employment that includes wholesale and retail trade, services, transportation, real estate, finance, insurance. In the terminology of agencies that collect and report data on employment, services is a subcategory of service-producing.

Services

Activities perceived to have monetary or exchange value, such as legal advice, health care, repair work, entertainment, transportation and business services.

Shopping Center

A group of buildings or spaces leased to commercial establishments, planned, developed, owned and managed as an operating unit.

Site

Land improved to the extent that it is ready to be used for a specific, planned purpose.

Site Analysis
An evaluation of the site itself, including zoning, title, CC&Rs (conditions, covenants and restrictions), soil analysis and utilities.

Smith, Adam
Author of *The Wealth of Nations* (1776). Written as a reaction against mercantilism, Smith's book marks the foundation of modern capitalist theory.

Socialism
Economic system under which the ownership, management and control of the means of production and distribution are held by the community; a command economy.

Socially Defined Needs
Those things not biologically necessary but deemed necessary for adequate life by a particular group or society.

Special Assessment
A tax on real estate by a public authority to pay for public improvements benefiting the property such as sewers, street lights and parks.

Specialization
Concentration on a particular sphere of activities. Not the same as division of labor, which involves splitting a process into very small steps and assigning individual workers to each step. A specialist goes beyond general knowledge with special knowledge and skills. Typically, the specialist is highly skilled and highly paid, while the divided-task worker is low-skilled and low-paid.

Specie
A form of money; minted metal coinage.

Square-Foot Cost

The cost of one square foot of an improvement.

Square-Foot Method

The appraisal method of estimating building costs by multiplying the number of square feet in the improvement being appraised by the cost per square foot for recently constructed similar improvements.

Standard of Living

A society's definition of the resources and facilities required to provide minimally acceptable material comfort and well-being.

Steering

The illegal practice of channeling home seekers to particular areas, either to maintain the homogeneity of an area or to change the character of an area. In either case, a limit on the buyers' choices of where to live.

Straight-Line Method

A method of calculating depreciation for tax purposes, computed by dividing the adjusted basis of a property by the estimated number of years of remaining useful life.

Straight (Term) Loan

A loan in which only interest is paid during the term of the loan, with the entire principal amount due with the final interest payment.

Subdivider

One who buys undeveloped land; divides it into smaller, usable lots; and sells the lots to potential users.

Subdivision

A tract of land divided by the owner, known as the subdivider, into blocks, building lots and streets according to a recorded subdivision plat, which must comply with local ordinances and regulations.

Substitution

An appraisal principle that states that the maximum value of a property tends to be set by the cost of purchasing an equally desirable and valuable substitute property, assuming that no costly delay is encountered in making the substitution.

Superfund

Popular name of the hazardous-waste cleanup fund established by the Comprehensive Environmental Response, Compensation and Liability Act (CERCLA).

Supply

The quantity of a product offered at various prices over a specified period of time. The amount of goods available in the market to be sold at a given price.

Supply and Demand

The twin forces that establish value for any product (including real estate) in the market.

Supply-Side Theory

Focuses on how government can encourage supply to fight inflation. The favored tool is the tax cut. The theory holds that low taxes stimulate production, supply outruns demand and the excess supply dampens inflationary pressures. The high level of business activity stimulated by tax cuts results in a higher national income, which in turn provides additional tax revenues to the government. Contrasts with the Keynesian emphasis on stimulation of demand to reenergize a weak, high-unemployment economy.

Syndicate

A combination of people or firms formed to accomplish a business venture of mutual interest by pooling resources. In a real estate investment syndicate, the parties own and/or develop property with the main profit arising from its sale.

Taking

The act of a government body seizing privately owned property for a public purpose through its police power. The owner is entitled to just compensation for the property seized. The term derives from the Fifth Amendment to the U.S. Constitution: "nor shall private property be taken for public use, without just compensation."

Tax

A compulsory payment of a percentage of income, property value or sales price for the support of services provided by a government.

Taxation

The process by which a government or municipal body raises money to fund its operation.

Tenant Improvements

Alterations to the interior of a building to meet the functional demands of the tenant.

Tight Money

A market condition in which loan funds are scarce and interest rates and discount points are high.

Transferability

One of the four essential elements of value. A commodity must be transferable as to use or title in order to be marketable.

Trend

Changes that have a long-term, consistent direction. In appraisal, a series of related changes brought about by a chain of causes and effects.

Trough

The bottom segment of the business cycle curve.

Truth-in-Lending Act

The Federal Reserve Board's Regulation Z, which requires disclosure of certain loan terms to the borrower.

Underground Economy

Unofficial market in which individuals trade goods and services while avoiding income taxation or as a means of using barter to obtain goods and services not otherwise affordable.

Unearned Increment

An increase in the value of property, not anticipated by the owner, due primarily to the operation of social forces, such as an increase in population.

Unit-in-Place Method

The appraisal method of estimating building costs by calculating the costs of all of the physical components in the structure, with the cost of each item including its proper installation or connection.

Upper Turning Point

The point on the business cycle curve at which contraction of the economy begins.

Utility

The ability of a product to create desire in consumers. One of the four essential elements of value.

VA Loan

A loan guaranteed by the U.S. Department of Veterans Affairs. A mortgage loan on approved property made to a qualified veteran and guaranteed by the VA in order to limit the lender's possible loss and extend the veteran's choices of housing.

Value

The worth of a thing in money or goods at a certain time. The power of a good or service to command other goods in exchange for the present worth of future rights to its income or amenities.

Wants

People are taught to want many of the goods and services they purchase. Wants are socially defined. These wanted goods and services may be viewed either as intrinsically desirable or as effective means to an end.

Wealth

Anything valued by more than one person and "in hand" (controlled by humans). Anything potentially subject to exchange. Something that is perceived by others as having value.

Wraparound Mortgage

A method of refinancing in which the new mortgage is placed in a secondary, or subordinate position; the new mortgage includes both the unpaid principal balance of the first loan plus whatever additional sums are advanced by the lender. In essence, it is an additional mortgage in which another lender refinances a borrower by lending an amount over the existing first mortgage amount without disturbing the existence of the first mortgage.

Yield

The ratio of annual net income from the property to its cost. The ratio of the annual interest and dividends from an investment to its cost.

Zoning

Governmental regulations relating to the use of land. An exercise of police power by a municipality to regulate and control the character and use of property in its jurisdiction.

APPENDIX	
II	# U.S. Population Projections to 2025

from

PPL-47: Population Projections for States by Age, Sex, Race, and Hispanic Origin: 1995 to 2025[*]

This report contains the State population projections descriptive text and methodology sections from the PPL-47 report. It excludes the detailed tables 1 to 7 and appendix table A-1. The complete PPL-47 report with detailed tables can be ordered from the Population Division Statistical Information Staff (phone 301-457-2422).

HIGHLIGHTS: POPULATION PROJECTIONS FOR STATES BY AGE, SEX, RACE, AND HISPANIC ORIGIN: 1995 TO 2025

Purpose of the Report

This report is intended to inform its users about evolving population trends which might affect the demographic landscape of the 50 States and the District of Columbia by age, sex, race, and Hispanic origin. It describes how States are projected to become more racially and ethnically diverse over the next 30 years.

The factors which significantly contribute to such changes (fertility, mortality, immigration, and interstate migration) are discussed.

---

[*]Paul R. Campbell, Population Projections Branch, Population Division, U.S. Bureau of the Census, October 1996

This report also describes how a State's age compositions shift as "baby boomers" (those persons born between 1946 and 1964) become eligible for retirement. These projections are used as the basic input to many federal, State, and local projection models that produce detailed education, economic, labor force, health care, voting, and other statistics. Thus the results are useful to planners in both the public and private sectors.

Users are provided with a description of the results, methodology, assumptions, and an evaluation of past errors in the projections. Official State agencies projections are presented for comparison.

Size and Growth of Regions and States

- Over the next 30 years the West is projected to grow nearly twice the national average, while the Northeast and Midwest grow at one-half the U.S. total rate.

- During the late 1990's international migration is expected to play a dominant role in the population growth of the West, while both international and domestic migration will be important contributors to growth of the South.

- The South will continue to be the most populous region of the Nation during the next 30 years. The Midwest, the second most populated region in the Nation in 1995, switches places with the third most populated region, the West, by 2005.

- **California**, the most populous State, contained 12 percent of the Nation's population in 1995. By 2025, **California** is expected to have 15 percent of the Nation's population.

- From 1995 to 2025 **California** adds 17.7 million people (equivalent to nearly the current population of New York State).

- **California** is projected to add the largest number of international migrants (8 million). This would be more than one-third of the immigrants added to the Nation's population over the 30 year period.

- **California** is expected to be the fastest growing State from 1995 to 2025 (56 percent). The first eight of the fastest growing States are Western States.

- After 2015, Florida is projected to replace New York as the Nation's third most populous State, with Texas ranked second.

Race and Hispanic Origin Distribution[1]

- The White population, the largest of the five race/ethnic groups, is projected to be the slowest-growing among the groups during the 1995 to 2025 projection period. During this period, the White population is projected account for at least one-fifth of the absolute increase in the Nation's population in all regions except in the Northeast (where this group declines in size). Sixty-seven percent of the 16 million Whites added to the U.S. population will be located in the South.

- Over the 30 years, the Black population is projected to be the second slowest-growing in all regions, except the South where it will rank third. Sixty-four percent of the 12 million Blacks added to the United States during 1995 to 2025 will be in the South.

- The Asian population is the fastest-growing group in all regions. Asians are the fourth largest of the race and Hispanic origin groups in all regions except the West where they rank third. The Asian population is projected to have the greatest gains in the West with an increase of 7 million persons (56 percent of the total added to the U.S. Asian population during 1995 to 2025) and in the Northeast with an increase of 2 million.

- The American Indian population, the least populous group, is projected to be the third fastest-growing population in all regions but the South during 1995 to 2025 where it ranked fourth. Nearly half of the 0.8 million American Indians added to the Nation's American Indian population will be located in the West.

- The Hispanic origin population is projected to increase rapidly over the 1995 to 2025 projection period, accounting for 44 percent of the growth in the Nation's population (32 million Hispanics out of a total of 72 million persons added to the Nation's population). The Hispanic origin population is the second fastest-growing population, after Asians, in every region over the 30 year period.

- In 1995, States with the largest share of the Nation's Whites were **California**, New York, Texas, Pennsylvania, and Florida. Among these five States in 2025 only Texas and Florida are projected to have a larger share of the Nation's White population than in 1995 (compared to almost no change for **California** and decreases for New York and Pennsylvania).

- The State of New York, with nearly 3 million Blacks, had the largest share of the Nation's Black population (8 percent) in 1995. Other States with large shares of the Nation's Black population are Texas, **California**, Georgia, and Florida. Texas (after 2005), Georgia (after 2010), and Florida (after 2020) are expected to have the largest population gains among Blacks and to replace New York as the State with the largest share of the Nation's Black population.

- In 2025, **California**, with an expected 41 percent of the Nation's 21 million Asians, is expected to remain number one with the largest share, followed by New York, Hawaii, New Jersey, and Texas. Together these States will account for   more than half of the Nation's Asian population in 2025.

- During 1995, Oklahoma had the largest share of the Nation's American Indians (257,000 or 13 percent). The other leading States with the largest proportion of the Nation's American Indian population in rank order are Arizona, **California**, New Mexico, and Alaska. By 2025, Oklahoma and Arizona still rank number one and two with the largest share of the Nation's American Indians. However, New Mexico moves ahead of **California**, and Washington moves up to be the fifth most populous State among American Indians. About 45 percent of the American Indian population is projected to reside in these five States by 2025.

- In 1995, 74 percent of the Nation's Hispanics resided in five States. **California** with 9 million had the largest share of the Nation's Hispanic population followed by Texas, New York, Florida, and Illinois. **California**'s Hispanic population will more than double over the projection period (21 million and represents 36 percent of the total Hispanic population in 2025).

Age Distribution

- In 2025, Alaska is the State with the highest proportion of its population under 20 years of age (34 percent), followed by **California** (33 percent).

  States projected to have the smallest proportion of population under age 20 are West Virginia and Florida (both with 21 percent).

- As the Baby Boom generation (those born between 1946 and 1964) reaches retirement age after 2010, the percentage of the population that is elderly will increase rapidly in the South and Midwest.

- In 1995, Florida had the largest proportion of elderly (19 percent) of any State, and Alaska had the smallest at 5 percent. By 2025, Florida (with 26 percent) would remain the leading State with more than a quarter of its population classified as elderly. Alaska would still rank as the youngest with 10 percent.

- Between 1995 and 2025 the number of elderly are projected to double in 21 States.

INTRODUCTION

This report presents population projections for the 50 States and the District of Columbia by age, sex, race, and Hispanic origin for 1995 through 2025.[2]

Projections are discussed for the White (non-Hispanic); Black (non-Hispanic); American Indian, Eskimo, and Aleut (non-Hispanic); Asian and Pacific Islander (non-Hispanic); and Hispanic origin populations which sum to the State totals.[3]

Cohort-Component Methodology

The projections use the cohort-component method.[4] The cohort-component method requires separate assumptions for each component of population change: births, deaths, internal migration[5], and international migration. These components, by race and Hispanic origin, come from various sources. State differentials in fertility are based on 1989 to 1993 births, 1994 estimated population distributions of females in childbearing ages for States, and 1994 national fertility data. State differentials in survival rates are based on 1989 to 1993 deaths, 1994 estimated population for States, and 1994 national life tables. The projections use Internal Revenue Service (IRS) data on interstate migration flows from 1975 to 1976 through 1993 to 1994. International migration for States was further disaggregated by age, sex, race, and Hispanic origin using the foreign-born population immigrating during the five year period 1985 to 1990 as enumerated in the 1990 census.

Consistency with Various Estimates and Projections

The projection's starting date is July 1, 1994. The July 1, 1994 State population estimates by age, sex, race, and Hispanic origin were derived from the 1990 enumerated census figures and annual population estimates.

The national population total is consistent with the middle series of the Census Bureau's national population projections for the years 1996 to 2025.[6]

The July 1, 1994 starting point estimates for State populations by single years of age and sex are consistent with previously released data from the U.S. Bureau of the Census. The 1995 State population projections were controlled first to the 1995 national population projections, by age, sex, race, and Hispanic origin, and second to the 1995 State population estimates, which were only available by age and sex.[7]

Technically, the 1995 results are still projections since race and Hispanic origin estimates were not available. These results are more consistent with State estimates than the national population projections for the year 1995.

The July 1, 1994 estimates are consistent with the 1990 count, but cannot be directly compared to the published results by age and race because modifications were made to the data to correctly place each person in an appropriate category. This was done to adjust for age misreporting and the reporting of an unspecified race in the 1990 census.[8]

Preferred and Alternative Series

This set of population projections provides a preferred series using a demographically based time series and an alternative series using an economically based set of assumptions. These series differ only in the internal migration assumptions. The two sets of projections available are as follows:

1. *Series A*, the Preferred Series, is a time-series model and uses State-To-State migration observed from 1975 to 1976 through 1993 to 1994

2. *Series B*, the Economics Model, uses the Bureau of Economic Analysis (BEA) employment projections.[9]

Users are likely to choose the demographic series — the time series — due to the series stability, long-term inertia, and no need for economic assumptions. However, there is no definitive set of projections and the economic model is an alternative. Given the sensitivity of internal migration to changes in economic conditions, internal migration changes can be rapid and sizable. Identifying a preferred series along with an alternative series, reflects a process of evaluating State population projection models used in previous Census Bureau State population projections.

The "Domestic Migration" section gives a detailed description of the two series. In the projections, race is cross classified by Hispanic origin and not of Hispanic origin. The Hispanic origin migration is based on domestic migration data only available for the 1988 to 1989 through 1993 to 1994 period.

Unless otherwise noted, the discussion in this report refers to the preferred series.

PROJECTED POPULATION TRENDS

The projections of State population by age, sex, race, and Hispanic origin shown in this report result from the methodology and detailed assumptions about each component of population change presented in the methodology section of this report.

Comparison of Series

The summary of regional projections provided in *Table A* shows the range of results when comparing the preferred with the alternative series.

Under both series, the South would continue to be the most populous region. More than one-third of the total United States population is projected to reside in the South during the 1995 to 2025 period under both series. Both series show net population gains in every region over the 30 years. However, growth in the South and West are rapid and above the national average. The population of the Northeast and Midwest decline as a share of the Nation's total population.

A summary comparison of the relative ranking of the State population size in the years 1995 and 2025 under the two projection series are provided in *Table B*.

TABLE A

Comparison of Population Projections by Region and Series: 1995 to 2025

Series and region	Percent of total			Average annual percent change	
	1995	2000	2025	1995-2000	1995-2025
Series A					
United States	100.0	100.0	100.0	0.9	0.9
Northeast	19.6	19.0	17.1	0.2	0.4
Midwest	23.5	23.1	20.7	0.5	0.4
South	35.0	35.5	36.2	1.2	1.1
West	21.9	22.4	26.0	1.3	1.7
Series B					
United States	100.0	100.0	100.0	0.9	0.9
Northeast	19.6	19.0	16.8	0.3	0.3
Midwest	23.5	23.1	21.6	0.6	0.6
South	35.0	35.6	37.0	1.3	1.2
West	21.9	22.3	24.6	1.3	1.4

Source: U.S. Bureau of the Census, Population Division, PPL-47, table 1.

TABLE B

Projections of the Top 10 States, Ranked by Population Size: 1995 and 2025

(In millions. As of July 1. Series A and B reflect different interstate migration assumptions.)

Rank	1995 Series A & B State	Pop.	2025 Series A State	Pop.	2025 Series B State	Pop.
1	**California**	31.6	**California**	49.3	**California**	41.5
2	Texas	18.7	Texas	27.2	Texas	28.2
3	New York	18.1	Florida	20.7	Florida	20.1
4	Florida	14.2	New York	19.8	New York	19.4

5	Penna.	12.1	Illinois	13.4	Illinois	13.7
6	Illinois	11.8	Penna.	12.7	Penna.	12.9
7	Ohio	11.2	Ohio	11.7	Ohio	12.3
8	Michigan	9.5	Michigan	10.1	Georgia	11.0
9	New Jersey	7.9	Georgia	9.9	Michigan	10.4
10	Georgia	7.2	New Jersey	9.6	N. Carolina	9.9

Source: U.S. Bureau of the Census, Population Division, PPL-47, table 1.

The relative ranking of population size of States varies under the two projection series. The first seven of the top 10 most populous States follow the same rank order under both series in 2025. **California** would continue to be the most populous State, however, growth is much slower under Series B. Among the top 10 most populous States, the 2025 projection totals are higher for more States in Series B than Series A.

A summary of the State projections results in *Table C* shows a comparison of the fastest growing States in the first and last quinquennials covered in the preferred and alternative projection series.

TABLE C

Projections of the 10 Fastest Growing States Ranked by Percent Growth for Each Series: 1995 to 2025

(Series A and B reflect different interstate migration assumptions).

RANK

	Series A	*Series B*
1995 to 2000		
1	Nevada	Nevada
2	Idaho	Arizona
3	Arizona	Idaho
4	Utah	Utah
5	Colorado	Colorado
6	New Mexico	New Mexico

7	Wyoming	Georgia
8	Georgia	North Carolina
9	Oregon	Oregon
10	Montana	Wyoming

2020 to 2025

1	**California**	New Mexico
2	Hawaii	Arizona
3	New Mexico	Utah
4	Texas	DC
5	Alaska	Alaska
6	Florida	Texas
7	Arizona	Hawaii
8	Washington	**California**
9	DC	Idaho
10	Oregon	Georgia

1995 to 2025

1	**California**	Nevada
2	New Mexico	Arizona
3	Hawaii	Utah
4	Arizona	Idaho
5	Nevada	New Mexico
6	Idaho	Colorado
7	Utah	Georgia
8	Alaska	Texas
9	Florida	Wyoming
10	Texas	Florida

Source: U.S. Bureau of the Census, Population Division, PPL-47, table 1.

The rankings of the fastest growing States by series vary by selected projection periods. In both Series A and B, and in both the 1995 to 2000 and 2020 to 2025 periods, Arizona and New Mexico are the only States consistently among the top 10 fastest growing States. Although the

District of Columbia is projected to be among the 10 fastest growing on Series A and B for the 2020 to 2025 period, it ranked 51st during 1995 to 2000.

The domestic migration assumptions accepted in these projections account for much of the dramatic shifts in population growth. For a discussion on the migration assumptions see the methodology section.

Size and Growth of the Total Population

In the following sections, projection results are only presented for Series A (labeled preferred series).

A brief discussion beginning with some short term results, those that cover 1995 to 2000, followed by long term results covering the 30 years ending in 2025. Results are shown for regions and States.

The short term results are likely to be more accurate than the long term projections. For a discussion on the decline in accuracy over the projection horizon, see the section on "Forecast Error in Past Projections". A long term summary of trends is provided for users who need lengthier projections.

Regional Population Growth. The South and West regions are projected to account for 80 percent of the 12 million persons added to the Nation's population between 1995 and 2000. States in those two regions accounted for 84 percent of the growth during the 1980's. The average annual change of more than one percent for each of these regions is above the national average of 0.9 percent.

During the late 1990's international migration is expected to play a dominant role in the population growth of the West, while both international and domestic migration will be important contributors to growth of the South. The South is the only region to show a net gain in the number of domestic migrants. The slow population growth of the Northeast and Midwest is attributed to net internal out-migration to other regions (see section on "Components of Population Change" below for details).

The fast growth projected for the initial five years in the South and West appears also for the long term. Over the next 30 years the West is projected to grow nearly twice the national average, while the Northeast and Midwest grow at one-half the U.S. total rate (refer to *Table A*). Growth in the South is expected to be slightly above the national average.

During the 1995 to 2025 period, the South and West are each expected to increase by more than 29 million persons. The South and West combined are projected to account for 82 percent of the 72 million persons added to the Nation's population over the next 30 years. This is essentially a continuation of trends began during the 1980's when the South and West accounted for 84 percent of the 22 million persons added to the Nation's population.[11] The Midwest is projected to add 7 million persons during the period 1995 to 2025, while the Northeast adds approximately 6 million persons.

The South will continue to be the most populous region of the Nation during the next 30 years. The Midwest, the second most populated region in the Nation in 1995, switches places with the third most populated region, the West, by 2005. Factors that contribute to the rapid growth or decline in regions are discussed below in the "Components of Population Change" section.

State Population Growth. The most populous State, **California**, contained 12 percent of the Nation's population in 1995. By 2025, **California** is expected to have 15 percent of the Nation's population (see Table B). From 1995 to 2025 **California** adds 17.7 million people (equivalent to nearly the current population of New York State). Besides natural increase, international migration is expected to account for **California**'s rapid growth, see table 2 and the "State Components of Change" section. In the year 2025, eight percent of the Nation's population is projected to reside in Texas compared to six percent in New York. Florida is projected to replace New York as the third populous after 2015, while Illinois replaces Pennsylvania in fifth place by 2005. Wyoming, currently with the smallest share of the Nation's inhabitants (0.2 percent), will be replaced by the District of Columbia shortly before the year 2000.

The rate of population change among the 50 States and the District of Columbia will vary during the late 1990's (see Table 6). Nevada is expected to have the most rapid growth (22 percent from 1995 to 2000) with the District of Columbia at the other end of the continuum with population loss (-6 percent). The most rapid rate of change is projected for the Mountain States (with the rate of population change ranging from 9 to 22 percent during the 1995 to 2000 period, see table 6). Georgia is the only other State with a projected rate of population change of nine percent or greater during this period.

After 2000, the rate of population change for the States will decline substantially for each quinquennial period, see table 6.

For example, during the 1995 to 2000 period, 25 States are projected to have their of population increase by 5 percent or more, compared with only six States during the 2020 to 2025 period.

The District of Columbia, with the least growth during the 1995 to 2000 period, is expected to show a reversal of trends (from a rate of population change at -6 percent during the 1995 to 2000 period to nearly 5 percent during 2020 to 2025). The District of Columbia's turn-around in growth is due to the projected decline of internal out-migration.

Californiais expected to be the fastest growing State from 1995 to 2025 (56 percent). The first eight of the fastest growing States are Western States (see table C).

Components of Population Change

Regional Components of Change. The South is projected to have more births (43 million) and deaths (32 million) in the population than any of the other three regions during the 1995 to 2025 period, see table 3. The West ranks second among the regions with the most births (36 million), and at the bottom with the smallest number of deaths (17 million).

Migration is projected to play a major role in regional differences in growth during the 30 year period. The South is projected to have the largest gains from net internal migration, while the Northeast and Midwest expect losses. Nevertheless, the losses through internal out-migration for these regions are projected to balance out due to gains from immigration.

Over the 1995 to 2025 period, population growth in the South is projected to increase rapidly. The components of this rapid change are high rates of natural increase (many births minus few deaths)[12], high net internal in-migration, and high immigration. Most of the growth in the West is projected to be due to natural increase and net immigration. Net internal migration is projected to be marginally negative in the West (-0.4 million).

State Components of Change. Table D shows the top five States with the largest components of population change for the period 1995 to 2025.

TABLE D

Top Five States with the Largest Components of Population Change: 1995 to 2025			

RANK	BIRTHS	DEATHS	NATURAL INCREASE
1	California	California	California
2	Texas	Florida	Texas
3	New York	Texas	New York
4	Florida	New York	Illinois
5	Illinois	Pennsylvania	Georgia

State-to-State Migration . . .

RANK	NET GAINS	NET LOSSES	INTERNATIONAL MIGRATION
1	Florida	New York	California

2	Texas	**California**	New York
3	North Carolina	Illinois	Florida
4	Georgia	Michigan	New Jersey
5	Washington	Massachusetts	Illinois

Net Population Change . . .

RANK	STATE
1	**California**
2	Texas
3	Florida
4	Georgia
5	Washington

Source: U.S. Bureau of the Census, PPL-47, table 2.

During the 1995 to 2025 period, five States are projected to have 5 million or more births: **California**, Texas, New York, Florida, and Illinois. Four of these States will have 5 million or more deaths: **California**, Florida, Texas, and New York. Among the five States, **California** and Texas are expected to have twice as many births as deaths. Furthermore, **California** and Texas alone are projected to account for 46 percent of the Nation's growth from natural increase.

During 1995 to 2025, West Virginia (with 160,000 more deaths than births) is expected to be the only State to have a deficit of births. However during 2020 to 2025, five other States are projected to have more deaths than births (Arkansas, Kentucky, Alabama, Maine, and Montana).

Three States will gain one million or more persons over the 30 year period through net internal migration: Florida with nearly 4 million; and both Texas and North Carolina with more than 1 million. Georgia and Washington had slightly less than 1 million. New York, **California**, Illinois, and Michigan will lose at least one million, see table D.

California is projected to add the largest number of international migrants (more than 8 million). This would be more than one-third of the immigrants added to the Nation's population over the 30 year period. Other States projected to have major gains of a million or more persons from immigration are New York, Florida, New Jersey, Illinois, and Texas, see table D.

Table E summaries the top 10 State with the largest net population gains and shows the few States where most of the growth will occur for the nation over the 30 year period.

TABLE E

Top 10 States with the Largest Net Population Gains: 1995 to 2025			

1995 to 2000		1995 to 2025	
Rank	**State**	**Rank**	**State**
1	Texas	1	**California**
2	Florida	2	Texas
3	**California**	3	Florida
4	Georgia	4	Georgia
5	North Carolina	5	Washington
6	Arizona	6	Arizona

7	Washington	7	North Carolina
8	Colorado	8	Virginia
9	Tennessee	9	New York
10	Virginia	10	New Jersey

Source: U.S. Bureau of the Census, PPL-47, table 1.

Over the next three decades, the net population change[13] will be most evident in 7 States gaining more than 2 million persons (**California**, Texas, Florida, Georgia, Washington, Arizona, and North Carolina). They will account for 58 percent of the net population change in the United States. The net population change for **California**, Texas, and Florida combined is expected to account for 45 percent of the Nation's total growth during this period.

Race and Hispanic Origin

This is the first State projection report to show separate race and Hispanic origin results that are additive or sum to the State totals. The descriptive analysis provided in this report covers the following five groups: White (refers to non-Hispanic White), Black (refers to non-Hispanics Black), American Indian (refers to non-Hispanic American Indian, Eskimo, and Aleut), Asian (refers to non-Hispanic Asian and Pacific Islander), and Hispanics origin.[14] The four non-Hispanic race groups plus the Hispanic origin group sum to the States totals.[15]

• • •

The White population, the largest of the five race/ethnic groups, is projected to be the slowest-growing among the groups during the 1995 to 2025 projection period. During this period, the White population is projected to account for more than one-sixth of the absolute increase in the Nation's population in all regions except in the Northeast (where this group declines in size).

Sixty-seven percent of the 16 million Whites added to the U.S. population will be located in the South. After the year 2005, the West will replace the Northeast as the third largest region for the White population. The South is expected to continue to have the largest share of the Nation's White population.

Over the 30 years, the Black population is projected to be the second slowest-growing in all regions, except the South where it will rank third. Sixty-four percent of the nearly 12 million Blacks added to the United States during 1995 to 2025 will be in the South.

In 1995, the Black population was the second most populous group in all regions but the West, where it ranks fourth. However due to the faster growth in the Hispanic origin population, by 2025, the proportion of Hispanics surpass the Black population share in the Northeast and the Nation.

The Asian population is the fastest-growing group in all regions. Asians are the fourth largest of the race and Hispanic origin groups in all regions except the West where they rank third. The Asian population is projected to have the greatest gains in the West with an increase of 7 million persons (56 percent of the total added to the U.S. Asian population during 1995 to 2025) and in the Northeast with an increase of 2 million.

The American Indian population, the least populous group, is projected to be the third fastest-growing population in all regions but the South during 1995 to 2025 where it ranked fourth. Nearly half of the 0.8 million American Indians added to the Nation's American Indian population will be located in the West.

The Hispanic origin population is projected to increase rapidly over the 1995 to 2025 projection period, accounting for 44 percent of the growth in the Nation's population (32 million Hispanics out of a total of 72 million persons added to the Nation's population).

The Hispanic origin population is the second fastest-growing population, after Asians, in every region over the 30 year period.

In 1995, the Hispanic origin population is the third most populous race/ethnic group in all regions except the West where it ranks second. The Hispanic population is expected to comprise a substantially larger share of the total population in 2025 than in 1995 -- up from 21 to 32 percent in the West, from 9 to 15 percent in the South and Northeast, and from 3 to 6 percent in the Midwest.

State Growth of Race and Hispanic Origin Groups. In 1995, States with the largest share of the Nation's Whites were **California**, New York, Texas, Pennsylvania, and Florida. Among these five States in 2025 only Texas and Florida are projected to have a larger share of the Nation's White population than in 1995 (compared to almost no change for **California** and decreases for New York and Pennsylvania).

Table I shows a summary comparison of the top five
States with the largest population gains by race/Hispanic
origin during the late 1990's and over the 30 year
projection period. Table J identifies the five most populous
States by race/Hispanic origin during 1995 and 2025.

TABLE I

Top Five States With the Largest Population Gains, Ranked by Race and Hispanic Origin: 1995 to 2025					
Rank	White	Black	American Indian	Asian	Hispanic origin
1995 to 2000					
1	NC	GA	NM	CA	CA
2	FL	TX	OK	NY	TX
3	TX	FL	AZ	NJ	FL
4	GA	NC	MN	TX	NY
5	AZ	MD	MT	WA	AZ
1995 to 2025					
1	FL	GA	NM	CA	CA
2	TX	TX	OK	NY	TX
3	WA	FL	AZ	NJ	FL
4	NC	MD	WA	TX	NY
5	GA	VA	MN	HI	AZ

Persons of Hispanic origin may be of any race.
Source: U.S. Bureau of the Census, Population Division, PPL-47, table 3.

TABLE J

Top Five States With the Largest Population, Ranked by Race and Hispanic Origin: 1995 and 2025					

Rank	White	Black	American Indian	Asian	Hispanic origin
			1995		
1	CA	NY	OK	CA	CA
2	NY	TX	AZ	NY	TX
3	TX	CA	CA	HI	NY
4	PA	GA	NM	TX	FL
5	FL	FL	AK	NJ	IL
			2025		
1	CA	TX	OK	CA	CA
2	TX	GA	AZ	NY	TX
3	FL	FL	NM	HI	FL
4	NY	NY	CA	NJ	NY
5	PA	CA	WA	TX	IL

Persons of Hispanic origin may be of any race.
Source: U.S. Bureau of the Census, Population Division, PPL-47, table 3.

Texas is the only State projected to rank among both the top five most populous States for Whites and the top five States with the largest net gain for the White population during 1995 to 2025. State with the largest net gains in rank order were Florida, Texas, Washington, North Carolina, and Georgia. Furthermore, Whites will have net population losses in 12 States.[16]

In 1995, New Mexico and Hawaii were the only States, along with the District of Columbia, to have 50 percent or less Whites (50, 30, and 28 percent, respectively). By the year 2000 **California**'s White population is projected to drop below half the State's total population (48 percent in 2000 down from 53 percent in 1995).

The State of New York, with nearly 3 million Blacks, had the largest share of the Nation's Black population (8 percent) in 1995. Other States with large shares of the Nation's Black population are Texas, **California**, Georgia, and Florida. Texas (after 2005), Georgia (after 2010), and Florida (after 2020) are expected to have the largest population gains among Blacks and to replace New York as the State with the largest share of the Nation's Black population. More than one-third of the Nation's Black population is projected to reside in these five States by 2025.

During 1995, Oklahoma had the largest share of the Nation's American Indians (257,000 or 13 percent). The other leading States with the largest proportion of the Nation's American Indian population in rank order are Arizona, **California**, New Mexico, and Alaska. Rankings of the most populous American Indians States will change among the latter three States. American Indians are projected to have the largest population gains in New Mexico and Oklahoma and the largest loss in **California** between 1995 and 2025. By 2025, Oklahoma and Arizona still rank number one and two with the largest share of the Nation's American Indians. However, New Mexico moves ahead of **California**, and Washington moves up to be the fifth most populous State among American Indians. About 45 percent of the American Indian population is projected to reside in these five States by 2025.

Among the States, the largest share of the Nation's Asians are projected to continue to reside in **California**. In 1995 39 percent of the Nation's nearly nine million Asians lived in **California**. Other States with high proportions of the Nation's Asian population in rank order are New York, Hawaii, Texas, and New Jersey. In 2025, **California**, with an expected 41 percent of the Nation's 21 million Asians, is expected to remain number one with the largest share, followed by New York, Hawaii, New Jersey, and Texas. Together these States will account for more than half of the Nation's Asian population in 2025.

In 1995, 74 percent of the Nation's Hispanics reside in five States. **California** with 9 million will have the largest share of the Nation's Hispanic population followed by Texas, New York, Florida, and Illinois. **California**'s Hispanic population will more than double over the projection period (21 million and represents 36 percent of the total Hispanic population in 2025).

While Texas will remain in second place with 17 percent of the Hispanics in 2025, New York is expected to decline from 9 to 6 percent and is expected to switch from third to fourth place with Florida. Illinois will remain in fifth place.

Age Distribution

Youth Population. Table K summaries the regional changes in the proportion of youth, adult, and elderly over the 30 year period.

Shifts in the age distributions will be fairly stable between 1995 and 2010, however, after 2010 there will a rapid increase in the percent elderly as the share of the adult population declines in all regions.

TABLE K

Percent Distribution of the Population by Age and Region: 1995, 2010, and 2025			
REGION	**UNDER 20**	**20 TO 64**	**65 AND OVER**
1995			
United States	28.8	58.4	12.8
Northeast	26.9	58.9	14.2
Midwest	29.0	57.9	13.1
South	28.8	58.5	12.7
West	30.4	58.3	11.3
2010			
United States	27.4	59.4	13.2
Northeast	26.2	60.1	13.7
Midwest	26.9	59.5	13.6
South	26.6	59.6	13.8
West	29.8	58.5	11.7
2025			
United States	26.8	54.7	18.5
Northeast	25.8	56.0	18.2

Midwest	26.1	54.8	19.1
South	25.3	54.7	20.0
West	29.9	54.0	16.1

Source: U.S. Bureau of the Census, Population Division, PPL-47, table 4.

Over the 30 year period, the Nation's youth population (ages 0 to 19 years) is projected to decline as a fraction of the total population. In 1995, the Nation's youth was 29 percent of the total population. A drop of two percentage points in the youth rate is expected over the three decades. During 1995 to 2025, all regions are expected to show a decline in the proportion of the population that is under 20 years of age. In 2025, the West (with a slight decline in the proportion of youth) will continue as the leader with the greatest proportion of population under 20 years of age, followed by the Midwest, and Northeast. The South will have the smallest proportion of youth.

All States follow the national and regional trends during the 1995 to 2025 period. Most States show a decline in the proportion of population that is under 20 years of age. The exceptions are projected to be **California**, Hawaii, New York, Rhode Island, and the District of Columbia. In 2025, Alaska is the State with the highest proportion of its population under 20 years of age (34 percent), followed by **California** (33 percent).

States projected to have the smallest proportion of population under age 20 are West Virginia and Florida (both with 21 percent).

Elderly Population. As the Baby Boom generation (those born between 1946 and 1964) reaches retirement age after 2010, the percentage of the population that is elderly will increase rapidly in the South and Midwest. Between 1995 and 2010 the proportion of elderly is expected to increase slightly in all regions, but the Northeast which will show a decline. After 2010, the proportion of elderly will increase rapidly as the share of the adult population declines.

The size of the elderly population is projected to increase in all States over the 30 years. During this period **California** and Florida would continue to rank first and second, respectively, in having the largest number of elderly. While New York and Pennsylvania ranked third and fourth, respectively in 1995, they are expected to drop to fourth and fifth place, by the year 2025. Texas would move from fifth place in 1995 to third place by the year 2025.

Although Alaska is projected to have the least elderly among the States over most of the 30-year period, it will have a high annual average increase in the elderly population (3.8 percent). In Alaska, the number of elderly persons is expected to triple over the 30-year period. By the year 2025 it ties with the District of Columbia for the least elderly population.

The population 65 plus is expected to double in the top seven States with the most rapid growth of the elderly population in rank order are: Alaska, Utah, Idaho, Colorado, Nevada, Wyoming, and Washington. These States are projected to have an average annual rate of change for the elderly that ranges from 5.1 to 6.9 percent between 1995 and 2025. About half the States are expected to have an average annual rate of change at 3 percent or greater during 1995 to 2025.

The aging of the Baby Boom population after 2010 will have a dramatic impact on the growth of the elderly population. By the year 2025, the survivors of the Baby Boom will be between the ages of 61 and 79. The average annual rate of change in the proportion of population 65 years and over for States shows only minor growth or loss during the periods 1995 to 2010. During the period 2010 to 2025 all States shows a rapid acceleration in the growth of the elderly population.

In 1995, Florida had the largest proportion of elderly (19 percent) of any State, and Alaska had the smallest at 5 percent. By 2025, Florida (with 26 percent) would remain the leading State with more than a quarter of its population classified as elderly. Alaska would still rank as the youngest with 10 percent. To further illustrate the rapid growth in elderly populations, only four States had at least 15 percent of their population in the elderly category in 1995. By 2025, that number would grow to 48 States. Only Alaska (10 percent), **California** (13 percent), and the District of Columbia (14 percent) would not meet this level.

Between 1995 and 2025 the number of elderly are projected to double in 21 States.

Dependency Ratio. Table L shows the range of variation between the five highest and lowest dependency ratios for States 1995 and 2025. Utah, Idaho and Arizona are the only States consistently among the top five with the highest ratios over the projection period, while Virginia and Maryland are consistently among the lowest five.

TABLE L

Ratio of Youth and Elderly Per 100 Adults, Five Highest and Five Lowest States: 1995 and 2025

	1995		2025	
Rank	**State**	**Ratio**	**State**	**Ratio**
1	Utah	90.1	Utah	97.7
2	South Dakota	84.5	North Dakota	96.5
3	Idaho	80.9	Montana	95.3
4	Florida	80.6	Arizona	94.5
5	Arizona	79.3	Idaho	94.1
		. . .		
47	Alaska	65.1	Georgia	76.0
48	Colorado	63.8	New Hampshire	75.8
49	Maryland	63.8	New Jersey	75.0
50	Virginia	61.7	Virginia	73.9
51	District of Columbia	57.6	Maryland	73.4

Ratio of youth (under age 20) and elderly (ages 65 and over) per 100 adults aged 20 to 64. Source: U.S. Bureau of the Census, Population Div., PPL-47, table 4.

The dependency ratio indicates the number of youth (under age 20) and elderly (ages 65 and over) there would be for every 100 people of working ages (20 to 64 years). In 1995, the dependency ratio for regions ranged from 70 to 73 per 100. By 2025 all regions show an increase in the dependency ratio, while the range among the regions widens. The West would have the highest dependency ratio (85 per 100 adults). Both the South and Midwest, are projected to have the mid-range dependency ratios (83 per 100 adults), while the Northeast (79 per 100 adults) has the smallest.

During 1995, the dependency ratio varied greatly, ranging from 90 per 100 in Utah to 58 per 100 in the District of Columbia. By 2025, the majority of the Baby Boomers will have joined the elderly population the dependency ratios increase for all State and the range of variation narrows. Utah is projected to have the highest ratio, 98 per 100, while Maryland will have the lowest, 73 per 100. Generally, States with the highest dependency ratios have slightly more than half their population in the adult age group and the remaining proportion in the youth and elderly categories.

DETAILED METHODOLOGY

Overview

The 1995 to 2025 State population projections were prepared using a cohort-component method. Each component of population change — births, deaths, State-to-State migration flows, international in-migration, and international out-migration — was projected separately for each birth cohort by sex, race, and Hispanic origin. The race/ethnic groups projected were non-Hispanic White; non-Hispanic Black; non-Hispanic American Indian[17]; non-Hispanic Asian[18]; Hispanic White; Hispanic Black; Hispanic American Indian; and Hispanic Asian (see Appendix C for detailed definitions). The basic framework was the same as in past projections.[19] Detailed components necessary to create the projections were obtained from vital statistics, administrative records, census data, and national projections.

The cohort-component method is based on the traditional demographic accounting system:

P1 = P0 + B - D + DIM - DOM + IIM - IOM

where:

    P1 = population at the end of the period
    PO = population at the beginning of the period
    B   = births during the period
    D   = deaths during the period
    DIM = domestic in-migration during the period
    DOM = domestic out-migration during the period
          (Both DIM and DOM are aggregations of
          State-to-State migration flows)
    IIM = international in-migration during the period
    IOM = international out-migration during the period

To generate population projections with this model, we first created separate data sets for each of these components. The assumptions and procedures by which these data were generated by single year of age, sex, race, and Hispanic origin are described in the following sections. In general, the assumptions concerning the future levels of fertility, mortality, and international migration are consistent with the assumptions developed for the national population projections released by the Census Bureau.[20]

Once the data for each component were developed, it was a relatively straightforward process to apply the cohort-component method and produce the projections.

For each projection year the base population for each State was disaggregated into race and Hispanic origin categories, by sex, and single year of age (ages 0 to 85+).

Classifying race by Hispanic origin results in eight race/ethnic groups: four Hispanic race groups and four non-Hispanic race groups.

The components of change are individually applied to each group to project the next year's population. The next step was to survive each age-sex-race/ethnic group forward one year using the pertinent survival rate.

The internal redistribution of the population was accomplished by applying the appropriate State-to-State migration rates to the survived population in each State. The projected out-migrants were subtracted from the State of origin and added to the State of destination (as in-migrants). Next, the appropriate number of immigrants from abroad were added to each group. The populations under one year of age were created by applying the appropriate age-race-specific birth rates to females of child-bearing age.

The number of births by sex and race/ethnicity were survived forward and exposed to the appropriate migration rate to yield the population under one year of age. The final results of the projection process were adjusted to be consistent with the national population projections by single years of age, sex, and race/ethnicity. The entire process was then repeated for each year of the projection.

. . .

NOTES

1. Projections are discussed for five groups that sum to the State totals: 1) White refers to non-Hispanic White; 2) Black refers to non-Hispanic Black; 3) American Indian refers to non-Hispanic American Indian, Eskimo, and Aleut; 4) Asian refers to non-Hispanic Asian and Pacific Islander; and 5) Hispanic origin may be any race.

2. Does not include the residents of Puerto Rico.

3. Eight race and Hispanic origin groups were projected and are presented in the detailed tables. These groups were non-Hispanic White; non-Hispanic Black; non-Hispanic American Indians, Eskimo, and Aleut; non-Hispanic Asian and Pacific Islander; Hispanic White; Hispanic Black; Hispanic American Indians, Eskimo, and Aleut; and Hispanic Asian and Pacific Islander.

4. For a definition of the cohort-component method see Shryock, Henry S. and Jacob S. Siegel, et al., *The Methods and Materials of Demography*, Vol. 2, U.S. Government Printing Office, Washington, DC, 1971, p. 778.

5. "Internal migration" means State-to- State, domestic or interstate migration.

6. Day, Jennifer Cheeseman, 1996, *Population Projections of the United States by Age, Sex, Race, and Hispanic Origin: 1995 to 2050*, U.S. Bureau of

the Census, Current Population Reports, Series P25-1130, Government Printing Office, Washington, DC.

7. U.S. Bureau of the Census, 1996a, PE-47, *Estimates of the Population of States by Age, Sex, Race, and Hispanic Origin: 1990 to 1994*, Diskettes (3); and U.S. Bureau of the Census, 1996b, PE-38 *Population of States by Single Years of Age and Sex: 1990 to 1995.*

8. U.S. Bureau of the Census, 1991, *Age, Sex, Race and Hispanic Origin Information from the 1990 Census: A Comparison of Census Results with Results where Age and Race have been Modified*, 1990 CPH-L-74, August.

9. U.S. Bureau of Economic Analysis, 1995, *BEA Regional Projections to 2045*, Volume 1: States, U.S. Government Printing Office, Washington, DC.

10. Campbell, Paul, *Population Projections for States, by Age, Sex, Race, and Hispanic Origin: 1995 to 2025*, U.S. Bureau of the Census, Current Population Reports, Series P25-1111, U.S. Government Printing Office, Washington, DC, 1994.

11. Based on 1980 and 1990 census figures reported in U.S. Bureau of the Census, *Statistical Abstract of the United States: 1992*, (112th edition), Washington, DC, 1992, table 23, p. 21. Also see Sink, Larry D., "Trends in Internal Migration in the United States," U.S. Bureau of the Census, Current Population Reports, Series P23, No. 175, *Population Trends in the 1980's*, U.S. Government Printing Office, Washington, DC, 1992.

12. The surplus of births over deaths in a population for a given time period is referred to as "natural increase".

13. Net population change refers to the number of persons added to (subtracted from) the base population (in this instance the July 1, 1995 State population and the ending point July 1, 2025) due to births, deaths, and net internal and international migration.

14. Hispanic origin is considered an ethnic group, not a race group. Therefore, persons of Hispanic origin may be of any race.

15. More detailed projections are available since race and Hispanic origin was classified into eight race and Hispanic origin groups (White, Black, American Indian, and Asian cross classified by Hispanic origin and not of Hispanic origin).

16. During 1995 to 2025, States with losses for the White population in rank order were New York, New Jersey, Pennsylvania, Massachusetts, Illinois, Michigan, Connecticut, Ohio, Rhode Island, West Virginia, and **California**.

17. "American Indian" represents American Indian, Eskimo, and Aleut.

18. "Asian" represent Asian and Pacific Islander.

19. Campbell, 1994, op.cit., p. xx.

20. See Day, 1996, op. cit.

Understanding the Consumer Price Index

adapted from the Bureau of Labor Statistics

INTRODUCTION

The continually growing number of uses and users of the **Consumer Price Index (CPI)** have generated an increasing number of questions about the CPI. Although the Bureau of Labor Statistics (BLS) has provided extensive material to the public describing the CPI, much of this material has been quite technical. BLS has developed this pamphlet, therefore, to

1. answer frequently asked questions about the CPI

2. familiarize users of the CPI with some of the most important of the new procedures introduced with the 1998 CPI Revision and

3. help users of the CPI better understand and use it.

1. What is the CPI?

The Consumer Price Index (CPI) is a measure of the average change over time in the prices paid by urban consumers for a fixed market basket of consumer goods and services. The CPI

440

provides a way to compare what this market basket of goods and services costs this month with what the same market basket cost, say, a month or year ago.

2. How is the CPI used?

The Consumer Price Index affects nearly all Americans, because of the many ways it is used. Three major uses are:

1. As an **economic indicator**. The CPI is the most widely used measure of inflation and is sometimes viewed as an indicator of the effectiveness of government economic policy. It provides information about price changes in the Nation's economy to government, business, labor, and other private citizens, and is used by them as a guide to making economic decisions. In addition, the President, Congress, and the Federal Reserve Board use trends in the CPI to aid in formulating fiscal and monetary policies.

2. As a **deflator of other economic series**. The CPI and its components are used to adjust other economic series for price changes and to translate these series into inflation-free dollars. Examples of series adjusted by the CPI include retail sales, hourly and weekly earnings, and components of the national income and product accounts.

   An interesting example is to use the CPI as a deflator of the value of the consumer's dollar to find its purchasing power. The purchasing power of the consumer's dollar measures the change in the quantity of goods and services a dollar will buy at different dates. In other words, as prices increase, the purchasing power of the consumer's dollar declines.

3. As a **means of adjusting dollar values**. As inflation erodes consumers' purchasing power, the CPI is often used to adjust consumers' income payments, for example, Social Security; to adjust income eligibility levels for

government assistance; and to automatically provide cost-of-living wage adjustments to millions of American workers.

The CPI affects the income of almost 80 million persons, as a result of statutory action:

- 47.8 million Social Security beneficiaries

- about 22.4 million food stamp recipients

- about 4.1 million military and Federal Civil Service retirees and survivors

Changes in the CPI also affect the cost of lunches for 26.7 million children who eat lunch at school, while collective bargaining agreements that tie wages to the CPI cover over 2 million workers.

Another example of how dollar values may be adjusted is the use of the CPI to adjust the Federal income tax structure. These adjustments prevent inflation-induced increases in tax rates, an effect called "bracket creep."

3. Is the CPI a cost-of-living index?

No, although it frequently (and mistakenly) is called a cost-of-living index. The Bureau of Labor Statistics (BLS or the Bureau) has for some time used a cost-of-living framework in making practical decisions about questions that arise in constructing the CPI. A cost-of-living index is a conceptual measurement goal however, it is not a straightforward alternative to the CPI.

A cost-of-living index would measure changes over time in the amount that consumers need to spend to reach a certain "utility level" or "standard of living." Both the CPI and a cost-of-living index would reflect changes in the prices of goods and services, such as food and clothing, that are directly purchased in the marketplace; but a complete cost-of-living index would go beyond this to also take into account changes in other governmental or environmental factors that affect consumers' well-being. It is very difficult to determine the proper treatment of public goods, such as safety and education, and other broad concerns, such as health, water quality, and crime, that would comprise a complete cost-of-living framework.

Another difference between the CPI and a cost-of-living index is that the CPI does not reflect the changes in buying or consumption patterns that consumers probably would make to adjust to relative price changes. For example, if the price of pork increases compared to that of other meats, shoppers might shift their purchases away from pork to beef, poultry, or fish. The ability to substitute means that the increase in the cost to consumers of maintaining their level of well-being tends to be somewhat less than the increase in the cost of the mix of goods and services they previously purchased. The current CPI does not reflect this substitution among items as a cost-of-living index would. Rather, the current CPI measures the cost of purchasing the same market basket of items, in the same fixed proportions (or weights) month after month.

Experimental projects that may move the CPI closer to a cost-of-living measure are underway. Nevertheless, the difficult problems of defining living standards and measuring changes in the cost of their attainment over time make it improbable that a true cost-of-living measure can be produced in the foreseeable future.

It is important to note that local area CPIs cannot be used to compare levels of living costs or prices across areas. (See Question 17)

4. Whose buying habits does the CPI reflect?

The CPI reflects spending patterns for each of two population groups: *All Urban Consumers* (**CPI-U**) and *Urban Wage Earners and Clerical Workers* (**CPI-W**). The CPI-U represents about 87 percent of the total U.S. population. It is based on the expenditures of almost all residents of urban or metropolitan areas, including professionals, the self-employed, the poor, the unemployed, and retired persons, as well as urban wage earners and clerical workers. Not included in the CPI are the spending patterns of persons living in rural nonmetropolitan areas, farm families, persons in the Armed Forces, and those in institutions such as prisons and mental hospitals.

The CPI-W is based on the expenditures of households that are included in the CPI-U definition that also meet two requirements: more than one-half of the household's income must come from clerical or wage occupations, and at least one of the household's earners must have been employed for at least 37 weeks during the previous 12 months. The CPI-W's population represents about 32 percent of the total U.S. population and is a subset, or part, of the CPI-U's population.

5. Does the CPI measure my experience with price change?

Not necessarily. It is important to understand that BLS bases the market baskets and pricing procedures for the CPI-U and CPI-W on the experience of the relevant average household, not of any specific family or individual. It is unlikely that your experience will correspond precisely with either the national indexes or those for specific cities or regions.

For example, if you or your family spend a larger than average share of your budget on medical expenses and medical care costs are increasing more rapidly than other items in the CPI market basket, your personal rate of inflation (or experience with price change) may exceed the CPI. Conversely, if you heat your home with solar energy and fuel prices are rising more rapidly than other items, you may experience less inflation than the general population.

This is one reason why people sometimes question the accuracy of the published indexes. A national average reflects all the ups and downs of millions of individual price experiences. It seldom mirrors a particular consumer's experience.

6. How is the CPI *market basket* determined?

The CPI market basket is developed from detailed expenditure information provided by families and individuals on what they actually bought. For the current CPI, this information was collected from the Consumer Expenditure Survey over the 3 years 1993, 1994, and 1995. In each of these 3 years, about 7,000 families from around the country provided information on their spending habits in a series of quarterly interviews. To collect information on frequently purchased items, such as food and personal care products, another 5,000 families in each of the 3 years kept diaries listing everything they bought during a 2-week period.

Altogether, about 36,000 individuals and families provided expenditure information for use in determining the importance, or weight, of the over 200 item categories in the CPI index structure.

7. What goods and services does the CPI cover?

The CPI represents all goods and services purchased for consumption by the reference population (CPI-U or CPI-W). BLS has classified all expenditure items into more than 200 categories, arranged into eight major groups. Major groups and examples of categories in each are as follows:

- **FOOD AND BEVERAGES** — breakfast cereal, milk, coffee, chicken, wine, full service meals and snacks

- **HOUSING** — rent of primary residence, owners' equivalent rent, fuel oil, bedroom furniture

- **APPAREL** — men's shirts and sweaters, women's dresses, jewelry

- **TRANSPORTATION** — new vehicles, airline fares, gasoline, motor vehicle insurance

- **MEDICAL CARE** — prescription drugs and medical supplies, physicians' services, eyeglasses and eye care, hospital services

- **RECREATION** — televisions, cable television, pets and pet products, sports equipment, admissions

- **EDUCATION AND COMMUNICATION** — college tuition, postage, telephone services, computer software and accessories

- **OTHER GOODS AND SERVICES** — tobacco and smoking products, haircuts and other personal services, funeral expenses

Also included within these major groups are various government-charged user fees, such as water and sewerage charges, auto registration fees, and vehicle tolls.

The CPI also includes taxes (such as sales and excise taxes) that are directly associated with the prices of specific goods and services. However, the CPI excludes taxes (such as income and Social Security taxes) not directly associated with the purchase of consumer goods and services.

The CPI does not include investment items, such as stocks, bonds, real estate, and life insurance. (These items relate to savings and not to day-to-day consumption expenses.)

For each of the more than 200 item categories, BLS has chosen samples of several hundred specific items within selected business establishments, using scientific statistical procedures, to represent the thousands of varieties available in the marketplace.

For example, in a given supermarket, the Bureau may choose a plastic bag of golden delicious apples, U.S. extra fancy grade, weighing 4.4 pounds to represent the "Apples" category.

8. How are CPI prices collected and reviewed?

Each month, BLS data collectors called economic assistants (formerly known as field representatives) visit or call thousands of retail stores, service establishments, rental units, and doctors' offices, all over the United States, to obtain price information on the thousands of items used to track and measure price change in the CPI. These economic assistants record the prices of about 80,000 items each month. These 80,000 prices represent a scientifically selected sample of the prices paid by consumers for the goods and services purchased.

During each call or visit, the economic assistant collects price data on a specific good or service that was precisely defined during an earlier visit. If the selected item is available, the economic assistant records its price. If the selected item is no longer available, or if there have been changes in the quality or quantity (for example, eggs sold in packages of 8, when previously they had been sold by the dozen) of the good or service since the last time prices were collected, the economic assistant selects a new item or records the quality change in the current item.

The recorded information is sent to the national office of BLS where commodity specialists, who have detailed knowledge about the particular goods or services priced, review the data. These specialists check the data for accuracy and consistency and make any necessary corrections or adjustments. These can range from an adjustment for a change in the size or quantity of a packaged item to more complex adjustments based upon statistical analysis of the value of an item's features or quality. Thus, the commodity specialists strive to prevent changes in the quality of items from affecting the CPI's measurement of price change.

9. How is the CPI calculated?

The CPI is a product of a series of interrelated samples. First, using data from the 1990 Census of Population, BLS selects the urban areas from which prices are to be collected and chooses the housing units within each area that are eligible for use in the shelter component of the CPI. The Census of Population also provides data on the number of consumers represented by each area selected as a CPI price collection area.

Next, another sample (of about 16,800 families each year) serves as the basis for a Point-of-Purchase Survey that identifies the places where households purchase various types of goods and services.

Data from the Consumer Expenditure Survey conducted from 1993 through 1995, involving a national sample of almost 36,000 families, provided detailed information on their spending habits. This enabled BLS to construct the CPI market basket of goods and services and to assign each item in the market basket a weight, or importance, based on total family expenditures.

The final stage in the sampling process is the selection of the specific detailed item to be priced in each outlet. This is done in the field, using a method called **disaggregation**. For example, BLS economic assistants may be directed to price "fresh whole milk." Through the disaggregation process, the economic assistant selects the specific kind of fresh whole milk that will be priced in the outlet over time. By this process, each kind of whole milk is assigned a probability of selection, or weight, based on the quantity the store sells. If, for example, vitamin D, homogenized milk in half-gallon containers makes up 70 percent of the sales of whole milk; and the same milk in quart containers accounts for 10 percent of all whole milk sales, then the half-gallon container will be seven times as likely to be chosen as the quart container. After probabilities are assigned, one type, brand, and size container of milk is chosen by an objective selection process based on the theory of random sampling. The particular kind of milk that is selected by disaggregation will continue to be priced each month in that outlet.

In summary, the price movement measurement (see Question 8) is weighted by the importance of the item in the spending patterns of the appropriate population group. The combination of all these factors gives a weighted measurement of price change for all items in all outlets, in all areas priced for the CPI.

10. How do I read or interpret an index?

An **index** is a tool that simplifies the measurement of movements in a numerical series. Most of the specific CPI indexes have a 1982-84 reference base. That is, BLS sets the average index level (representing the average price level)—for the 36-month period covering the years 1982, 1983, and 1984—equal to 100. The Bureau measures changes in relation to that figure. An index of 110, for example, means there has been a 10-percent increase in price since the reference period; similarly an index of 90 means a 10-percent decrease.

Movements of the index from one date to another can be expressed as changes in index points (simply, the difference between index levels), but it is more useful to express the movements as percent changes. This is because index points are affected by the level of the index in relation to its reference period, while percent changes are not.

BLS usually updates reference periods every 10 years or so, to make it easier for people to relate changes in the CPI to other economic and cultural changes. Through the release of the

December 1998 index, the CPI standard reference period will be 1982-84=100. Effective with the release of the January 1999 CPI, the standard reference period will be changed to 1993-95=100. That is, for most of the specific CPI indexes, BLS will set the average index level—for the 36-month period covering the years 1993, 1994, and 1995—equal to 100.

11. Is the CPI the best measure of inflation?

Inflation has been defined as a process of continuously rising prices, or equivalently, of a continuously falling value of money.

Various indexes have been devised to measure different aspects of inflation. The CPI measures inflation as experienced by consumers in their day-to-day living expenses; the Producer Price Index (PPI) measures inflation at earlier stages of the production and marketing process; the Employment Cost Index (ECI) measures it in the labor market; the BLS's International Price Program measures it for imports and exports; and the Gross Domestic Product Deflator (GDP-Deflator) measures combine the experience with inflation of governments (Federal, State and local), businesses, and consumers. Finally, there are specialized measures, such as measures of interest rates and measures of consumers' and business executives' inflation expectations.

The "best" measure of inflation for a given application depends on the intended use of the data. The CPI is generally the best measure for adjusting payments to consumers when the intent is to allow consumers to purchase, at today's prices, the same market basket of goods and services that they could purchase in an earlier period. It is also the best measure to use to translate retail sales and hourly or weekly earnings into real, or inflation-free, dollars.

12. Which index is the "official CPI" reported in the media?

Each month, BLS releases thousands of detailed CPI numbers to the media. However, the media usually focuses on the broadest, most comprehensive CPI. This is *The Consumer Price Index for All Urban Consumers (CPI-U) for the U.S. City Average for All Items, 1982-84=100.* (After 1998, the reference period will be 1993-95=100.) This data is reported on either a seasonally adjusted or not seasonally adjusted basis. Often, the media will report some, or all, of the following:

- Index level, not seasonally adjusted (For example, August 1997=160.8.)

- 12-month percent change, not seasonally adjusted (For example, August 1996 to August 1997 = 2.2 percent.)

- 1-month percent change on a seasonally adjusted basis (For example, from July 1997 to August 1997 = 0.2 percent.)

- Annual rate of percent change so far this year (For example, from December 1996 to August 1997, if the rate of increase over the first 8 months of the year continued for the full year, after the removal of seasonal influences, the rise would be 1.6 percent.)

- Annual rate based on the latest seasonally adjusted 1-month change (For example, if the July 1997 to August 1997 rate continued for a full 12 months, the rise, compounded, would be 2.3 percent.)

13. What index should I use for escalation?

The decision to employ an escalation mechanism, as well as the choice of the most suitable index, is up to the user. When drafting the terms of an escalation provision for use in a contract to adjust future payments, both legal and statistical questions can arise. While BLS cannot help in any matters relating to legal questions, it does provide basic technical and statistical assistance to users who are developing indexing procedures.

Some examples of technical or statistical guidelines from BLS follow:

- BLS strongly recommends using indexes unadjusted for seasonal variation (i.e., not seasonally adjusted indexes) for escalation. (See Question 14 for a further explanation of seasonally adjusted indexes and why BLS doesn't recommend seasonally adjusted indexes for use in escalation.)

- BLS recommends using national or regional indexes for escalation, due to the volatility of local indexes. (See Question 15 for an explanation of this point.)

If you have further questions, the Bureau has prepared a detailed report, *Using the Consumer Price Index for Escalation*. This information is also available on the CPI home page at `http://stats.bls.gov/cpihome.htm` or write or call the nearest BLS regional office listed in the answer to Question 21.

You may also call the BLS national office at (202) 606-7000.

14. When should I use seasonally adjusted data?

By using seasonally adjusted data, economic analysts and the media find it easier to see the underlying trend in short-term price change. It is often difficult to tell from raw (unadjusted) statistics whether developments between any two months reflect changing economic conditions or only normal seasonal patterns. Therefore, many economic series, including the CPI, are seasonally adjusted to remove the effect of seasonal influences.

Seasonal influences are those that occur at the same time and in about the same magnitude every year. They include price movements resulting from changing climatic conditions, production cycles, model changeovers, and holidays.

BLS annually reestimates the factors that are used to seasonally adjust CPI data, and seasonally adjusted indexes that have been published earlier are subject to revision for up to 5 years after their original release.

Therefore, unadjusted data are more appropriate for escalation purposes.

15. What area indexes are published, and how often?

Besides monthly publication of the national (or U.S. City Average) CPI-U and CPI-W, monthly indexes are also published for the four regions: Northeast, Midwest (formerly North Central), South, and West. Monthly indexes are also published for urban areas classified by population size: all metropolitan areas over 1.5 million; metropolitan areas smaller than 1.5 million; and all nonmetropolitan urban areas. Indexes also are available within each region, cross-classified by area population size. For the Northeast and West, however, indexes for nonmetropolitan areas are not available.

BLS also publishes indexes for 26 local areas. Local area indexes are byproducts of the national CPI program. Each local index has a much smaller sample size than the national or regional indexes and is, therefore, subject to substantially more sampling and other measurement error. As a result, local area indexes are more volatile than the national or regional indexes. Therefore, BLS strongly urges users to consider adopting the national or regional CPIs for use in escalator clauses. If used with caution, local area CPI data can illustrate and explain the impact of local economic conditions on consumers' experience with price change. Local area data are available on the following schedule.

BLS publishes three major metropolitan areas monthly:

Chicago, IL/Gary, IN/Kenosha, WI
Los Angeles/Riverside/Orange County, CA
New York, NY/Northern NJ/Long Island, NY/NJ/CT/PA

Data for an additional eleven metropolitan areas are published every other month [on an odd (January, March, etc.) or even (February, April, etc.) month schedule] for the following areas:

Odd Cycle
Baltimore, MD
Boston/Lawrence/Salem, MA/NH
Cleveland/Akron/Lorain, OH
St. Louis/East-St. Louis, MO/IL
Washington, DC/MD/VA

Even Cycle
Dallas/Fort Worth, TX
Detriot/Ann Arbor, MI
Houston, TX
Miami/Fort Lauderdale, FL
Pittsburgh/Beaver Valley, PA

(Note: The designation *even* or *odd* refers to the month during which the area's price change is measured. Due to the time needed for processing, data are released two to three weeks into the following month.)

Data are published for another group of 12 metropolitan areas on a semiannual basis. These indexes, which refer to the arithmetic average for the 6-month periods from January through June and July through December, are published with release of the CPI for July and January, respectively, in August and February for:

Anchorage, AK
Pittsburgh, PA
Cincinnati/Hamilton,OH/KY/IN
Portland/Salem, OR/WA

Denver/Boulder/Greely, CO
St. Louis, MO/IL
Honolulu, HI
San Diego, CA
Kansas City, MO/KS
Tampa/St. Petersburg/Clearwater, FL
Milwaukee/Racine, WI
Minneapolis/St, Paul, MN/WI

16. What area CPI should I use, if there is no CPI for the area in which I live?

Although BLS can provide some guidance on this question, users must make the final decision.

As noted in the answers to Questions 13 and 15, BLS strongly urges the use of the national or regional CPIs for use in escalator clauses. These indexes are more stable and subject to less sampling and other measurement error than are local area indexes and, therefore, more statistically reliable.

17. Can the CPIs for individual areas be used to compare living costs among areas?

No, an individual area index measures how much prices have changed over a specific time period in that particular area. It does not show whether prices or living costs are higher or lower in that area relative to another. In general, the composition of the market basket and relative prices of goods and services in the market basket during the expenditure base period vary substantially across areas.

18. What types of data are published?

There are many types of data published as outputs from the CPI program. The most popular are indexes and percent changes.

Requested less often are relative importance (or relative expenditure weight) data, base conversion factors (to convert from one CPI reference period to another), seasonal factors (the monthly factors used to convert unadjusted indexes into seasonally adjusted indexes), and average food and energy prices.

Index and price change data are available for the U.S. city average (or national average), for various geographic areas (regions and metropolitan areas), for national population-size classes of urban areas, and for cross-classifications of regions and size classes. Indexes for various groupings of items are available for all geographic areas and size classes.

There are individual indexes available for more than 200 items (e.g., apples, men's shirts, airline fares), and over 120 different combinations of items (e.g., fruits and vegetables, food at home, food and beverages, and All Items), at the national or U.S. city average level.

BLS classifies consumer items into eight major groups: Food and beverages, housing, apparel, transportation, medical care, recreation, education and communication, and other goods and services. (Some indexes are available as far back as 1913.)

Each month, indexes are published along with short-term percent changes, the latest 12-month change and, at the national item and group level, unadjusted and (where appropriate) seasonally adjusted percent changes (and seasonal factors), together with annualized rates of change. These annualized rates indicate what the rate of change would be for a 12-month period, if a price change measured for a shorter period continued for a full 12 months.

The answer to Question 15 provides information about the areas and size classes for which indexes are published. For areas, BLS publishes less-detailed groupings of items than it does for the national level. Annual average indexes and percent changes for these groupings are published at the national and local levels.

Semiannual average indexes and percent changes for some of these groupings are also published.

Each month, BLS publishes average price data for some food items (for the U.S. and four regions) and for some energy items (for the U.S., four regions, three size-classes, ten cross-classifications of regions and size-classes, and fourteen metropolitan areas).

19. What are some limitations of the CPI?

The CPI is subject to both limitations in application and limitations in measurement.

Limitations in Application

1. The CPI may not be applicable to all population groups. For example, the CPI-U is designed to measure the experience with price change of the U.S. urban population and, thus, may not accurately reflect the experience of people living in rural areas.

2. The CPI does not produce official estimates for the rate of inflation experienced by subgroups of the population, such as the elderly or the poor. (BLS does produce and release an experimental index for the elderly population. However, because of the significant limitations of this experimental index, it should be interpreted with caution.)

3. As noted in the answer to Question 17, the CPI cannot be used to measure differences in price levels or living costs between one place and another; it measures only time-to-time changes in each place. A higher index for one area does not necessarily mean that prices are higher there than in another area with a lower index. It merely means that prices have risen faster since their common reference period.

4. The CPI cannot be used as a measure of total change in living costs, because changes in these costs are affected by factors (such as social and environmental changes and changes in income taxes) that are beyond the definitional scope of the CPI and so are excluded.

Limitations in Measurement

Limitations in measurement can be grouped into two basic types: sampling errors and nonsampling errors.

1. **Sampling Errors.** Because the CPI measures price change based on a sample of items, the published indexes differ somewhat from what the results would be if actual records of all retail purchases by everyone in the index population could be used to compile the index. These estimating or sampling errors are limitations on the precise accuracy of the index, not mistakes in index calculation.

    The CPI program has developed measurements of sampling error, which are updated and published annually in the CPI Detailed Report. An increased sample size would be expected to increase accuracy, but it would also increase CPI production costs. The CPI sample design allocates the sample in a way that maximizes the accuracy of the index, given the funds available.

2. **Nonsampling Errors.** These errors occur from a variety of sources. Unlike sampling errors, they can cause persistent bias in index measurement. Nonsampling errors are caused by problems of price data collection, logistical lags in conducting surveys, difficulties in defining basic concepts and their operational implementation, and difficulties in handling the problems of quality change.

    Nonsampling errors can be far more hazardous to the accuracy of a price index than sampling errors. BLS expends much effort to minimize these errors. Highly trained personnel insure comparability of quality of items from period to period (see answer to Question 8), collection procedures are extensively documented, and recurring audits are conducted. The CPI program has an ongoing research and evaluation program, to identify and implement improvements in the CPI.

20. Will the CPI be updated or revised in the future?

Yes. The CPI will need revisions, as long as there are significant changes in consumer buying habits or shifts in population distribution or demographics. The Bureau, by developing annual Consumer Expenditure Surveys and Point-of-Purchase Surveys, has the flexibility to monitor changing buying habits in a timely and cost-efficient manner. In addition, the census conducted every 10 years by the Department of Commerce provides information that enables the Bureau to reselect a new geographic sample that accurately reflects the current population distribution and other demographic factors.

As a matter of policy, BLS is continually researching improved statistical methods. Thus, even between major revisions, further improvements to the CPI are made.

For example, until recently, the Bureau would continue to price the brand-name version of a prescription drug even after it lost its patent protection, if the brand-name drug was still sold in the selected outlet. Starting in January 1995, BLS changed this policy. Now, six months after a drug loses its patent protection, a unique item to be priced is reselected from all therapeutically equivalent drugs (including the original) sold in the selected retail outlet. This gives generic versions of the drug a chance to be selected as a substitute.

BLS waits until six months after the patent expires to give the emerging generic drugs time to gain market share, because the chance of selection is proportional to the sales of each version of the drug in the retail outlet. This new procedure provides a better reflection of consumers' experience with prescription drug prices, since many consumers switch to generic versions of drugs, as they become available.

21. How can I get CPI information?

CPI information is available from BLS electronically, through subscriptions to publications, and via telephone and fax, through automated recordings. Information specialists are also available in the national and regional offices to provide assistance.

Electronic Access to CPI Data

BLS on the Internet. Through the Internet, BLS provides free, easy, and continuous access to almost all published CPI data and press releases. The most recent month's CPI is made available immediately at the time of release. Additionally, a database called LABSTAT, containing current and historical data for the CPI is accessible. Data and press releases from other BLS surveys are also available. This material is accessible via the World Wide Web (WWW), Gopher, and File Transfer Protocol (FTP), as described below. For help using any of these systems, send e-mail to `labstat.helpdesk@bls.gov`

World Wide Web. BLS maintains a Web site at `http://stats.bls.gov` The BLS home page provides easy access to LABSTAT, as well as links to program-specific home pages. In addition to data, the CPI home page at `http://stats.bls.gov/cpihome.htm` provides other CPI information. This includes a brief explanation of methodology, frequently asked questions and answers, contacts for further information, and explanations of how the CPI handles special items, like medical care and housing. In addition, CPI press releases and historical data for metropolitan areas can be accessed, by linking to the regional office home pages from the main BLS Web site listed above.

FTP and Gopher. These tools provide access to CPI LABSTAT data, as well as documentation and press release files organized in hierarchical directories. Connect to `stats.bls.gov` using FTP or Gopher, log on as ANONYMOUS and use your complete Internet e-mail address as the password.

Subscriptions to CPI Publications

Summary Data. A free, monthly, 2-page publication containing one- and twelve-month percent changes for selected U.S. city averages; Consumer Price Index for All Urban Consumers (CPI-U) and Consumer Price Index for Urban Wage Earners and Clerical Workers (CPI-W) index series. The All Items index data for each local area are also included. To be added to the mailing list, write to: Office of Publications, Bureau of Labor Statistics, 2 Massachusetts Avenue, NE., Room 2850, Washington, DC 20212-0001, or call (202) 606-7828 or any of the BLS regional offices listed below.

CPI Detailed Report. Most comprehensive report of the Consumer Price Index. This publication may be ordered by writing to: New Orders, Superintendent of Documents, P.O. Box 371954, Pittsburgh, PA, 15250-7954, or by calling (202) 512-1800. [There is an annual subscription charge for this publication.]

Monthly Labor Review (MLR). The MLR provides selected CPI data included in a monthly summary of BLS data and occasional articles and methodological descriptions too extensive for inclusion in the CPI Detailed Report. This publication may be ordered by writing to: New Orders, Superintendent of Documents, P.O. Box 371954, Pittsburgh, PA, 15250-7954, or by calling (202) 512-1800. [There is an annual subscription charge for this publication.]

Recorded CPI Data

Summary CPI data are provided 24 hours a day on recorded messages. Detailed CPI information is available by calling (202)

606-7828. A Touch-Tone™ telephone is recommended, as this system allows the user to select specific indexes from lists of available data.

Recorded summaries of CPI are available by calling any of the area CPI hotlines listed below. These summaries include data for the U.S. city average, as well as the specified area. Recordings are approximately 3 minutes long, and are available 24 hours a day, 7 days a week.

Area	*Hotline*
Anchorage	(907) 271-2770
Atlanta	(404) 562-2545
Baltimore	(410) 962-4898
Boston	(617) 565-2325
Chicago	(312) 353-1883
Cincinnati	(513) 684-2349
Cleveland	(216) 522-3852
Dallas	(214) 767-6971
Denver	(303) 844-1735
Detroit	(313) 226-7558
Honolulu	(808) 541-2808
Houston	(713) 718-3753
Indianapolis	(317) 226-7885
Kansas City	(816) 426-2372
Los Angeles	**(310) 235-6884**
Milwaukee	(414) 276-2579
Minneapolis-St.Paul	(612) 290-3996
New York	(212) 337-2406
Philadelphia	(215) 596-1156
Pittsburgh	(412) 644-2900
Portland	(503) 231-2045
St. Louis	(314) 539-3527
Salt Lake City	(801) 485-6582
San Diego	**(619) 557-6538**
San Francisco	**(415) 975-4406**
Seattle	(206) 553-0645
Washington, DC	(202) 606-6994
Washington, DC	(202) 606-7828

Other Sources of CPI Data

Technical information is available during normal working hours, Monday through Friday (Eastern Time), by calling (202) 606-7000 or any of the regional offices listed below.

Fax-on-Demand. A wide variety of BLS information and data, including CPI, are available from the BLS Ready Facts catalog via fax-on-demand. CPI documents from Ready Facts that are available around the clock include the monthly CPI press release, selected national, regional and metropolitan area historical summaries, and some technical information. The latest CPI information is posted during the morning of release day.

To have the latest Ready Facts catalog sent to you, call (202) 606-6325, then follow instructions. Each regional office also has a fax system in place; these systems include all information available from the national catalog, in addition to region-specific information on the CPI.

Phone and fax-on-demand numbers for the eight regional offices are:

Washington, DC
Bureau of Labor Statistics
Office of Prices and Living Conditions
2 Massachusetts Avenue, NE.
Washington, DC 20212-0001
(202) 606-6325
(202) 606-7000

Boston
Bureau of Labor Statistics
JFK Federal Bldg., E-310
Boston, MA 02203
(617) 515-9167
(617) 565-2327

Philadelphia
Bureau of Labor Statistics
Gateway Building, Suite 8000
P.O. Box 13309
Philadelphia, PA 19101-3309
(215) 596-4160
(215) 596-1154

New York
Bureau of Labor Statistics
Economic Analysis and Information
201 Varick Street, Room 808
New York, NY 10014-4811
(212) 337-2412
(212) 337-2400

Atlanta
Bureau of Labor Statistics
Economic Analysis and Information
61 Forsyth Street, SW.,
Room 7T50
Atlanta, GA 30303
(404) 562-2545
(404) 562-2463

Chicago
Bureau of Labor Statistics
Economic Analysis and Information
230 S. Dearborn Street,
9th Floor
Chicago, IL 60604
(312) 987-9288
(312) 353-1880

Kansas City
Bureau of Labor Statistics
Economic Analysis and Information
1100 Main Street, Suite 600
Kansas City, MO 64105-2112
(816) 426-3152
(816) 426-2481

Dallas
Bureau of Labor Statistics
Economic Analysis and Information
525 Griffin Street, Room 221
Dallas, TX 75202
(214) 767-9613
(214) 767-6970

San Francisco
Bureau of Labor Statistics
Economic Analysis and Information
P.O. Box 193766
San Francisco, CA 94119-3766
(415) 975-4567
(415) 975-4350

Historical Tables. These include all published indexes for each of the detailed CPI components. They are available via the Internet, by calling (202) 606-7000 in the national office, or by contacting any of the regional offices listed above.

Descriptive Publications. These publications describe the CPI and ways to use it. They include simple fact sheets discussing specific topics about the CPI, this pamphlet with its broad, non-technical overview of the CPI in a question and answer format, and a quite technical and thorough description of the CPI and its methodology. These publications are available upon request by calling (202) 606-7000, and many are included on the CPI home page on the Internet.

Special Publications. Also available are various special publications, such as Relative Importance of Components in the Consumer Price Index, and materials describing the annual revisions of seasonally adjusted CPI data. For more information, call (202) 606-7000.

Further information may be obtained from the Office of Prices and Living Conditions, Bureau of Labor Statistics, 2 Massachusetts Avenue, NE., Room 3615, Washington, DC, 20212-0001, telephone (202) 606-7000, or by calling any of the regional offices listed above.

A Answers to Chapter Quiz Questions

The following are the correct answers to the Chapter Quiz questions. The number in parentheses after each answer refers to the page number on which the answer (or an explanation of the answer) can be found.

CHAPTER 1

1. B (1)
2. D (4)
3. C (8)
4. B (9)
5. B (14)
6. C (15)
7. D (16)
8. B (16)
9. D (17)
10. C (19)

CHAPTER 2

1. D (25)
2. A (25)
3. B (26)
4. D (27)
5. C (30)
6. B (31)
7. D (32)
8. B (32)
9. B (34)
10. A (38)

CHAPTER 3

1. C (43)
2. C (45)
3. B (46)
4. D (47)
5. D (48)
6. A (52)
7. B (56)
8. C (58)
9. A (60)
10. B (63)

CHAPTER 4

1. D (69)
2. C (73)
3. C (74)
4. D (76)
5. B (77)
6. A (79)
7. B (79)
8. D (81)
9. A (82)
10. B (85)

466

CHAPTER 5

1. C (92)
2. B (93)
3. C (94)
4. D (96)
5. B (97)
6. D (99)
7. B (100)
8. A (99)
9. C (100)
10. C (101)

CHAPTER 6

1. B (108)
2. B (109)
3. C (110)
4. D (112)
5. D (113)
6. A (115)
7. B (115)
8. A (117)
9. A (121)
10. B (122)

CHAPTER 7

1. C (135)
2. C (135)
3. A (136)
4. D (137)
5. A (139)
6. C (140)
7. B (142)
8. C (145)
9. B (146)
10. D (148)

CHAPTER 8

1. B (158)
2. A (159)
3. A (163)
4. C (160)
5. D (161)
6. A (163)
7. C (165)
8. B (169)
9. C (172)
10. A (180)

CHAPTER 9

1. B (188)
2. D (190)
3. B (194)
4. A (195)
5. A (196)
6. D (198)
7. D (200)
8. C (200)
9. B (203)
10. B (208)

CHAPTER 10

1. C (215)
2. D (216)
3. D (217)
4. B (219)
5. A (221)
6. D (228)
7. C (233)
8. D (233)
9. C (233)
10. B (232)

CHAPTER 11

1. D (242)
2. C (243)
3. B (244)
4. D (246)
5. A (249)
6. B (251)
7. C (252)
8. C (253)
9. D (260)
10. C (267)

CHAPTER 12

1. A (277)
2. B (278)
3. D (281)
4. C (282)
5. C (283)
6. C (283)
7. D (286)
8. B (286)
9. C (286)
10. B (287)

CHAPTER 13

1. B (294)
2. C (295)
3. C (297)
4. B (297)
5. C (298)
6. C (300)
7. D (300)
8. B (301)
9. D (304)
10. D (307)

CHAPTER 14

1. D (317)
2. D (319)
3. C (321)
4. D (325)
5. B (326)
6. D (326)
7. C (328)
8. A (329)
9. C (330)
10. B (330)

CHAPTER 15

1. C (338)
2. C (338)
3. B (339)
4. D (340)
5. D (340)
6. B (343)
7. B (344)
8. B (344)
9. B (347)
10. C (349)

Index